SHIPS FROM HELL

'The first men died, I think, of broken hearts; died knowing that cruelty has no frontier, and that though God wept for a fallen sparrow, the Japanese had in them so little of the milk of human kindness that they could leave a thousand men in the vastness of the China Sea to die in certain and terrible agony.'

Alfred G. Allbury, survivor of the torpedoed hellship
Rakuyo Maru.

SHIPS FROM HELL

Japanese War Crimes on the High Seas

Raymond Lamont-Brown

SUTTON PUBLISHING

First published in the United Kingdom in 2002 by
Sutton Publishing Limited · Phoenix Mill
Thrupp · Stroud · Gloucestershire · GL5 2BU

Reprinted in 2002

British Library Cataloguing-in-Publication Data
A catalogue record for this book is available from the British Library.

ISBN 0-7509-2719-4

Typeset in 12/13.5pt Bembo Mono.
Typesetting and origination by
Sutton Publishing Limited.
Printed and bound in England by
J.H. Haynes & Co. Ltd, Sparkford.

CONTENTS

Hana wa sakuragi; hito wa bushi.
[The cherry is the first amongst blossoms;
the warrior is first amongst men.]
Service personnel motto, 1941

Since the end of the war I have read that inhuman deeds have been committed by the Army and Navy of Japan. That was certainly not the intention of the authorities, namely the *Sanbo Hombu* (General Staff), the *Rikugunsho* (Ministry of War), the *Kaigunsho* (Navy Ministry), and myself. We did not even suspect that such things were occurring; the *Tenno-Heika* (His Majesty the Emperor) in particular, should, considering his humane observances, inspire the contrary sentiments. Such deeds are not tolerated in Japan. The character of the Japanese people is such that neither in *ten-chi* (heaven nor earth) should such things be tolerated. It would be very bad if men elsewhere in the world should believe that these inhuman deeds arise from the Japanese character.

Declaration by former Minister of War and Prime Minister, General Hideki Tojo, during interrogation at Sugamo Prison, March 1946.

Over a period of several months the tribunal has listened to witnesses who have described in detail cruelties committed on all war fronts and on such a large scale and indeed with such a fixed pattern that only one conclusion is possible. Those cruelties were authorised in secret either by or with the approval of Japanese Government, by individual members thereof and by commanders of the armed forces.

Statement from the judgment of the International Military Tribunal, November 1946.

The evil inspiration behind Japan's war atrocities, General Hideki Tojo, was executed for war crimes at 1.30am on 23 December 1948.

On 28 May 1959 Emperor Hirohito gave a personal order to the Shinto priests who administer the *Yasukuni-jinja* – Japan's main war memorial – to inscribe the names of all Japan's war criminals on the scrolls of the 2,500,000 immortal military dead commemorated at the shrine. In benediction he uttered words deemed blasphemous to the memories of the murdered PoWs: 'I have a special appreciation for the families of our war criminals. I know what they have done for Japan. They were among our greatest leaders.'

In 1998 the Japanese film *Pride – The Fatal Moment* was issued for public release, praising General Hideki Tojo as a heroic *samurai* in the Japanese tradition and a war hero.

CHRONOLOGY

1941

7 Dec.	*Chujo* Chuichi Nagumo's carrier-based planes attack Pearl Harbor.
8 Dec.	Ships of the Imperial Japanese Navy sink or capture British and American warships at Hong Kong and Shanghai.
9 Dec.	Surrender of Siam (Thailand).
	Japanese occupy Makin Island, Gilbert Islands.
10 Dec.	Japanese capture Guam.
	Japanese land-based planes of the 22nd Air Flotilla sink British battleships HMS *Prince of Wales* and HMS *Repulse*.
23 Dec.	Japanese capture Wake Island.

1942

19 Jan.	British Borneo surrenders.
23 Jan.	Japanese occupy Rabaul, New Britain, and Kavieng, New Ireland.
	First slave-labour gangs of US personnel arrive in China aboard the hellship *Nitta Maru*.
4 Feb.	First major massacre of civilians by naval staff at Amboina.
15 Feb.	Capitulation of Singapore, which becomes transportation port for PoWs.
17 Feb.–1 Mar.	Battle of the Java Sea.
28 Feb.–1 Mar.	Battle of the Sunda Strait.
8 Mar.	Surrender of Netherlands East Indies.
	Japanese occupy Lae and Salamaua, New Guinea.
	Japanese capture Rangoon, Burma.

8 Mar.	Plans to use PoWs to build railway from Bangkok to Rangoon launched.
23 Mar.	Japanese occupy Andoman and Nicobar Islands.
28 Mar.	Japanese occupy the whole of Sumatra.
Mar.–Apl	Japanese occupy Admiralty Islands and other key islands in Bismarck Sea, and Halmahera.
Apl	Transportation of Netherlands East Indies PoWs.
30 Apl	Japanese occupy Tulagi.
7 May	US Navy carrier planes attack Close Support Force of Port Moresby invasion fleet, and sink the light carrier *Shoho* (ex-*Tsurugizaki*). Battle of the Coral Sea.
8 May	Carrier battle in the Coral Sea. Heavy carrier USS *Lexington* sunk.
15 May	*Toyohashi Maru*, the first hellship to be sunk, by HMS *Trusty*.
4 Jun.	*Chujo* Chuichi Nagumo's carrier force attacked; *Akagi*, *Kaga* and *Soryu* sunk.
5 Jun.	Japanese occupy Altu Island.
7 Jun.	Japanese submarine *I-168* sinks the crippled USS *Yorktown*.
1 Jul.	First hellship to be sunk by US 'friendly fire': *Montevideo Maru* sunk by USS *Sturgeon* (SS187).
29 Jul.	Japanese capture Kokoda.
9 Aug.	US Marines eliminate Japanese at Tulagi.
4 Oct.	Hellship *Lisbon Maru* sunk after torpedoed by USS *Grouper* (SS214).
15–27 Oct.	Carrier battle of Santa Cruz Islands.

By the end of 1942 some fifty-four hellships had transported around 50,000 PoWs for slave labour.

1943

3 Jan.	Imperial Japanese Army eliminated at Buna, Gona.
Feb.	Beginning of Japanese evacuation from sites like Guadalcanal.
3–4 Mar.	Battle of the Bismarck Sea.
18 Mar.	Massacre of civilians aboard the destroyer *Akikase*.

18 Apl	USAAF P-38 intercepts and kills *Shosho* Isoroku Yamamoto near Buin.
Jul.–Aug.	Japanese evacuate Solomon Islands.
Oct.	Imperial Japanese Navy personnel begin slaughter of civilians at Kavieng.
	Massacre of Pan-American Airways employees at Wake Island.
Sept.–Nov.	Severe Japanese losses at Villa Lavella and Rabaul.
24 Nov.	Japanese lose Tarawa.

By the end of 1943 around forty hellships have transported a further 24,000 PoWs.

1944

	Imperial Japanese Navy involved in transporting biological warfare materials and personnel to the Pacific.
Feb.	Heavy Japanese losses in Marshall Islands.
	Japanese abandon Truk as main naval base.
Mar.	Transhipment by sea of PoWs from Bangkok–Rangoon railway site.
Apl	Japanese lose New Guinea.
	Last Japanese mass atrocity carried out on Allied merchant seamen following the sinking of MV *Behar*.
19–20 Jun.	Battle of the Marianas.
7 Oct.	Massacre of PoWs by naval personnel, Wake Island.
24 Oct.	Battle of Sibuyan Sea; loss of Japanese battleship *Musashi*.
25 Oct.	Battle of Surigao Strait.
	Battle off Sanar and Cape Engaro.

1945

19 Jan.	Moji, the PoW port of entry into Japan, suffers major Allied attacks.
17 Apl	Battleship *Yamato* lost.
5 May	Results of 'civilian atrocity' Operation FUGO discovered in USA.

| 17 May | Last sea battle. Heavy carrier *Haguro* sunk by Royal Navy destroyers off Penang, Malaya. |
| 2 Sept. | Formal surrender of Japanese accepted by General Douglas MacArthur aboard the battleship USS *Missouri* in Tokyo Bay. |

1946

1 Jan.	Establishment of the International Military (War Crimes) Tribunal for the Far East.
	Thames Maru first hellship to be mentioned in war crimes trial (in the Gozawa Trial, Singapore).
	War Crimes Tribunals uncover evidence that some 127,000 PoWs were transhipped during the war period in various hellships; deaths estimated at some 21,000, making a death-rate of around 16 per cent.

ACKNOWLEDGEMENTS

Text

Every effort has been made to trace literary heirs and successors for every quotation used in this book. The passage of time, the death of copyright holders and the moving of address by literary custodians all contribute to the difficulty of tracing copyright ownership, especially those that have reverted from publishers to authors. Nevertheless each quotation is individually acknowledged, where possible, in text and notes.

Special thanks are given to the following for helping to trace rights of ownership and specific quotations and sources: Kelvin Smith; Peter Elphick; Syd Sanders, Victoria, Australia; Lance and Mary Gibson, Victoria, Australia; Jim Barnes, Aspley, Australia; Don Wall, New South Wales, Australia; Dr John L. Weste, University of Durham; T.R.J. Coles, Southwest Wales Far East PoW Club; Carol Cooper, Children and Families of the Far East PoWs Association; Catherine Trippett, Permissions Manager, Random House Group Ltd; Florence Pinard, Subsidiary Rights Manager, Robert Hale; and Myrto Tzanatou, Rights Assistant, Little Brown. Extracts have been taken, with permission, from the following publications: Eric S. Cooper, *Tomorrow You Die*, E.S. Cooper & Sons, 1995; James D. McEwan, *The Remorseless Road*, Airlife Publishing, 1997; A.G. Allbury, *Bamboo and Bushido*, Robert Hale, 1955; and John and Clay Blair, *Return from the River Kwai*, Futura Publications, 1980. And thanks also go to the estate of the late Lord Russell of Liverpool and Messrs Cassell for permission to use extracts from *The Knights of the Bushido*, 1958.

Documentation

Assistance in tracing relevant documents for research for this book is gratefully acknowledged to the following: Dr A.P. van Vliet, Director,

Instituut voor Maritieme Historie, The Hague; Dr R.C.C. Pottkamp, Nederlands Instituut voor Oorlogsdocumentatie, Amsterdam; Dr Peter Liddle, Director, The Second World War Experience Centre, Leeds; Dr Rick D.H. van Velden, Algemeen Rijksarchief, The Hague, M. Kakinoma, Japan Information and Cultural Centre, Embassy of Japan, London; Captain Keeichi Kuno, Japanese Defence Attaché, Embassy of Japan, London; Stephen Walton, Archivist, Dept of Documents, Imperial War Museum, London; and Kiri Ross-Jones, MSS Dept, National Maritime Museum, London.

Photographs
Each photograph is individually acknowledged where it occurs for source and ownership. Particular thanks are due to Terence Kelly for supplying a rare photograph of Hellship survivors, and to William Hodge for the trial site and defendant illustrations, Singapore.

PREFACE

On 5 March 1942 my late father was arrested in his room at the Palace Hotel, Shanghai, on the orders of *Shosho* Koneshita, head of the Shanghai *Kempeitai*. The *Kempeitai*, by the by, were the dreaded Japanese military police. At the time my father was working as a civil engineer in the employ of the British firm Babcock & Wilcox Ltd, who had electric power contracts with General Chiang Kai-shek's Kuomintang Government in what was then dubbed the 'intelligence capital of the Far East'. At 4am – the *Kempeitai* liked to make their arrests at 03.00hrs Tokyo time – he was taken to the already notorious Bridge House Prison. This was the *Kempeitai* HQ fronting on to Soochow Creek, a part of the Shanghai waterfront known as the Bund of the Whangpoo River. There he was placed in one of the seventeen barred and bolted steel 'cages', some 9ft 4in by 20ft, with around forty other detainees, to await interrogation.

Shosho Koneshita, who had established his reign of terror as soon as the Imperial Japanese Army's occupation of Shanghai had been secured by 2 December 1937, was arresting foreign nationals on trumped-up charges of espionage and anti-Japanese propaganda. Under a programme of dehumanising beatings and torture, confessions were extracted when the victims had been pushed to the fringe of insanity. The horrors of interrogation went on for hours, the sound of screaming victims forming a horrific background for those waiting their turn.

At that time the Shanghai office of Britain's Consul-General, Sir Herbert Phillips, had been closed, but the Swiss tried to monitor what happened to the Allied civilians who suddenly disappeared into Bridge House Prison. After brutal interrogation to no avail my father was released as a part of the August 1942 repatriation programme for 225 British and Allied civilians, brokered between the Japanese and the British Government with the help of the Swiss Consul-General M. Emile Fontanel. But father's trials were not finished.

He was taken, with other prisoners, to the Shanghai docks on a stretcher, as he was unable to walk unaided following his beatings by *Kempeitai* 'liaison officer' *Tai-i* Hirano. Once at the docks the prisoners were embarked aboard the 17,256-ton liner *Kamakura Maru* (ex-*Chichibu Maru*). The ship soon became overcrowded with foreign nationals for repatriation; the tortured victims, sick deportees and assorted 'enemies of the Emperor' were given no medical care. Within months of the repatriation trips the cruise liner was to enter a new role as a PoW 'hellship', and soon *Kamakura Maru* was to be joined by another soon-to-be-notorious hellship, the 16,975-ton liner *Tatsuta Maru*.

While my father was being abused by the *Kempeitai*, the British Ambassador to Japan Sir Robert Leslie Craigie and his staff had been interned from the outbreak of the war at the embassy compound in Tokyo.

Their release was negotiated on 30 July 1942 by the Swiss Minister M. Camille Gorgé. All the while the *Kempeitai* made it as difficult as possible for the staff, hounding them at every opportunity, totally against international diplomatic law. Craigie and his staff were eventually taken to Yokohama and locked below decks in the *Tatsuta Maru*. The midsummer sun had made the ship into an oven. Overcrowded with repatriated foreigners, *Tatsuta Maru* left Yokohama for Ito on the Sagami Nada, thence to Shanghai, to rendezvous with *Kamakura Maru*.

One after the other the two liners set off for Lourenço Marques (modern Maputo), the neutral Portuguese port in Mozambique on the Indian Ocean. Here an exchange of evacuees was to be effected, with calls at Singapore and Saigon. After ten days at Lourenço Marques, the Far Eastern evacuees boarded the Khedevial Line's SS *El Nil* and the P&O Line vessel SS *Narconda*; my father was a passenger on the latter. On 9 October 1942 the vessels docked at Liverpool to a civic welcome.

Just as the British Embassy staff had been hassled and impeded on their way to the *Tatsuta Maru* by the *Kempeitai*, on 9 December 1941 life for the US Ambassador to Japan Joseph C. Grew and his staff also became unpleasant – until the Swiss Minister M. Gorgé effected their repatriation in June 1942 aboard another Japanese Trans-Pacific liner, the 16,975-ton *Asama Maru*. Before sailing from Yokohama to Hong Kong the Americans were locked up in the sweltering ship for hours.

For a while both the *Kempeitai* and the *Tokkeitai* (the Imperial Japanese Navy equivalent of the *Kempeitai*) illegally treated the US diplomats as PoWs.

At Hong Kong the ship took on more evacuees and sailed by way of Saigon and Singapore to join the Italian vessel *Conte Verde*, which had been stuck in Shanghai since the beginning of the war, and a rendezvous at Lourenço Marques. Thereafter the Americans were embarked on the US-chartered Swedish vessel *Gripsholm*, bound for New York. *Asama Maru* returned to Singapore and Yokohama to take up a role as a hellship.

During his repatriation my father first encountered the vessels that would later be transformed into the hellships in which thousands of Allied PoWs would be subjected to Imperial Japanese Forces atrocities. Through my father's diaries of his captivity I too gained my first knowledge of Japanese naval war crimes in the Second World War. These nautical atrocities are much less well-known than those perpetrated by the Imperial Japanese Army, but they deserve an equal airing. My further research into this branch of Japanese war crimes introduced me to the naval equivalent of the *Kempeitai*, the shadowy but equally bestial and zenophobic *Tokkeitai*. Just as *Kempeitai* officers had disappeared, reinvented themselves and merged with the Japanese populace after the Second World War so the *Tokkeitai* personnel were equally difficult to trace. But this book contains a part of their story, as revealed in the war crimes tribunals.

My father's story, and other eye-witness accounts of atrocities, were dismissed as *uso wo* (lies) by such men as Chief of Intelligence and Propaganda Taro Terasuki. Today, many Japanese still deny that any war crimes ever took place, and there is a renewed attempt in the Japanese media to portray the Japanese as the 'liberators' of the Far East.

Just three years after a film called *Jiman* ('Pride – The Fatal Moment') offered a sympathetic portrayal of Hideki Tojo, hanged for war crimes in 1948, a movie from the Toho Studios was launched in Japan in March 2001 called *Merdeka* ('Independence'). It glorifies the troops of the Japanese Imperial Army as liberators of fellow Asians, in particular freeing the people of Indonesia from Dutch colonial rule. The irony is, of course, that the same soldiers murdered both Dutch and Indonesians in well-attested incidents during the war.

This propaganda line is in keeping with the revived trend among historians of such groups as the Japanese Society for History Textbook Reform, and politicians like those of the ruling Liberal Democrat party, to rewrite history for schoolchildren, glossing over Japanese army and navy war crimes. This rewriting has been endorsed by the Japanese *Mombusho*, the Ministry of Education. The revised version has been met with dismay in countries that suffered under Japanese occupation, and both the Foreign Minister of the Republic of Korea and the Chinese Ambassador to Japan went public to express their 'deep concerns'.

This book is dedicated to the author's late father and his fellow sufferers of the Bridge House Prison, and to all those PoWs, civilian and service, who were murdered by Imperial Japanese Forces in the Second World War. While factions in Japan are intent on rewriting and falsifying history, this book aspires to right the balance.

SAMURAI OF THE SEA

'You are all *Samurai no Umi* [Samurai of the Sea], rid the waves of the
Emperor's enemies. Execute the trespassers of the Emperor's oceans at
dawn, let their blood honour the Nation of the Rising Sun.'
Katei-kyoshi no aisatsu (Tutor salutation to graduating naval officers).

PUBLIC REVELATIONS

During December 1941 and March 1942 offices were established in
Tokyo within the *Heimu Kyoku* (Military Administration Bureau) of the
Rikugunsho (Ministry of War) to oversee the handling of *furyo* (PoWs)
and log their numbers. Although the *Dai Nippon Teikoku Rikugun*
(Imperial Japanese Army) was to handle such prisoners from captured
territories from North China to what the Japanese called *Nan 'yo*
(Southern Region), the *Dai Nippon Teikoku Kaigun* (Imperial Japanese
Navy) was to administer those in the Celebes, part of Borneo, the
Moluccas, Timor, the Lesser Sundas, New Guinea, Rabaul, the
Bismarck Archipelago, Guam and Wake. The navy was also to oversee
the transport of prisoners by sea between captured territories and work-
camps.

Within their remit, personnel of the Imperial Japanese Navy
contributed to some of the worst atrocities of any war, past or present,
and from the very first days of the Allied surrender members of the
Imperial Japanese Navy, of all ranks, were slaughtering, abusing,
torturing and humiliating prisoners of war.

Within the hundred-plus volumes of the *Senshi Sosho* (Japan's official
military history) there is no mention of their infamy. A huge raft of
incriminating evidence was 'deliberately' destroyed on direct orders (by
telegram) from the *Rikugunsho* as early as 1944, when the Allies retook
the Philippines. Many senior Japanese naval officers committed suicide
when they heard they were to be arrested, but first they burned their

records.[1] Yet from the files of the *Kyokuto Kokusai Gunji Saiban* (International Military (War Crimes) Tribunal of the Far East), which held its hearings at Tokyo from 4 May 1946 to 16 April 1948, a horrified world began to learn of the atrocities at sea. For example, one early summation revealed this concerning the Imperial Japanese Navy's conserving of space on their PoW ships:

> Wooden stages or temporary decks were built in empty coal bunkers and holds, with a vertical space of only three feet between. The space allotted to prisoners on these decks was an area six feet per fifteen prisoners. They were compelled to sit crosslegged during the entire voyage. Space was conserved also by the elimination of proper sanitary facilities. Those provided consisted of buckets or boxes which were lowered into the hold or bunker with ropes, and were removed in the same manner for emptying over the side. Drippings from these containers added to the general insanitary conditions. Many prisoners were suffering from dysentery . . . their excreta fell freely through the cracks in the wooden stages upon their comrades below.[2]

The PoWs' food was also served pre-prepared on shore and cold in order to conserve space that would have been needed for a separate galley. Water rations were restricted for the same reason.

TRAINING FOR INFAMY

As international correspondents filled notebook after notebook with such material a broader picture of the cruelties enacted by the Imperial Japanese Navy began to emerge. The source of the training and inculcated philosophy which had produced the officers who conducted such barbarities, and condoned them in subordinates, lay far to the south-west on the Japanese main island of Honshu. It was the *Kaigun heigakko* (Naval College) at Etajima.

By ferry, the island of Etajima ('Water ricefield island') is some 25 minutes' sea journey from Kure, the former great Japanese naval port from which the Second World War Imperial Fleets set out to conquer the Pacific. Situated in Hiroshima Bay, Etajima remains famous

JAPANESE SHIP DESIGNATIONS AND NAMES

Maru: All Japanese merchant ships are given the suffix *Maru*, the written ideographic character meaning 'round'. It is generally supposed that this custom dates back to medieval times when the *daimyo* named their vessels after their castles – wherein the central part is the *Hon-maru*.

Ships of the Imperial Japanese Navy were designated *Ken*, while foreign ships were called *Go*.

Naming of vessels:

Carriers:	After animals, birds and flying objects.
Battleships:	After provinces of ancient Japan. Purists might like to note that there were four exceptions, all battle-cruisers, *Haruna*, *Hiei*, *Kirishima*, and *Kongo*, which were named after mountains.
Heavy cruisers:	After mountains.
Light cruisers:	After rivers.
Destroyers:	Poetic names of climatic conditions, such as *Shigure* ('Drizzling Autumn Rain'). Again for the purists, after 1944 the shortage of war materials obliged the Japanese to build smaller destroyers, which had the names of flowers, fruit and trees.
Submarines:	There were three classes of submarine denoted phonetically I, RO and HA (corresponding to A, B and C).

as the 'Cradle of the Imperial Japanese Navy'. For the Japanese, the Meiji Restoration of 1868 has something of the significance of the French Revolution for the French. The Emperor Meiji (r. 1867–1912) took over the rule of the country after centuries of military dictatorship by the *Shogun* (generalissimos). As Japan entered a period of westernisation in all aspects of government, establishments such as the *Kaigun heigakko* were one consequence.

ETAJIMA KENJI NO UTA

(Anti-western Song of *Kaigun heigakko* – the 'Etajima Strong Ones')

On the ocean surge and break big waves
Where stands *Akitsushima*[a] our beautiful country
Adorned with evergreen pines.
Her history is thousands of years old,
Her Imperial Policy is great and noble.

There stands the beautiful *Fuji-San*[b]
High up on the *Tokaido*[c].
Our hearts throb more and more with the hot blood
Of the sons of the Sacred Land.
We shall never stop sacrificing ourselves
To defend the glorious foundations of our country.

At the foot of *Furutaka*[d] the water is clear
And the wind-kissed pines make sweet music.
At daybreak *Nomishima*[e] looms hazy amid purple shadow.
Here hoisting the flag of daring and bravery
We spend four years.

We launch out cutters on the sea
Our strong arms bend even the oars
When we land armed with bayonets
We look grim and severe and all silent.
Now let us be wonderfully high spirited,
And let us cultivate an indomitable spirit.

Behold! in the West, blooming proudly, there lie
Hidden blights under its civilisation.
Look! the Pacific Ocean is stormy
And dark clouds hover over East Asia.
Who will shoulder the duty of defending our country?

Oh! strong ones of Etajima!
You are just like dragons who hide in a lake
Who, if a chance comes when storm clouds gather
Dash up into the sky.
To fight till we fall
Is the sincere cry of our hearts!

a. *Akitsushima*: Ancient name for Japan, derived from its resemblance to the body of a dragonfly.
b. *Fuji-San*: Sacred Mount Fuji.
c. *Tōkaido*: The road along the eastern coast of the main island of Honshu, from Tokyo to Kyoto.
d. *Furutaka*: Mountain on Etajima used for training purposes.
e. *Nomishima*: Island off Etajima.

The appearance of foreign war vessels off the coast of Japan in the nineteenth century underlined their realisation that only a powerful navy could ensure national defence. This was a fact made more evident when an American squadron under Commodore Matthew Perry forced open the isolationist gates of Japan in 1854 – gates that had been shut to foreigners since the seventeenth century. Indeed, there are those who argue that Perry's success was to lead to the logical and inevitable Japanese retaliation at Pearl Harbor as a delayed rejoinder to the unwanted intrusions by the West.

A naval school was first opened at Nagasaki in 1855 and soon afterwards a shipyard (Mitsubishi Dock) was established there. A little later, a training centre for seamen opened in Edo (the old name for Tokyo) and the gift from the Netherlands of the training ship *Kanko Maru* led to more gifts of vessels from other countries. The importance of sea defence, and Japan's impotence to respond, was underlined in 1863 when a British squadron bombarded Kagoshima (after the murder of a British citizen). When Meiji took over the reins of government the Imperial Japanese Navy consisted of nine vessels, all under 1,000 tons, and the dockyards were only capable of building wooden ships.

In 1887 Japan launched its first ironclad and a fleet of ships was ordered from abroad; they came mostly from Britain and sailed under

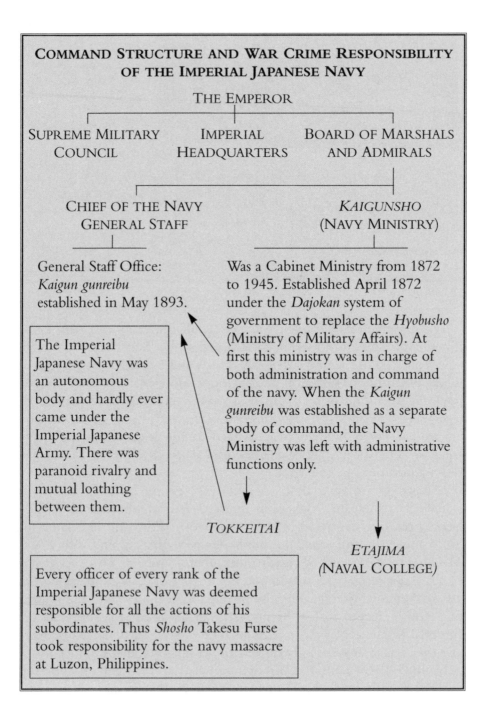

COMMAND STRUCTURE AND WAR CRIME RESPONSIBILITY
OF THE IMPERIAL JAPANESE NAVY

THE EMPEROR

SUPREME MILITARY   IMPERIAL   BOARD OF MARSHALS
COUNCIL   HEADQUARTERS   AND ADMIRALS

CHIEF OF THE NAVY   *KAIGUNSHO*
GENERAL STAFF   (NAVY MINISTRY)

General Staff Office: *Kaigun gunreibu* established in May 1893.

Was a Cabinet Ministry from 1872 to 1945. Established April 1872 under the *Dajokan* system of government to replace the *Hyobusho* (Ministry of Military Affairs). At first this ministry was in charge of both administration and command of the navy. When the *Kaigun gunreibu* was established as a separate body of command, the Navy Ministry was left with administrative functions only.

The Imperial Japanese Navy was an autonomous body and hardly ever came under the Imperial Japanese Army. There was paranoid rivalry and mutual loathing between them.

TOKKEITAI

ETAJIMA (NAVAL COLLEGE)

Every officer of every rank of the Imperial Japanese Navy was deemed responsible for all the actions of his subordinates. Thus *Shosho* Takesu Furse took responsibility for the navy massacre at Luzon, Philippines.

the guidance of British naval advisers. By 1889 the naval stations at Kure and Sasebo had been established.

On 4 January 1882 an Imperial Rescript was promulgated for the Japanese Imperial Navy and its personnel (*Keigun-guntia*, 'Soldiers of the Sea'), exhorting them to carry out five major instructions: to be loyal to the divinely succeeded Emperor; to be courteous to each other – those who had no respect for their superiors were dubbed *uragirimono* (traitor); to engender courage; to be faithful and conscientious; and to be simple and frugal in habits. This Rescript became the Japanese sailor's Bible and led to a devotion marked by the fanaticism of their fighting in the Second World War.

During 1892 the Japanese Government began a new naval programme, issued under Imperial Rescript, and to which Emperor Meiji contributed personally from his own funds; government officials too contributed 10 per cent of their salaries to the building up of the navy. The Japanese Navy was first tested in a theatre of war against China between 1 August 1894 and 17 April 1895; this war startled the West, with Japan quickly and utterly defeating a superior force. After the Russo-Japanese War of 1904–5, wherein Japan challenged and neutralised Imperial Russia for the control of Korea and Manchuria, Japan became one of the Great Sea Powers. The Imperial Japanese Navy increased in strength and efficiency and rendered significant service to the Allies during the First World War by taking over Tsintao and the German South Sea Islands, and convoying troopships from Australia and New Zealand to France. All the lower deck ratings of the Imperial Navy were composed of conscripted men and volunteers.

In its first form the Officer Cadet College was founded at Tsukiji, Tokyo, in 1869. As the Meiji Revolution modelled all the new state governmental institutions on western originals, the Japanese Navy was inaugurated on occidental principles. A British Navy Mission of thirty-four officers and other ranks, under the command of Captain A. Lucius Douglas RN, arrived in Japan in 1873 to supervise the development of the college.

The college was moved to Etajima in August 1888 and renamed 'The Imperial Naval Academy'. It was located on a site overlooking an almost landlocked bay called Etajima. Today the oldest building remaining is the *Suikokan*, erected in 1888. Once the Imperial Navy Officers' Club,

THE IMPERIAL JAPANESE NAVY, 7 DECEMBER 1941

Vessel manifest: 235 ships. Largest naval force in the Far East.
10 battleships, 18 heavy cruisers, 20 light cruisers, 6 heavy carriers, 4 light carriers, 111 fleet destroyers, 1 escort carrier, 65 submarines

Combined Fleet Commanders: 6 Fleets, 2 Air Fleets
1. Battle Fleet. *Chujo* Isoroku Yamamoto. Hiroshima Base. Yamamoto was born in 1884, and shot down at Buin, 18 April 1943.
2. Scouting Fleet. *Chujo* Nobutake Kondo. Hainan Island Base. Kondo became a businessman after 1945.
3. Blockade and Transport Fleet. *Chujo* Ito Takahashi. Formosa Base. Takahashi was arrested as a war crimes suspect, 2 December 1945.
4. Mandates Fleet. *Chujo* Shigeyoshi Inouye. Truk Base, Caroline Isles. Inouye survived the war.
5. Northern Fleet. *Chujo* Boshino Hozogaya. Maizuru and Ominato Base. Hozogaya was relieved of his command after 1943.
6. Submarine Fleet. *Chujo* Teruhisa Komatsu. Kwajalein Atoll Base, Marshall Islands. A cousin of the Empress, he was in government after 1945.
1st Air Fleet. (Carriers) *Chujo* Chuichi Nagumo. Kure Base. Nagumo committed suicide, 7 July 1945.
11th Air Fleet. *Chujo* Nishio Tsukahara. Formosa and Indo-China Base.

Naval Districts: 4 – Kure; Maizuru; Sasebo; Yokosuka.

Naval Guard Districts: 6 – Chinkai (Korea); Hainan (S. China); Ominato; Osaka; Ryojun (Port Arthur, Manchuria); Takao (Formosa).

this building is now used for formal receptions and college functions. The *Akarenga* (Main Building) was built in 1893 and was constructed of red bricks imported from Britain.

During the 1930s, when Japan was guided by politico-military rulers bent on imperial conquest, the Naval College was greatly expanded and offered a four-year training course for some 250 entrants a year. Until the 1930s all practical training and technical naval subjects were taught on the *Chihaya*, an old dispatch boat of pre-Russo-Japanese War vintage, or on the light cruiser *Oi*. An important part of the college training before the Second World War was the teaching of *Bushido*, 'The Way of the *Samurai* (warriors)': this was a code of selfless honour upon which every *samurai* was expected to base his actions; loyalty, veracity, sincerity and readiness to die for honour were the main virtues required.

An examination of the code of *Bushido* has always perplexed westerners, as it appears to be entirely at odds with Japanese actions during the war. Like Imperial Japanese Army recruits, the Imperial Japanese Navy trainees were taught that *death before surrender* was the ultimate achievement, as death in the Emperor's service guaranteed that the soul would go to dwell with the pantheon of the *Kami* (Japanese gods). Thus an enemy who surrendered rendered himself 'inhuman', and the atrocious bestiality and cruelty meted out to Allied PoWs in the war was the consequence of this *Bushido* training philosophy. To add to the mystery, the code of *Bushido* was virtually gone from the Japanese class system by around 1877, although its ethics were still incorporated into the Army and Navy training programmes. Most of the senior officers of the Imperial Japanese Navy in 1941 were not of the *samurai* class, but had learned their cruelty to PoWs in the China campaigns from the late nineteenth century to the 1930s.[3]

The 'religious spirit' of the Naval College at Etajima was fundamentally focused in 1928 on a small Shinto shrine called the *happoen*, which means, literally translated, 'the eight-points-of-the-compass-garden'. The strong focus of 'ancestor worship' engendered by Japan's national Shinto religion, and underlined in *Bushido*, led to close links between the Naval College and the Japanese imperial family. Before the Second World War all *shiki* (ceremonies, such as the Emperor's birthday parade) commenced at college assemblies in the *daikodo* (main assembly building) with ritual bowing to the portraits of the Emperor and Empress.

Each year the passing out ceremony was attended by *Gensui* (Admiral of the Fleet) HIH Prince Hiroyasu Fushimi, Chief of the General Staff, and on rare occasions by Emperor Hirohito himself. Fushimi, by the by, was the Emperor's cousin and had served as a *Shosa* (Lieutenant-Commander) in the Russo-Japanese War; as the most senior of all naval officers he knew about Imperial Japanese Navy war crimes, condoned them, and promoted the use of suicide weapons (such as *Kamikaze*) when the war went against Japan. He died, unpunished, in 1947. During the period 1888 to 1939 eighteen imperial princes underwent training as cadets at Etajima; indeed, when HRH Edward, Prince of Wales, visited Etajima in May 1922 he was hosted by cadet HIH Prince Takamatsu, the Emperor's youngest brother.

Discussing the pre-1939 cadets at the college, Cecil Bullock, who taught there, described them as 'magnificent persons' physically, but 'rather dull' intellectually, a state he put down to 'an overloaded curriculum' and 'too much physical exercise' cutting down concentration.[4] Discipline was also brutally severe.

The Imperial Japanese Navy conducted a disciplinary system known as *tekken seisai* (the iron fist), in which cadets were physically mistreated for mistakes, or sometimes for no reason at all. This was euphemistically called *ai-no-muchi* (the whip of love), the Japanese equivalent of the occidental phrase 'cruel to be kind'. *Tekken seisai* was later to be vigorously meted out to PoWs by Imperial Japanese Navy personnel.

The insistence on blind obedience to their superiors made the cadets susceptible to the bad influence of dominant leaders. One example of this blind loyalty leading to violence was the murder on 15 May 1932 of *Sori-daijin* (Prime Minister) Tsuyoshi Inukai by *Chu-i* (sub-lieutenants) led by *Shosa* Hitoshi Fuji. Devotion to the *Hakko ichiu* principle ('the whole world under one roof', with Japan as leader under the Emperor) led to the officers' assassination of Inukai, who was deemed to have gone soft on this policy. All through the 1930s young officers of Etajima continually criticised men such as *Kaigun-daijin* (Navy Minister) Mineo Osumi for their 'non-imperial policies'.

Another aspect of the training which was to have some relevance in the war crimes trials was the Naval College's classes in international law, a subject instituted at the turn of the nineteenth century. Consequently all naval cadets were aware of the legislation laid down for the proper treatment of PoWs as specified by the Hague Convention (1907) and the Geneva Convention (1929). The Japanese Government had ratified the former and signed the latter, although it was never ratified because of the Imperial Japanese Army's opposition to it. After the outbreak of war, the numbers of hours devoted to the study of international law, and its relevance to a war situation, was reduced and more time was spent on the Japanese constitution and its relevance to the *Dai Toa Kyozonken* (Great East Asia Co-Existence Sphere), on Japanese naval law, and on how international law could be manipulated or ignored by seamen for Japan's advantage. In particular the pleading of *kyoku no tsukemasu* (superior orders) for atrocities committed while on naval duties was seen at work with reference to the *Tokkeitai*.

TOKKEITAI – SPECIAL JAPANESE NAVAL POLICE

The *Law Reports of the Trials of War Criminals* brought to light misdeeds perpetrated by the *Tokkeitai*. The *Tokkeitai* were the Imperial Japanese Navy equivalent of the Imperial Japanese Army's military policemen, the *Kempeitai*, and they were equally loathed and feared in the areas of Japanese military occupation and in the Naval Control Areas.

One trial gives an example of their infamy. The following charges were brought against sixteen *Tokkeitai* officers who had served in Makassar. The indictment read that they had: 'contrary to the laws and customs of war, carried out unlawful mass arrests and/or exercised systematic terrorism [ie, torture] against persons suspected by the Japanese of punishable acts . . .'[5] A distinguishing feature of this trial was that the *Tokkeitai* personnel were tried as a group, rather than as individuals. All sixteen were found guilty of war crimes in varying degrees: nine were executed, and the others received sentences from one to twenty years' imprisonment.

At this trial the usual defence plea of *kyoku no tsukemasu* brought out the court ruling that 'no subordinate may be successful with this plea if the orders were clearly criminal in themselves'.[6]

The *Tokkeitai* emerged from the *Dai Nippon Teikoku Kaigun*'s need for a special police force of their own. Jealousy between the army and navy

TOKKEITAI ARMBAND INSIGNIA

特警隊

The Japanese Kanji calligraphy spells out *Tokubetsu Keisatsutai* ('Special Police Force').

SECOND WORLD WAR IMPERIAL JAPANESE NAVY ADMINISTRATION AREAS

The *Tokkeitai* had a specific role in Celebes; Lesser Sunda Islands; Moluccas; and South Borneo.

Gilbert Islands: Some of these sixteen islands were occupied by the Japanese until they were liberated by US forces in 1943.
Herein command was in the brief of the 4th Fleet and the Central Pacific Area Fleet.
Makin was specifically commanded by *Chu-i* Ishikawa and *Chu-i* Kurokawa.
The *Tokkeitai* also had groups in Abaiang; Marakei; Abemama; and the capital of Tarawa under *Chu-i* Shibasaki.

Marshall Islands: In 1914 the Japanese seized these islands which had been mandated to them in 1920 by the League of Nations. Japan claimed absolute sovereignty in 1935. They were taken by US forces during 1943–4. Naval Commander was *Shosho* Teruo Akiyama, who died in his destroyer *Niitsuki* in 1943.

caused resentment that the *Dai Nippon Teikoku Rikugun's Kempeitai* might police their officers and ratings. Unlike the *Kempeitai*, the *Tokkeitai* did not have their own sophisticated training schools with courses in such subjects as terrorism and espionage. *Tokkeitai* officers had only their Etajima College training and, like the junior ranks of the Special Police Force, they were recruited as required from naval personnel.[7] The *Tokkeitai* did not have the Gestapo-style role that the *Kempeitai* carried out.

As the Special Japanese Naval Police, the *Tokkeitai* were commanded by a *Taisa*, and were divided into *Buntai* (Sections) and *Bunkantai* (Detachments). Their orders came directly from their Naval Area HQs which were linked to their homeland HQ at Yokosuka Naval Base.

When outside their administration areas the duties of the *Tokkeitai* were to pursue a general policy of *chian-iji* (maintenance of order). PoWs would often see them at transhipment ports supervising the loading and unloading of cargoes (usually by impressed native recruits) and ensuring that PoWs and others did not pilfer. In some cases *Tokkeitai* personnel would travel on PoW hellships, but usually these were vessels that were in the direct control of the Imperial Japanese Navy and not army requisitions.

Inside their administration areas the *Tokkeitai* expanded their duties to include the detection and suppression of anti-Japanese elements, secure PoWs, recruit labour, issue travel permits, requisition supplies, promote propaganda programmes and carry out reprisals against rebellious ethnic groups and monitor political subversives. It is known that the *Tokkeitai* were used in areas outside their administration brief. The occupying Japanese had particular problems in Malay, where around half the population were Chinese; native-born Straits Settlements Chinese were British subjects and loyal, but the rest were supporters either of Chiang Kai-shek's Kuomintang or of the Chinese Communists. *Tokkeitai* were used to round up Communists[8] and liaise with the pro-Japanese supporters of Wang Ching Wei. This was an unusual instance of the *Tokkeitai* being involved in political issues outside their remit.

It is known, too, that the *Tokkeitai* were involved, although to a very much lesser extent than the *Kempeitai*, in the recruitment of *ianfu* (comfort women), the transportation of *karayuki* (Japanese travelling prostitutes) and the transhipment of victims for bacterial warfare and medical experiments in mainland China. Their record of massacres of PoWs and native populations was equally as savage as those of the *Kempeitai*.

NON-NAVY TRANSPORT OF HUMAN CARGOES

The Imperial Japanese Army's movement of human cargoes by sea was handled by the 3rd Bureau's (Transport and Communications) 8th Section of the General Staff. In wartime orders came directly from Imperial HQ, via the Vice-Minister of War through the *Seibe Kyoku* (Economics Mobilisation Bureau). The Imperial Japanese Army, therefore, had its own Transport and Shipping Units which could ferry slave labour, comfort women and PoWs as needed, in addition to requisitioning merchant shipping. As Japan's successful invasion of south-east Asia grew apace the transport regiment (two battalions) could not cope with the quantity of human cargoes and any Imperial Japanese Army unit was tasked to deal with captives of all kinds passing through a particular area. So PoWs in particular became used to being 'handled' by both army and navy personnel and their respective police, the *Kempeitai* and the *Tokkeitai*.

Each principal base port in Japanese theatres of war and occupation had shipping transport commands that were responsible for fuelling vessels, storing and loading cargoes and planning sea routes (in cooperation with the navy). Thus PoWs also got used to being treated as freight, and stowed-away on vessels among cargoes of all kinds. Cargoes could include dangerous explosives and ammunition, which were unstable in storms.

RESCUE AND ESCAPE

From the beginning of the Second World War the British were intercepting and decoding the *tasogare* (basic naval reporting codes) as used by the Imperial Japanese Navy from bases such as the main Tokyo Naval Control *musen-denshin kyoku AB* (Radio Station AB). The *tasogare* detailed ship movements, and the information was processed via Hong Kong and Singapore to the desks of the British codebreakers at Bletchley Park, in the small Buckinghamshire market town of

Bletchley.[9] Such broadcasts were also intercepted by Australian wireless units at Canberra, Townsville and Darwin. (Certain sections of the US Navy refused to cooperate with British intelligence.) From these signals, the use and routes of hellships were monitored by the Allies.

However, knowledge of hellship movements was of little use to Allied vessels in mounting rescue missions. Early in the war it was realised that the Japanese were entirely ruthless in their dealings with PoWs. For instance, the *Manchester Guardian* had reported to a shocked British readership that soon after the Crown Colony of Hong Kong surrendered on 25 December 1941 to *Chujo* Takashi Sakai and the 23rd Army, atrocities against civilians and PoWs were perpetrated. Attempts, therefore, to rescue men from hellships would only trigger orders to slaughter PoWs. Nevertheless, decoded *tasogare* helped to identify hellship convoys which could be avoided by Allied hunter-killer submarines. Again escape was difficult from the hellships or slave-labour holding ports. Those of European descent were easy to spot, and the huge territory under Japanese Occupation was hard to escape from, to say nothing of the inhospitable tracts of jungle.

Recently released decoded papers on the Imperial Japanese Navy's activities regarding the shipment of PoWs have added more angles to the seaborne atrocities of the Second World War. The data underlines the deliberateness of Japanese cruelty towards helpless prisoners. The War Office files studied by Foot and Langley in the 1970s threw up such evidence: 'A Japanese crew . . . tossed some grenades down the hold [*of a PoW transport ship*] before they battened it down and took to the boats; whence they fired on prisoners swimming in the water.'[10] This led to a study of why Japan as a nation could be so bestial.

All Japanese naval and military personnel were raised to believe that surrender meant mindless dishonour to nation and family. Should someone surrender, ran the credo, they could not be accepted back into any normal Japanese community. They would be shunned by family and peers alike. Thus a surrendering PoW was so dishonoured that what happened to them was of no relevance; consequently Japanese personnel shot PoWs as they would rats. Yet there was more to it than that. In the First World War the Japanese had behaved humanely to their German Imperial Army captives, honouring the 1882 Imperial Rescript of the reforming Emperor Meiji to treat PoWs as guests. By the 1930s a radical new system of education was in force at all levels of administration and society. Just as the seeds of honour, respect and humanity towards defeated foes had been expunged from the *Bushido* code by the military cadres that now influenced Japanese Government, so, when Japan announced in 1933 that she would leave the League of Nations, propaganda against *gaijin* (foreigners) was stepped up. Cinema films depicted the Japanese nation as superior to all others. Thus when the Imperial Japanese Army marched into central eastern China in 1937, the Japanese personnel – brought up on discipline through brutality – considered all enemies as *chancorro* (sub-human). The scene was set, too, for atrocities at sea.

INTRODUCTION

PORTS OF TRANSPORTATION

The Imperial Japanese Forces had two main focal points for the transportation of PoWs. On 6 May 1942, when Lieutenant-General Jonathan M. Wainwright surrendered the garrison at Fort Mills (the HQ of the US Forces in the Philippines), Corregidor, to *Chujo* Masaharu Homma's 14th Army, the Japanese controlled the entire Philippines. Thus Manila became the HQ of the 3rd Southern Expeditionary Fleet (31st Naval Special Base Force of the South-west Area Fleet) and the prime transportation base for PoWs taken in the Philippines. They were mostly US PoWs to be routed to Japan (and elsewhere) via Formosa (modern Taiwan).

On 17 February 1942 Lieutenant-General A.E. Percival officially surrendered (after the capitulation of 15 February) his command of Singapore to *Chujo* Tomoyuki Yamashita, Commander of the 25th Army. Thereafter Singapore – known as *Shonan*, 'The Radiant South', to the Japanese – became the second principal transportation base for PoWs taken mainly in South-east Asia, and mostly under the administration of *Shosho* Osamu Imamura, Commander of the 10th Naval Special Base Force. The PoWs here were mostly Australians, Dutch and US personnel of the 131st Field Artillery, as well as the survivors of the 9050-ton heavy cruiser USS *Houston* of the US Asiatic Fleet, which Captain A.H. Rooks and his crew had abandoned during the Battle of Sunda Strait on 1 March 1942.[1] Singapore was an important collection point for transhipment to Japanese-occupied Sumatra, Borneo, Burma, Ambon, Haraku, Timor and New Britain. PoW shipping routes were through the South China Sea, via Saigon and Formosa from Keppel Harbour.

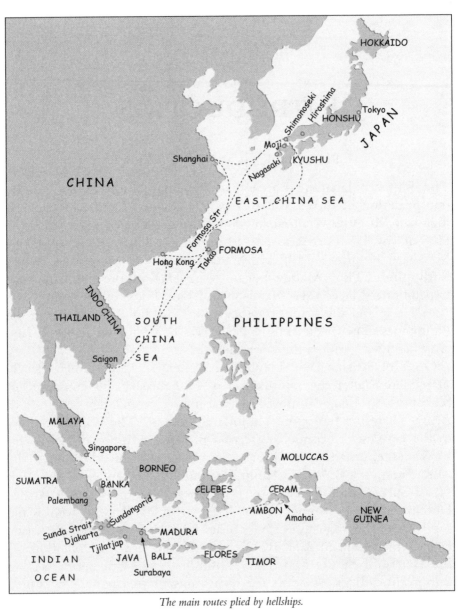

The main routes plied by hellships.

MAIN PORT OF ENTRY FOR POWS IN JAPAN

Moji lies at the northernmost tip of the Japanese main island of Kyushu, fronting the windy, treacherous mile-wide Shimonoseki strait. Today it is within the industrial region of Kita-Kyushu City. Moji was an important base for the transhipment of coal and steel from the turn of the nineteenth century, but in the Second World War it became an import-export port of strategic importance, shipping slave-labour to places as far off as Hokkaido, the northernmost main island of Japan. From 19 January 1945 Moji suffered major Allied air attacks.

In all weathers PoWs would be lined up ashore, where they were sprayed with a de-lousing agent. Visits to the *benjo* (latrine) were not allowed, even for those with raging dysentery. A *shoban* (orderly officer) would order a ludicrous *kanzei* (customs) inspection, wherein naval and army guards would rummage through the meagre packs the PoWs were carrying; tempers would fray as the guards found nothing to purloin – anything worth taking had already been removed by other guards en route. Depending on the nitpicking attitude of the *shoban* an even more ridiculous *imin* (immigration) inspection might then take place; this meant another pack examination. A third rifling would occur under the guise of an *igakuteki* (medical) examination. Thereafter the dead would be trundled off in the same wagons as the sick to what passed as a military hospital.[2] A key propaganda factor in the further transhipment of PoWs was their humiliation. Both army and naval guards encouraged schoolchildren and adult civilians to verbally abuse, hit and spit on PoWs as they passed.

The *Netherlands Instituut voor Oorlogsdocumentatie* in Amsterdam details one 'historic embarkation' worthy of mention in this connection. On 10 January 1943 the 11,409-ton liner *Aki Maru* (ex-*Mishima Maru*), built in 1942 and now converted as a troop transport, set sail for Formosa. The twenty-day PoW voyage had a roster of seventy-four high-ranking Allied prisoners, all glittering 'propaganda prizes'. They included Tjarda van Starkenborg Stachouwer, Governor-General of the Dutch East Indies; Lieutenant-General Hein Ter Poorten, Dutch C.-in-C. land forces; Sir Thomas Shenton Whitelegge Thomas, Governor and C.-in-C. Straits Settlements, and High Commissioner of Malay States; Air Vice Marshal (Sir) Paul C. Maltby, Singapore; A.I. Spito, Governor of

Sumatra; and Sir Mark Young, Governor of Hong Kong. With the
Netherlands Instituut documents is filed this diary entry of a Dutch field
officer, describing the transport link from Batavia to *Aki Maru*:

Wednesday, 30 December 1942: On Monday, 28 December by truck to
Batavia harbour. Speech by transport commander [a *Tokumu socho*].
The Governor-General of the Dutch East Indies [*Stachouwer*] and
generals placed in automobiles – other officers in three trucks. We
were allowed to take all our bedding and luggage with us.

In the harbour, [*Chujo*] Yaheita Saito [Commander of the 25th
Army in Sumatra and Malaya, later head of all PoW camps in Malaya;
cited as war criminal] himself was present, together with a number of
other officers.

The ship was an old, rusty steamer, about 4,000 BRT. Saito had a
few presents for the Governor-General: mosquito coils, 25 cigars,
Eau de cologne. He conversed with many of us. All very friendly. We
talked about corresponding with our families. – 'War is not pleasant,'
they said.

We went aboard. On the 1st level of the hold, in two layers were
the Japanese. On the 2nd level also in two layers we were located –
also the Governor-General. Forward hold: two layers thick.
Everything too low to stand straight up. Cramped sleeping places.
Japanese soldiers were in the same situation. No angry mood. Food
the same for everybody: rice, three times a day. Latrines were a joke –
transparent wooden huts – urinating done in public view – difficult
for some. Stinking mess. We washed ourselves with our own sweat.

The Governor-General holds himself up quite well, considering
the circumstances.

The Japanese extracted the maximum propaganda value from the
embarkation. The Dutch exited in ignominy after 300 years of colonial
rule.

MODE OF TRANSPORT: THE 'HELLSHIPS'

PoWs bound for slave-labour were transported by ferries, small cargo
boats, freighters, and junks between islands, and on larger army, navy

and Merchant Marine ships on the longer routes to Japan. The larger vessels were usually specially converted for the role. The upper decks held Japanese nationals, as well as administrators, educators, economists, agricultural specialists and their families who worked within the Japanese *Dai Toa Kyozonken* (Great Co-Prosperity Sphere). The lower decks held Japanese soldiers and *jugun ianfu* (comfort women), while in the hold would be the *Kamotsu* ('freight' – the PoWs).

An example of a 'hellship' was the 4,000-ton cargo vessel *Byoke Maru*, which transported 1,250 PoWs from Singapore to Moji between 1 July and 8 September 1944. The voyage was described by Australian Ray Parkin, the last serviceman off HMAS *Perth*, which was sunk with USS *Houston*. Parkin was one of a group of PoWs selected on 21 June 1944 for shipment to work at the *tanko* (coal mines) of the Ohama Mining Company on Honshu main island. Parkin and his fellow PoWs were brought by rail to River Valley Camp, Singapore, for onward transportation.[3]

The *Byoke Maru* was a rotting ship with a roofless bridge space. Rusted gear, broken tackle and a myriad of junk lay everywhere. Because of the number of PoWs aboard men made their billets among cargoes. En route the empty coal barrows on deck filled with rain, and the PoWs used them as baths. The ship was riddled with nits and flies; the Japanese set each PoW the task of catching ten flies a day. Each evening the dead flies were counted by a *Chu-i*; those who were short on their tally were beaten.

Illness was rife on board *Byoke Maru*, with many prisoners suffering from beri-beri, pellagra and cerebral malaria.[4] But as they travelled in convoy, illness and the Japanese were not the only enemies as *Byoke Maru* was buffeted by storms; there was also the constant fear of attack by Allied submarines.

At the War Crimes tribunals the Japanese war criminals testified that PoWs were transported in no worse conditions than their own Imperial Forces. Indeed, one example cited was the strategy of *Taisa* Masaharu Tsuji before his invasion of Malaya. He deliberately subjected his infantrymen to days on end in steaming hot holds to prepare them for transhipment to the tropics.

Transhipped PoWs were expected to exist on raw fruit rather than use cooking facilities. Thus they dubbed their vessels *Banana Maru*. Some

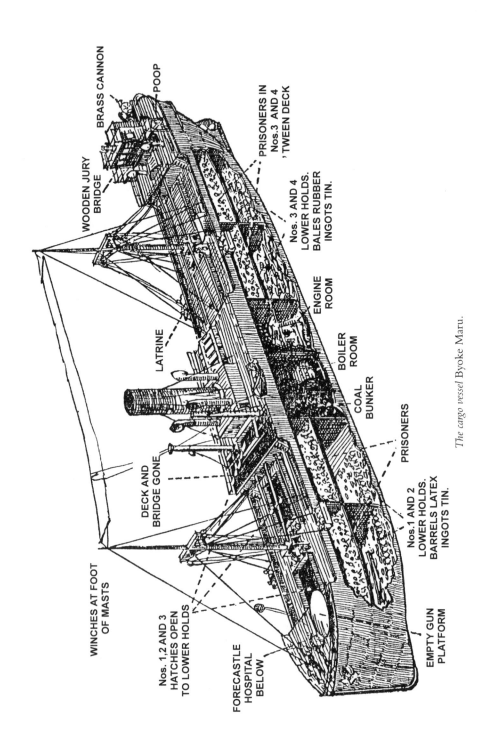

BRASS CANNON

POOP

PRISONERS IN
Nos. 3 AND 4
'TWEEN DECK

Nos. 3 AND 4
LOWER HOLDS.
BALES RUBBER
INGOTS TIN.

WOODEN JURY
BRIDGE

ENGINE
ROOM

LATRINE

BOILER
ROOM

COAL
BUNKER

PRISONERS

DECK AND
BRIDGE GONE

Nos. 1 AND 2
LOWER HOLDS.
BARRELS LATEX
INGOTS TIN.

WINCHES AT FOOT
OF MASTS

Nos. 1, 2 AND 3
HATCHES OPEN
TO LOWER HOLDS

FORECASTLE
HOSPITAL
BELOW

EMPTY GUN
PLATFORM

The cargo vessel Byoke Maru.

ship's officers were allowed other meagre rations, which will be described later (see p. 34).

In loading the hellships the Japanese pursued what they called the rule of *Chomansai*. *Mansai* means 'full capacity' – and *Cho* in this instance means 'ultra' or 'super'. From the Russo-Japanese War onwards the Imperial Japanese Navy had used two rules of thumb for loading personnel, and a similar system was then used in an extreme way to calculate PoW loading. Originally they allowed 1 man per *tsubo* (3.95 sq. yd). By 1941, this was reduced to 1 man per two-thirds of a *tsubo*; and by 1944 to 1 man per one-third of a *tsubo*.

Testimony from PoWs shows that civilian (Merchant Marine) ships captains were the most humane when conditions permitted. Merchant seamen were notably less racist and less anti-Caucasian. Imperial Japanese Navy officers, following orders, wanted to keep prisoners alive for slave work, but rabid anti-Caucasians deliberately let prisoners die.

As the number of PoWs increased the Japanese local occupation staff established a routine for embarkation that was followed by most commands. The process is neatly summed up in the memories of Anthony Cowling. At the outbreak of the Second World War Cowling was a 17-year-old civilian living in Singapore. He volunteered for the RAF, lying about his age. He was inducted into the RAF as an Aircraftsman (Second Class) at Seletar camp and was informed that he would be posted to South Africa for flying training. Instead he was evacuated as the Imperial Japanese Army pushed down the Malaya peninsula to Singapore. After the fall of Singapore Cowling moved with his unit to Batavia in Java, and they became PoWs at Tasik Malaja when the Dutch C.-in-C. surrendered to the invasion forces of the 48th Infantry Division and the Sakaguchi Detachment of the 56th Regimental Group. The prisoners were moved from Semarang PoW Camp to Jaar Market camp (an old Dutch Army barracks) and thence to the work-camp on the island of Haruku in the Moluccas archipelago. Haruku camp was notorious: it had the highest PoW mortality rates in the Japanese Empire.

On 19 April 1943, 2,071 officers and men mustered for embarkation on their hellship. They were embarked on the 3,700-ton troop transport vessel *Amagi Maru*. Once on board they were paraded at attention while

Japanese wearing face-masks and spray canisters on their backs sprayed them with disinfectant. Peeling off in ranks, they were then made to walk through a tray of disinfectant. Requests to fall out to use the *benjo* were refused and beatings were regularly administered for slow movement.

The *Amagi Maru* carried war materials. The Geneva Prisoner of War Convention of 1929 forbade the use of slave-labour for war work, but the Japanese had never signed it. And even though they were morally bound by the Fourth Hague Convention of 1907, which said much the same, the Japanese forced these PoWs to load and unload the *Amagi Maru*.[5]

British PoWs considered it ironic that some of the hellships had been built in the most prestigious UK shipyards. Don Peacock, a former trainee journalist on the *Northern Despatch*, now served in the RAF at Seletar, Singapore.[6] Like Anthony Cowling he was a prisoner at the Jaar Market PoW camp at Surabaya. He remembers being marched to Tandjong Priok docks. His hellship was the 8,000-ton *Cho Saki Maru*. One thousand fellow prisoners were boarded, with around four hundred men crammed into each shelved hold of 40 by 50 feet. To their dismay they saw that their vessel was British-built: she had been sold to the Japanese for scrap in the 1930s. The prisoners spent sixteen days aboard *Cho Saki Maru* bound for the Haruku labour camp; as Peacock vividly describes, it was a new life of 'disease, despair and death'.[7]

DEATHS BY 'FRIENDLY FIRE'

Early in the war PoWs were not likely to be killed by Allied attacks as the Imperial Japanese Navy had control of the seas. For example, on 10 January 1942, only weeks after 5,000 troops of the Japanese South Seas Detachment, 144th regiment of *Chujo* Takashina Takeshi's 29th Division, had landed on the eastern and northern shores of Guam and overcame the 300-strong garrison of US Marines (plus native police), the 12,755-ton liner *Argentine Maru* sailed out of Port Inarajan with a full load of PoWs led by Commander Donald T. Giles, Vice-governor of Guam. There were no attacks on the ship and no fatalities. Most deaths by 'friendly fire' resulted from submarine attacks. On 1 July

1942 the 1926-built Mitsubishi passenger–cargo vessel *Montevideo Maru*, out of Rabaul (Papua New Guinea) and bound for Hainan, was attacked and sunk off Luzon in the Philippines by the submarine USS *Sturgeon* (SS1 87): 840 Australian PoWs and 160 civilians died.

On 25 September 1942 a company of 1,816 British PoWs marched from their prison camp at Hong Kong for transportation to Japan. Their embarkation aboard the *Lisbon Maru* was under the supervision of *Tsuyaku* Nimori, formerly the camp interpreter. The PoWs were divided into three holds: no. 1 (under the forecastle) held members of the Royal Navy; no. 2 (forward of the bridge) housed men from the 2nd Battalion Royal Scots, the 1st Battalion Middlesex Regiment and a number of smaller units; no. 3 (aft) housed (mostly) men of the Royal Artillery.

Also aboard the *Lisbon Maru* were 2,000 Japanese soldiers of *Chujo* Takashi Sakai's conquering 23rd Army. Sakai had forced the British garrison to surrender through Major-General C.M. Maltby on 25 December 1941. This shipment of soldiers and PoWs was dispatched on the orders of the new *Chiji* (governor) of Hong Kong, *Shosho* Rensuke Isogai.[8]

As the *Lisbon Maru* began her voyage the PoWs had adequate drinking water and passable food, but there were no washing facilities. Each unit worked out shifts whereby each man had allotted times for standing, sitting and lying down in the cramped conditions. At intervals the PoWs were allowed to go on deck to join the latrine queues.

Just before *tenko* on the morning of 1 October the ship was rocked by a loud explosion; the engines stopped and the lights went out. The PoWs did not know what had happened, but observed that the sentries at each hatch were doubled. The hatches were not battened down, but were covered with tarpaulin secured with ropes.

Through *Tsuyaku* Nimori, the senior British officer, Lieutenant-Colonel Stewart, repeatedly appealed for the hatches to be opened as the PoWs were suffocating. Further, the drinking water had run out. In response, *Tsuyaku* Nimori had a bucket of urine lowered into Stewart's hold. The men began to succumb more rapidly to the effects of their diphtheria in the foul conditions, and many fainted rapidly after beginning the forced labour of pumping out no. 3 hold, which was making water.

On the night of 2/3 October the Japanese troops of the 23rd Army were taken off the sinking *Lisbon Maru* and moved on to a transport tow vessel, while the PoWs remained in the crippled ship. Soon the *Lisbon Maru* began to settle more rapidly in the water and Lieutenant-Colonel Stewart supervised a small group trying to break out of the hold. As they worked the vessel came to a stop. Slowly a small aperture was made in one hatch and Lieutenants Potter and Howell squeezed through to the deck, together with a colleague who could speak Japanese. As they walked towards the bridge to request a parley with the captain, the Japanese guards opened fire on them. Howell died later of his wounds. Potter and the interpreter managed to scramble back to Stewart, reporting that the *Lisbon Maru* was now sinking even more rapidly.

As the prisoners regrouped once more in the hold, Japanese guards under *Tai-i* (Lieutenant) Wado poked their rifles into the hold and fired, killing two officers. As the cordite drifted away, the *Lisbon Maru* lurched violently and settled further into the sea at the stern. Water began to pour into no. 2 hold. Lieutenant G.C. Hamilton of the Royal Scots left this account of what happened next:

> As soon as the ship settled the men stationed at the hatch cut the ropes and the canvas tarpaulin, and forced away the baulks of timber, and the prisoners from my hold formed into queues and climbed out in perfect order.
>
> The men from the other two holds broke out at the same time, but many in the aftermost hold were trapped by the inrushing sea and drowned before they could get out.
>
> When we emerged on to the deck the Japanese opened fire at us, and continued firing after the men had jumped over the rails into the sea.
>
> When I came on to the deck there were no Japanese left on the ship at all, although when the first lot of prisoners reached it some half dozen guards were still there. All the prisoners in the three holds, who had not been suffocated or drowned, managed either to climb up on deck themselves or were hauled up by others.
>
> About three miles away I could see some islands and a swift current was running in their direction. Four Japanese ships were standing by,

but they appeared to be as inhospitable as the rocky islands for they showed no signs of wanting to pick up any of us. Ropes were dangling from these ships into the water but any prisoners who tried to climb up them were kicked back into the sea.

I stuck out for the islands, but after swimming for about half an hour I saw that the Japanese had changed their tune and were beginning to pick up the prisoners. Being still a long way from land I turned and swam for one of the Japanese ships. When I reached it someone threw me a rope and some of our own men helped me aboard. A few prisoners managed to reach the islands, but many were lost on the rocky coast.

There were a number of Chinese junks and sampans about. These had come from the islands. The Chinese in them picked up several of our men and treated them with great kindness, gave them food and clothing from their meagre supplies, and looked after them until the Japanese landing parties came to recover them.

The ship that picked me up was a small patrol vessel which carried on with its patrol for about three days and then put into Shanghai when the picked-up survivors were landed. There all the survivors were eventually assembled on the quayside. Many were completely naked and most of us only had shorts or a shirt. During the time I was on the patrol vessel we were kept on deck under a tarpaulin which leaked badly, and food consisted of four hard-tack biscuits and two small cups of watered milk per day, with bowl of soup on the third day. Two men died during this time . . .[9]

There is no doubt that the Japanese intended the remaining PoWs to drown, or die in the water. There were several more Japanese vessels in the area but none made a move to rescue PoWs until the Chinese started to drag the stricken men into their sampans. Only then did the Japanese act. Back in Japan the English language newspaper *Nippon Times* reported the *Lisbon Maru* sunk, with the inference that the Allies had killed their own servicemen.

On the morning of 5 October the Japanese assembled the survivors on the docks at Shanghai for a *tenko*: 970 men responded to their names, but as many as 840 failed to answer, including 6 who had escaped with the help of the Chinese. As the PoWs waited for onward transportation to Japan aboard the *Shinsei Maru*, they were starved, beaten and abused, their guards being goaded to excesses by the loathsome *Tsuyaku* Nimori.

The name *Tsuyaku* Nimori was soon to appear again. Months later he was aboard the hellship *Toyama Maru*, taking Canadian PoWs from Hong Kong to Japan. With him went his philosophy: *Kono shosen ni dorobo nezumi ga imasu. Bassuru.* ('There are thieving rats – ie, PoWs – aboard this ship. Punish.') Incensed that the PoWs were bartering sweaters – given to them by the Red Cross – for food among the Japanese guards, Nimori made an example of one opportunistic 'salesman', Rifleman Doucet of the Royal Rifles of Canada. Doucet died later at Marumi prison camp from the beating that Nimori and a *gocho* (corporal) gave him.[10]

OTHER CAUSES OF DEATHS AT SEA

Torture (thereby murder), starvation, suffocation and disease were the main causes of PoW and civilian deaths at the hands of the Japanese at sea. All of these were exacerbated by the slowness of hellships. Many of the PoWs transhipped were aboard freighters. By late 1942 the Imperial Japanese Navy's grip on the seas was slackening and PoW ships were forced to go more slowly, hugging coastlines and making many stops. Thus on 20 October 1942 the *Tottori Maru* set out from the Philippines bound for Pusan in Korea via Formosa. The journey took thirty days. More than a dozen PoW cadavers were thrown overboard and there was widespread illness. Eighty deaths were recorded on the *Dai Ichi Maru*, which set out on 30 October 1942, reaching Japan on 25 November.

Survivors of the *Maros Maru* told a harrowing tale. This vessel was one of the 'little ships' that island-hopped for protection against Allied air attacks. It plied the Moluccas and Java routes, but on one trip was stuck for forty days off Makassar. Aboard were 500 British and Dutch PoWs from Haruku and Ambon, along with another 150 men who had been 'rescued' from a hellship sunk by a PB4Y Liberator. Starving and parched, more and more PoWs started to hallucinate, while others were pushed over the edge of insanity by the daily cruelties. The PoWs began to die by the dozen.

To dispose of the bodies the Japanese ordered the ambulant PoWs to throw their dead fellows overboard. But most of the bodies, bloated, just floated. Some PoWs were then delegated to row out to the purple and yellow bodies, slit them open to release the putrifying gases, and then weight them with ballast so they would sink.

POW 'RESCUE', JAPANESE-STYLE

When a hellship was hit by 'friendly fire' and was sinking, the PoWs had a 50–50 chance that the Japanese would unbatten the holds to let them escape. Lesser odds were on offer for life jackets being available. Even if the PoWs made it over the side, there was little chance of being picked up by a Japanese lifeboat or liferaft. Some of the PoWs from the *Jun'yo Maru*, for instance, who tried to scramble aboard liferafts, had their heads sliced off by the raft *tosotsusha* (leader). If Japanese ships came to the aid of a stricken hellship it was solely to rescue Japanese personnel. Some PoWs were hauled on deck and shot for sport, while others were used for target practice (as on the *Lisbon Maru*). Some were just machine-gunned in the water, as witnessed in the *Shin'yo Maru* incident.

CHAPTER ONE

EARLY SHIPMENTS OF THE DAMNED

'A day which will live in infamy' was how US President Franklin Delano Roosevelt described the events that began at 07.55hrs on 7 December 1941 – when Pearl Harbor Striking Force Commander *Chujo* Chuichi Nagumo launched Japan's sudden and devastating attack on Pearl Harbor on Oahu, Hawaii. In all, 31 vessels and 432 planes took part in the attack. Back in Japan the government of *Taisho Sori-Daijin* Hideki Tojo hailed the event as *Shinjuwan Kogeki*. A total of 2,403 US Forces personnel and civilians were killed, half of them when the battleship USS *Arizona* blew up. The Japanese losses were logged by the *Rikugunsho* (Ministry of War) in Tokyo at around 60 personnel.[1]

Because of the time zones Japan's *Dai ni-ji Sekai Taisen* (Second World War) had already begun elsewhere. At 02.15hrs on the morning of 8 December 1941 advance troops of the Japanese 25th Army, led by *Taisho* Hirofumi Yamashita, landed at Kota Bharu on the east coast of Malay Peninsula, bent on seizing Singapore. This was more than an hour *before* the attack on Pearl Harbor Pacific Time. The landing was the next vital step in Japan's grand plan of *Hakko Ichiu* ('The World under One Roof'), and provided the means to make Japan an independent *Dai Nippon Teikoku* ('Empire of Great Japan').

When these attacks took place Japan had already been at war for four years on the mainland of China. Following the amputation of Manchuria from China in 1932 and the formation of the puppet state of *Manchuquo* under the quisling monarch Henry Pu Yi (the former Emperor of China), the Imperial Japanese Forces had conducted a large-scale rape, pillage and annexation of China proper. By 1941 a Japanese army in excess of a million strong occupied China's largest cities and huge swathes of the interior. Despite this the Chinese

National Government of General Chiang Kai-Shek (1887–1975) refused to sue for peace, so Japan was forced to keep pouring manpower and supplies into what was a bottomless pit.

Then as now, Japan was very heavily dependent on sources of minerals, petroleum and other raw materials outside its homeland. So Japan's *Hakko Ichiu* programme was intended to make China into an economic milch-cow, one of a whole herd of South-east Asian states keeping *Dai Toa Teikoku* alive and its satellites of the proposed *Dai Toa Kyozonken* in good health. Japan needed coal from Sakhalin, China, Korea and Manchuquo; oil from Borneo, Sumatra, Java and Burma; rubber from the Philippines, French Indo-China and Timor; and tin from Malaya and Siam (Thailand). To tap these resources, and exploit what coal and oil reserves could be found in the homeland, the Japanese needed a new work-force. This was to be drawn from the myriad prisoners who were surrendering to the Imperial Japanese Forces every day, and it would be a work-force based on *dorei-seido* (slavery). And so a new phase of administration began along the eastern edges of the 1920s Mandated Territories.

Wake Island is a 2,600-acre V-shaped atoll consisting of three islands, and it lies some 700 miles north of Kwajalein in the Marshall Islands. American territory since 1899, it played an important part in US military plans as a way station for aircraft en route to the Philippines. It was also an important reconnaissance base for monitoring the Japanese-held Marshall Islands.

Japan had been drawn into international affairs from the days of the First World War, when they fought on the Allied side against the Germany of Kaiser Wilhelm II. As a consequence of this cooperation Japan had won a permanent seat on the new League of Nations, established by the Treaty of Versailles on 29 June 1919. From that point, though, the Japanese had swerved away from peaceful expansion through trade and friendly diplomacy to outright military aggression. By the late 1930s confrontation with the West was growing and America in particular was aiming to keep one step ahead. Hence the importance of Wake Island.

Since early 1941 more than a thousand construction workers had grafted on gruelling shifts to transform the atoll into a military base. On Wake itself, the longest of the islands, the Americans constructed a

5,000ft-long runway. Meanwhile on Peale Island a seaplane base was scheduled, and on Wilkes Island there was to be a submarine base.

In the days before the Japanese attack on Pearl Harbor the Wake theatre was commanded by US Navy Commander Winfield Scott Cunningham, with a defence force of 450 men of the 1st Marine Defense Battalion under Major James P.S. Devereux, and a marine fighter squadron, VMF-211, under Major Paul A. Putnam. The whole command was seriously under strength. They possessed only a dozen anti-aircraft guns and had no radar for either fire-power control or warning systems. Their dozen FWF-3 Wildcat fighters were obsolete, and their pilots only desultorily trained to fly them.

The Japanese plan for the invasion of Wake was assigned to the Imperial Japanese Navy's 4th Mandates Fleet under the command of *Chujo* Shigeyoshi Inouye. His forces were responsible for defending Japan's possessions in the south-west and central Pacific. *Chujo* Inouye had a base at Kwajalein, the world's largest atoll, in the Ralik Chain, some 280 miles north-west of Majuro in the Marshall Islands. From this base Japanese bombers had already set out to 'soften up' the Wake defences at the time of the attack on Pearl Harbor.

As the Japanese bombers approached Wake, some of the US Wildcats were out on patrol. The aircraft missed one another because of the weather, but the remaining Wildcats were destroyed on the ground along with vital fuel supplies. Air raid followed air raid to destroy Wake's hospital and the fire control systems of some of the coastal defence guns. However, these remained substantially intact until the Japanese land invasion.

The Japanese commander of the 450-man Wake Island Invasion Force was *Shosho* Sadamichi Kajioka. His flagship, the 2,890-ton light cruiser *Yubari*, built in 1923, was escorted by a destroyer force and invasion transports.[2] The first attempt to land was made on 11 December. When the Japanese fleet was only 500 yards from the shore, Wake's 5-inch batteries opened fire. *Yubari* was forced to retreat in the blistering barrage as the 1925-built 1,270-ton destroyer *Hayate* was blown out of the water. This was the first Japanese surface warship to be lost in the Second World War. *Shosho* Kajioka ordered a withdrawal to Kwajalein under sustained fire from the four surviving Wildcats.

A second attack on Wake was now attempted with Kajioka's fleet reinforced by *Shosho* Hiroaki Abe's 8th Cruiser Squadron, ripe from its success in the Pearl Harbor attack. This time the Wake invasion was successful and on Tuesday 23 December 1941 Major J.P.S. Devereux surrendered the command to *Shosho* Kajioka.

In all, 1,600 Americans fell foul of the Imperial Japanese forces for the first time. It seems that the senior army officer leading the occupying force at Wake wanted a mass execution of survivors; *Shosho* Kajioka opposed him.[3] He had orders to take the new prisoners to Japan. Naked and bound, the American prisoners sat it out in their own filth as the Japanese built a barbed-wire pound for them on Wake airfield.

At last, when secured within the compound, the new PoWs were untied and left without food, shelter or water for 24 hours. On 25 December they were given water in 55-gallon drums and a little later some mouldy bread with a hint of jam from what had been the base kitchens was handed round. Groups were formed among the prisoners to bury the rotting dead, and those who worked were able to salvage a few small items which the looting Japanese soldiers had left behind in the old living quarters.

Testimony about the conditions on the first prisoner sea transports to Japan was given by Harry Jeffries and Oklahoma Atkinson. Both were ne'er-do-well building labourers who had worked on the base at Wake.

Some 1,300 of the American prisoners were given one hour's notice, on 11 January, that they were to move to the shore to be shipped out of Wake. Rumour spread like wildfire that their destination was mainland Japan. As they waited, the men were handed out copies of the *Kisoku no furyo* (Regulations for PoWs). *Shikei* (the death penalty) was promised for a dozen or so offences, ranging from disobeying orders to talking without permission, and from raising the voice to Japanese personnel to walking about restricted areas. The Regulations went on to promise 'good treatment' to all who obeyed the rules of the Imperial Japanese Navy, or cooperated in constructing any part of the *Dai Toa Kyozonken*.

As the men gathered on the beach the Japanese guards searched each prisoner individually, confiscating anything that had been retained. All the best pickings, from Rolex watches to Parker pens, had long since been filched, now pathetically guarded combs, pencils, photographs and coins were all removed. The prisoners were then taken by lighter over the choppy seas to a navy vessel standing offshore. Jostled, kicked, beaten and bayoneted, the prisoners painfully scrambled up the rope ladders leading to the heaving deck. Once on board they were searched once more by the Japanese *suifu* (seamen). When the new guards found that the prisoners had already been picked clean there were more beatings to endure. The shuffling line of prisoners was pushed between rows of ratings who beat them with heavy 4ft-long bamboo staves as they moved along. Blows rained down on them as the prisoners were hustled into forward cargo holds until all 1,300 men were battened down.

The prisoners' new home was a 1939-built Japanese liner, the 17,830-ton *Nitta Maru* of the *Nippon Yusen Kaisha* (Japan Mail Steamship Company) shipping line. Her log-book recorded that she had won, and still held, the trans-Pacific speed record.[4] But for the prisoners it was to be no luxury cruise. They were packed in to suffocation point and anyone caught moving was beaten. At last their transport got under way, but the air remained foul and the heat unbearable.

Drinking water was refused, but the thirsty prisoners nearest the ship's metal sides were able to lick the moisture condensing on the metal from sweating bodies and foetid breath. Every 24 hours buckets of thin *miso-shiru* (in this case a poor soup made with inferior rice), infrequently with slivers of *tsukemono* (pickled vegetables), were lowered into the hold. Occasionally too, rotting *tai* (sea bream) was added. Many prisoners had developed dysentery while still on Wake, and as conditions aboard the *Nitta Maru* worsened so did the dysentery and other ailments. Many prisoners too weak to move lay in their own filth. There was an *eiseitai* (medical unit) aboard the ship but the *Kaigun Shikan Itakuteki* (Navy Medical Officer) refused to treat prisoners whether they were wounded or sick.

Slowly the hot conditions in the ship's holds cooled as the vessel moved across the North Pacific deep into Japanese waters. After a week or so the *Nitta Maru* and her helpless cargo arrived at the Japanese main island of Honshu to dock at the snow-covered port of Yokohama. Here at the *chinjufu* (naval district) of the 1st Naval District of the Japanese Empire, the vessel tied up for coaling and supplies. To celebrate their return to the sacred soil of Japan, the ratings opened the hatches and pelted the freezing prisoners with snowballs.[5]

The *Nitta Maru* left Yokohama the following morning, and a few days later a new form of horror was introduced. Already the prisoners had got used to a selected few of their number being taken from the hold to be interrogated, while others had judo throws practised on them by the ratings. The more observant among the prisoners noticed how the chosen men always seemed to include red-headed victims. There is something about red hair that triggers both fear and loathing in the Japanese psyche; when the Japanese think of demons and hobgoblins they always picture them with red hair. So those with red, or golden, hair always seemed to suffer the worst in Japanese camps and hellships. Even so, this time the selections were to be different.

On this particular occasion five men were picked out. They were taken on deck and lined up in front of a crowd of Japanese naval personnel. The commander of the prisoner detail stepped forward, while a group of *kashikan* (petty officers) fell in behind him, swords in hand. The commander, *Chu-i* Toshio Saito, pulled a paper from his pocket and recited in Japanese a terrifying dirge that was to be repeated to prisoners wherever they were captured in the Japanese Empire:

> You have murdered many Japanese soldiers.
> For what you have done you will now suffer death.
> It is the just recompense of the Japanese people.
> You are here as representatives of the [US Navy] and will die.
> You can now pray to be happy in the next world.[6]

To which he added: 'When you are born again I hope you will become peace-loving citizens.'

Finishing, *Chu-i* Saito bowed and the *kashikan* stepped forward. *Tokumu socho* (Warrant Officer) Yoshimura was selected to behead the first prisoner, who was blindfolded and forced to his knees on a small *tatami* (straw mat). It took three blows for Yoshimura to sever the American's head. Next to step forward was *Kashikan* Takamura, who severed his prisoner's head with one blow. He was followed by Chief *Kashikan* Kohara, who left this record of his actions:

> [*Chu-i* Saito] called out '*Gocho*'. I answered '*Hai*' [yes]. I was scared and shaking. I stepped forward to where the third American prisoner

of war was kneeling on the deck. I raised my sword to strike him. Being unable to bring myself to deliver the stroke, I lowered my sword. I opened my eyes, and I saw the red hair above the eye bandage. As *Chu-i* Saito was standing right beside me and had ordered me to do this duty I raised my sword again and attempted to strike. A second time I could not, so I lowered my sword once more.

Then realising that I was acting on orders from the *Tenno* [Emperor], I closed my eyes, raised my sword and brought it down . . . When I opened my eyes the body of the American prisoner was lying at my feet. His head severed from his body. I had carried out *Chu-i* Saito's orders.[7]

The assembled navy and army personnel applauded as each head hit the deck. Following the last execution the corpses were used for bayonet practice. In the officers' mess that evening, *Chu-i* Saito celebrated with libations of *sake* (rice wine) to salute the Emperor and rewarded the executioners with watches and jewellery taken from the prisoners.[8]

On 23 January 1942 the *Nitta Maru* docked at the Chinese port of Shanghai. When Japan had declared war, this former International City, secured for them earlier by *Shireichokan* of the Central China Area Army *Chujo* Iwane Matsui – the infamous 'Butcher of Nanking' – was sealed off. The port was to have been the scene of a triumphal march of defeated western PoWs to show the Chinese that their Japanese neighbours were omnipotent. The winter of 1941/2, however, had been savage and the Japanese garrison commanders at Shanghai could not guarantee that the Chinese would turn out to see the spectacle. Instead the *Nitta Maru* steamed up the Huangpu Jiang (then known to westerners as the Whangpoo River) to Woosung. Under naval armed guard the freezing prisoners were marched the 5 miles to the Shanghai War Prisoners Camp. The first slave-labour gangs had been safely delivered, courtesy of the Imperial Japanese Navy.

From the beginning of 1942 a definite policy of slave-labour recruitment among PoWs was in place. For instance, on 6 July 1942 *Shokan* Maraharu Yamada was sent from Kuching HQ, Borneo, to Changi prison, Singapore, to select likely workers. From Lieutenant-Colonel A.W. Walsh's Australian 2/10 Battalion he selected 1,500 personnel and boarded them on the 5,859-ton (coal) cargo vessel *Ume Maru*, built at Kawasaki in 1919. In three cramped holds they began a slow journey via Miri to Sandakan in Borneo. There the PoWs were set to work on the airfield and road system of Sandakan port. The hellship *Ume Maru* was subsequently torpedoed by USS *Seahorse* on 3 November 1943.

The Japanese Government also saw the propaganda value of these early shipments of PoWs. On 4 March 1942 *Taisho* Seishiro Itagaki, Commander of the *Chosen* Army, sent this telegram to the *Rikugunsho*:

As it would be very effective in stamping out the respect and admiration of the Korean people for Britain and America, and also in establishing in them a strong faith in [our] victory, and as the Governor-General [*Taisho* Jiro Minami] and the Army are both strongly desirous of it, we wish you would intern 1,000 British and 1,000 American prisoners of war in Korea. *Yoko kangaete kudasai . . .* Kindly give this matter special attention.

The *Rikugunsho* replied that the required number of *shiroi* (white) PoWs would be so recruited.

It is known that 1,100 PoWs were loaded on the 3,829-ton British-built cargo vessel *Fukkai Maru* at Singapore for this very purpose. Travelling via Takao, where the prisoners were forced to load and unload cargo, the *Fukkai Maru* landed at Pusan in Korea. An anonymous British soldier left this record of the incident:

As they disembarked [from *Fukkai Maru*] the prisoners were sprayed with disinfectant, photographed by Japanese pressmen and then mustered on the wharf for inspection of kit by the *Kempeitai*. During the inspection watches, wedding and signet rings and personal photographs were taken by the *Kempeitai* and never returned to their owners.

After the search, all prisoners, including those who were sick, were made to fall in, in columns of four, and were marched round the streets of Pusan between the marshalled Korean inhabitants of the city, with the Japanese officer at the head of the column on horseback and Japanese guards on either side.

The *Kempeitai* were reckoned to have amassed a crowd of 120,000 Koreans and 57,000 Japanese nationals to view the spectacle. The anonymous PoW continues:

> The march went on all day under a hot sun with only two halts in the playgrounds of two schools where the children were allowed to come close up to the prisoners to jeer and spit at them.
>
> The march ended about 5pm at the railway station where each prisoner was given a small oblong box containing cold boiled rice, a piece of dried fish and a few pieces of pickled cucumber. They were allowed to eat this on the platform as it was the first meal they had eaten since 8am. Before entering the train each man was given another similar box of food to last the next 24 hours which was to be spent on the train from Pusan to Seoul.
>
> On arrival at Seoul the prisoners were again marched round part of the town before finally entering the prisoner of war camp which was to be their home for the next two years. As a result of this propaganda march, and the long train journey on starvation rations, several of the prisoners died a few days after arriving at Seoul.

The proceedings were carefully recorded by an army film crew as propaganda films to be shown all over the area of the *Dai Toa Kyozonken*. The boxes mentioned were the traditional Japanese *bento* lunch boxes which were often issued on the hellships instead of organising PoW galleys. The boxes were loaded in advance and often rancid.

As the pattern of PoW transhipment began to settle, PoWs were soon to realise that their captors' organisation of the hellships was incompetent. Shipments were regularly disrupted by bad weather, chaotic loading and unloading, and poor administration. The Japanese high command now began to look for technical experts among the PoWs to work for the *Dai ichi* (no. 1) great plan of Japanese suzerainty of the East. For example, after the fall of Corregidor on 6 May 1942 to *Chujo* Masaharu Homma, personnel of Captain Alfred B. Dreher's 440th Ordnance Company were gathered up and boarded on the 6,780-ton, 1919-built passenger-cargo vessel *Tamahoko Maru* (ex-*Yone Maru*) for the short trip to Manila and transhipment to the 5,973-ton

Clyde-built *Tottori Maru* of the NYK Line, built in 1913. Here they merged with other PoWs to form a 'technical skills work-force' of around 1,930 men and 31 officers bound for the Manchuquo Machine Tool Company.

Tottori Maru was also carrying Japanese service personnel who had been arrested by the *Kempeitai* for various misdemeanours. The PoWs were now able to witness at first hand how the Japanese treated their own. A number of Japanese prisoners jumped into the sea to certain suicide rather than face the shame of court-martial. Bad weather was to cause disruption to the ship's planned routes, and the PoWs had to endure the foul weather mostly on deck. But for a while their predicament was eased when Korean forced labour scoured the ship of its urine and excrement while she was in dock at Takao.

Tottori Maru docked at Pusan on 9 November. Most of the PoWs were sent north to Mukden in Manchuquo, while the rest were transported to Moji to work in chemical plants and steelworks. *Tottori Maru* is known to have been torpedoed in the Gulf of Thailand by USS *Hammerhead* on 15 May 1945.

The very last of the early shipments to Japan began on 28 November 1942. The Japanese had amassed a group of some 2,200 American, Australian, Dutch and British prisoners at Singapore. Their hellship was the Yokohama Dock Company's 1930-built 17,256-ton *Kamakura Maru*. Now owned by NYK, the vessel was the former *Chichibu Maru*. The ship was so overloaded, some said with pillaged goods from occupied territories, that the PoWs had to remain on deck. Much hardship was suffered when the vessel moved from the tropics into storms of sleet. Several Dutch PoWs died from pneumonia. On 7 December 1942 the *Kamakura Maru* docked at Nagasaki.

As 1942 came to a close hellships were regularly attached to convoys. On 21 December, for instance, an eleven-ship convoy was mustered at Shanghai to form the *Dai-roku-bamme GO*. This was a Transportation Operation numbered 6. Among the vessels was a hellship, the 5,289-ton *Panama Maru*. She carried some 130 Chinese PoWs destined for the construction gangs at Truk. This transhipment also brought to light the transportation of non-Caucasian PoWs.

The first British War Crimes Trial to be held in the Far East highlights the early transportation of non-Caucasian PoWs. Known colloquially as the 'Gozawa Trial', it began on Monday 21 January 1946 at the Supreme Court Buildings, Singapore, with Lieutenant-Colonel Leon George Coleman, Solicitor of the Supreme Court of Judiciary, as President. The trial proceedings included testimony concerning the hellship *Thames Maru*, which sailed on its slave-labour journey from Singapore on 5 May 1943.[9]

The *Thames Maru* was a 5,000-ton military transport vessel with an estimated passenger manifest of around 3,000 men, whose destination was the island of Babelthuap, the largest of the Palau Islands, some 600 miles north of New Guinea. Here, in modern Belau, the Japanese were to lose 13,600 personnel in the final battle. The passengers comprised 2,000 Indian and 150 Indonesian PoWs, the personal staff of *Shosa* Suzi and 61 men of the Imperial Japanese Army's 7th Special Service Company, the *Gozawa Butain*. The PoWs were bound for the Yamato work-camp on Babelthuap, to toil on road-making, aerodrome construction and the loading and unloading of war supplies. This was an early example of the misuse of PoW labour by the Japanese.

The *Gozawa Butai* was commanded by *Tai-i* Sadaichi Gozawa, with his three section leaders *Sho-is* Ryuichi Kajino, Ryoichi Seki and Kaniyuki Nakamura. At Surabaya *Thames Maru* took on further passengers, including *Tai-i* Ken Okusawa as Medical Officer for the *Gozawa Butai*. This quartet were to be key prosecutees in the trial of 1946.

The Indian PoWs were made up of members of the 1st Battalion of the Hyderabad Infantry of the Indian States Forces. The Gozawa Trial brought to the western public's wider attention the presence of Indian soldiers in Singapore. Following the fall of Singapore, the Japanese endeavoured to recruit Indians for their new Indian National Army. The Indians were promised 'liberation' from British rule with the help of the Japanese Government when Japan won the war.[10] Those who refused to join were beaten and tortured. Thus the Japanese authorities did not consider the Indians aboard *Thames Maru* to be PoWs. Instead they were dubbed members of the *Heiho*, 'volunteers' who collaborated with the Japanese.

Thames Maru's voyage to Babelthuap lasted one month and four days, with meagre accommodation, bedding, water, food (rice and rotten *daikon*) and practically no hygiene. There were two *benjo* for 2,000

PoWs.[11] Dysentery was rife and a considerable number of PoWs died during and immediately after the voyage.

These appalling conditions and resulting deaths were a major part of the case for the prosecution in the eleven-day Gozawa Trial, led by Lieutenant-Colonel Robert Stephen Lazarus and Captain Alan Ashton Hibbert, although the whole case also concerned overworking, murder by flogging of eight PoWs, starvation and general maltreatment of PoWs. The charges also included the illegal execution by beheading of an Indian PoW without trial. The responsibility for the conditions aboard the *Thames Maru* were ascribed to *Tai-i* Gozawa by the prosecution witnesses.

The defence was conducted by Lieutenant-Colonel Stuart Colin Sleeman and Major Alan Fairbairn, and the trial duly took its course. The outcome resulted in *Sho-i* Nakamura being condemned to death; he was executed by hanging on Thursday 14 May 1946. *Tai-i* Gozawa was sentenced to twelve years' imprisonment, and *Sho-i* Okusawa to two years. *Sho-i* Nakamura was the first war criminal to be sentenced to death and the *Thames Maru* was the first hellship to be mentioned in a war crimes trial. This gave it international publicity.

Records at the *Rikugunsho* in Tokyo begin to show the first entries for hellships in 1941–2. During this period, fifty-four vessels had carried just under 50,000 PoWs. The death rate among prisoners was calculated at 4.5 per cent. Hellship losses amounted to only two, *Montevideo Maru* and *Lisbon Maru*. In the margin of his briefing *Kaigun-daijin Taisho* Shigetaro Shimada pencilled the calligraphy for *manzoku-na*, 'satisfactory'.

CHAPTER TWO

WORKERS FOR THE DIVINE EMPEROR

Some 1,200 men were captured by the Japanese in the Netherlands East Indies (Java) following the Dutch C.-in-C. General ter Poorten's surrender of the island to the Japanese 16th Army. The deaths of scores of these PoWs while being shipped to Japan at the end of October 1942 formed a test case for the *Rikugunsho*. The ministry was greatly dismayed at the loss of potential slave-workers for the Japanese war effort. Accordingly, on 10 December 1942 they issued *Rikugun (Ajiya) Himitsu-no-kunrei* (Army Asia Secret Order) 1504:

> Recently, during the transportation of prisoners of war to Japan, many of them have been taken ill or have died, and quite a few of them have been incapacitated for further work due to their treatment on the journey, which at times was inadequate.[1]

The order emphasised that all prisoners should arrive 'in a condition to perform work'.

However, as the order had been issued by the *Rikugunsho* and not the *Kaigunsho*, the Imperial Japanese Navy officers on the sea transportation runs took little notice. On 3 March 1944 deaths had become so prevalent that *Rikugun Daijin Chujo* Kyoji Tominaga sent an order to 'all units concerned' which contained these observations:

> In announcements by the *Furyo Gunsei* [PoW Administration] the use of prisoners for labour has already been stressed. Although this has directly helped to increase our fighting strength, the average prisoner of war's health condition is hardly satisfactory. Their high death rate must again be brought to your attention. In the light of the recent

intensified enemy propaganda warfare, if the present conditions continue to exist, it will be impossible for us to expect world opinion to be what we would wish it.

But in any event, it is absolutely necessary to improve the condition of the prisoners of war from the point of view of using them satisfactorily to increase our fighting strength. It should be added that although efforts must be made to utilise the space in ships for transporting war prisoners, it is necessary that the purport of 'Army Asia Secret Order no. 1504' of 1942 be thoroughly understood in handling war prisoners at this juncture.[2]

The prisoners in the earlier test case had been embarked on the 5,800-ton cargo vessel *Singapore Maru* under *Sencho* Yoshimara Nishimi, and had begun their journey at Singapore. At the trial of *Sencho* Nishimi for war crimes the senior British officer on board, Lieutenant-Colonel E.R. Scott, testified that prisoners began to die as soon as the overcrowded ship left port. At Cap St Jacques (Saigon) he had requested that all sick prisoners be disembarked. His request was ignored by Nishimi, who did nothing to improve sanitation, food or medical supplies.

On arrival at Takao in Formosa, Scott made a further request that one hundred sick prisoners be taken ashore. Nishimi indicated that he would allow some twenty to disembark, but in a cruel twist the hated British must choose who should win the disembarkation lottery.

At this point another 600 Imperial Japanese Army passengers joined the *Singapore Maru*; this brought the number of Japanese troops on board to 1,200. The journey continued into Japanese home waters, through the *Bungo Suido* into the *Seto Naikai* and Moji. Here, with the authority of the land commander, *Sencho* Nishimi was to allow eighteen PoWs, again selected by lottery, to go to hospital.

James McEwan remembers what happened. He was an Intelligence Officer with 36 and 100 RAF Squadrons, then flying Vickers Vildebeest MkII torpedo-bombers operating out of Seletar air base, north of the island of Singapore. He served also at Air HQ at Sime Road, Singapore, and on the night of 10 February he flew to Batavia (modern Jakarta) with secret papers. When Allied resistance in Java collapsed he was captured along with 1,200 men of the RAF and RAAF. They were assembled at Makasura camp, some 6 miles south of Batavia. The Japanese divided the PoWs into three groups. McEwan's group was shipped out to Singapore on the coaster *Yoshida Maru* on 21 October 1942, to join the hellship *Singapore Maru*.

As Orderly Officer of the Day, McEwan had gone to the British adjutant aboard *Singapore Maru* for his duties the morning after the ship dropped anchor in Moji roads. There he was informed that the Japanese had agreed to let eighteen men go to hospital. As there were thirty PoWs in the ship's bilges 'in a pretty bad way', they were the selected group for the eighteen passes issued by the Japanese. The passes, by the by, were yellow tabs like luggage labels. Reluctant to condemn twelve men to probable death by failing the lottery selection, McEwan went below with an orderly sergeant. He was horrified by what he encountered:

Climbing down the narrow companion-way to the bilges we were met by a heavy, sickening stench which was drifting upwards. When we got to the door the sergeant clicked forward the button of his torch and thrust it into my hand.

'Have a good look round first,' he warned, 'before you go in!'

I moved the probing yellow beam across the floor of the low-roofed bilges, trying to make out what was there. As I did so I became aware of a soft, swilling sound which made me stop. Across the stationary beam of the torch there passed a low but very definite brown wave which was urged on by the gentle rocking of the vessel on its keel.

'It's *benjo* [human waste]', explained the sergeant, seeing my bewilderment. 'The volunteers used to come down and empty the *benjo* buckets. But now they're all flat on their backs themselves and there's nobody to come. Not that it would matter much anyway for the buckets were too full and capsized. That's what's on the floor.'

Slowly I moved the beam across the floor, looking along the narrow wedge of light. From side to side, in time with the ship's motion, swilled a shallow surge of ordure. A few wooden buckets were at the back, all lying on their side. Between them and me lay the men, their clothing, the blankets which one or two of them possessed, everything about them saturated with the vile sludge. Some had a shirt and shorts; some had only a pair of shorts. A few were naked, apart from a singlet. Most likely they had fallen from a bucket when the ship rolled, and being too weak to pull up their shorts had let them slip off. The faces of most were blotched and polluted where soiled hands had touched them. Swallowing my horror, I turned the beam of the torch on the sheet of paper in my hand and ran my eyes down the names . . .[3]

Sick at heart McEwan made the 'hateful selection'.

Soon after docking the Japanese authorities ordered that all fit men were to muster on deck. The *tenko* was recorded thus:

PoWs aboard *Singapore Maru* at embarkation:	1,080
Disembarked sick at Takao, Formosa:	29
Died on board and buried at sea:	62
Left sick on vessel:	280
Mustered on deck:	709
	1,080

By January 1943 127 of the remaining men had died of malnutrition, dysentery or pellagra.[4]

As the war steadily turned against the Japanese the once rigid obedience to orders among Imperial Japanese Services officers was becoming more lax. Order no. 1504 therefore did not help the PoWs aboard another hellship, the *Maros Maru*. At the beginning of September 1944 Allied aircraft attacked Ambon, an island in the Molucca group, south of the Philippines. The prison camp of Weijami on Amboina Island was within the remit of *Chusa* Anami, who decided to move some 500 British and Dutch prisoners aboard the 600-ton former Dutch vessel *Maros Maru*, which the Japanese Navy had salvaged after it had been scuttled in 1942. It was now crewed by Javanese, under the command of *Chu-i* Kurishima.

The senior officer of the PoWs was Flight-Lieutenant W.M. Blackwood RAF, who left this account in the form of an affidavit at the International Military Tribunal in Tokyo:

On the morning of embarkation it rained for the first time for many days. My party marched barefoot, some had wooden sandals, in a glutinous sea of liquid mud which covered the sharp coral surface of the road. With guards harassing us to hurry, the beri-beri crippled being pushed and bullied, and the stretcher-bearers being goaded into a shambling trot, we made the jetty in about half an hour. There the stretchers were laid in the mud, fully exposed to the pitiless rain, although there were some empty huts available close by. After everybody was soaked, a few straw mats were produced and draped over those who were the most ill, and whose delirious groans fell without response upon the ears of our guards.

After a wait of nearly three hours, barges were brought alongside and we were ferried across the creek to where our transport lay at anchor.

When we drew alongside I could scarcely believe that all five hundred of us were expected to get aboard. When I realised that the holds were full and battened down, and we were to travel as deck passengers, I was staggered.

First of all the baggage was dumped on the hatch covers and an attempt was made to distribute the fit men, walking patients, and stretcher cases in the gangways and narrow deck spaces. The effect was like a London tube train in the rush hour. No level space could be found for the stretchers, and the sick men were subjected to acute discomfort, and an ordeal which it was at once obvious they could not sustain for a long sea passage. After protest, the baggage was removed from the hatch covers, but settling into this terribly cramped space with sodden kit bags was almost impossible.

Worse was to come. Firewood for the cookhouse fires on the voyage was brought alongside. Picture a small ferry boat, with a maximum beam of not more than 30 feet, and a space of about 45 feet from the after bulkhead of the forecastle to just abaft amidships, available for our whole party. The remainder of the deck, all the decks works and housings were out of bounds, so the measure of the overcrowding can be gauged. When the firewood had been brought on board and stacked the deck space was full to the gunwale . . . two wooden boxes slung over the ship's sides were all the latrine accommodation provided. Into these boxes our palsied men had to drag themselves after climbing over piles of wood, a journey fraught with difficulty for a fit man, let alone one who was ill.[5]

Through rough seas the *Maros Maru* made an erratic passage, with prisoners bearing the brunt of the conditions. Only after thirty had died were they allowed any shelter on deck. Drinking water was strictly rationed, but the PoWs watched helpless as the Korean guards showered with drums of drinking water. When one prisoner fell overboard, the officers and NCOs among the PoWs were lined up and beaten for not being more diligent in their discipline. The *Dai Shigoto* (Great Work, or Mission) of the Emperor had been thwarted by the ship having to be stopped to pick him up.

On 21 September *Maros Maru* docked at Raha Moenu Island in the Celebes. A Japanese freighter drew alongside and some 150 prisoners, under Captain van der Loot, clambered aboard the hellship with difficulty. Mostly Dutch and British, the new prisoners were naked and many were already incapacitated with beri-beri. These men were a nuisance to the Divine Emperor's warriors; they had been saved from the sea when a Consolidated Liberator had bombed and sunk their Japanese transport, and they were to repay their saviours by grafting for the *Dai Shigoto*.

Conditions on the *Maros Maru* worsened. There was now hardly any room to stand, let alone sit. Blackwood takes up the story again:

All the men lay spread out on the uneven bundles of firewood, blistering horribly in the tropical sun. Tongues began to blacken, raw shirtless shoulders to bleed, and all vestige of sanity deserted many. The night air was filled with the yells and screams of the dying, the curses of the worn-out trying to get some sleep, and the chronic hiccoughing that afflicts a man about to die from beri-beri.

Scenes of indescribable horror became commonplace. Picking their way through the tangled mass of humanity lying about on the narrow ship, orderlies carried the naked wasted bodies of the dead to the ship's side where, unheard except by those on the spot, the burial service for those who die at sea was read before casting the body with its sandbag overboard. One youngster, delirious with sunstroke, shouted the thoughts of his disordered mind for thirty hours before he became too weak to utter another word. Just before he died he grabbed a full tin that was being used as a bed-pan and drank the contents greedily, thinking it was water, before he could be prevented.[6]

As the *Maros Maru* touched the north end of the Gulf of Boni her elderly engines gave up. Frustrated by the fact that none of the Japanese personnel or Javanese crew had much engineering experience, *Chu-i* Kurishima of the PoW detail appealed to the prisoners to help make essential repairs. Realising that the death rate was escalating to eight per day at sea, a trio of PoWs led by Petty Officer Platt RN volunteered to repair and supervise the engines until the voyage was over.

Maros Maru reached Makassar safely and remained in harbour for forty days, while those PoWs who were fit enough unloaded the cargo. Food supplies for the PoWs improved but while the ship was at Makassar forty prisoners a day died. To the PoWs' despair, *Maros Maru* hove to for another forty days, with a further ninety deaths. All the while *Chu-i* Kurishima and his command treated the PoWs with unremitting bestiality. Blackwood attested to this:

One night, as a sick Dutchman lay dying, he began hiccoughing loudly at regular intervals. *Gunso* Mori appeared on the bridge and threatened to beat all sick men unless the dying man was given an injection to keep him quiet. This was done but within half an hour he was awake again and hiccoughing as before. *Gunso* Mori repeated his threat and another injection was given. Yet a third time the hiccoughing started. The [*Gunso*] came back on to the bridge and, yelling at the top of his voice, threatened to come down and lay about him with a stick among the stretcher cases. A third injection was given but the Dutchman was never heard again for he died.[7]

Sixty-seven days out of Amboina *Maros Maru* docked at Surabaya, Java. In all, 320 human beings had survived – half-starved, half-demented, filthy and crawling with vermin – to work as slaves for the Emperor's *Dai Shigoto*.

Yorkshireman Eric S. Cooper remembers his journey on a hellship to slave-labour in Japan. Cooper was serving in the RAF at Seletar in Singapore when the Japanese offensive began with the invasion of north-east Malaysia in December 1941. Seletar airfield was a regular target for bombings and strafings by Mitsubishi A6M *Reisen* Zeros. As the Imperial Japanese Army made its unstoppable advance across Singapore, Cooper and other RAF personnel effected an escape in a river gunboat on 12 February 1942. They made it to Sumatra and Batavia, only to be stranded in Java. Cooper was stricken with a burst appendix and was operated on at a hospital in Bandung. From there, with a group of RAF personnel, he made a run for the south coast of Java, where they hoped to find the American cruiser USS *Houston*. By that time, however, *Houston* had been sunk in the Sunda Strait. En route they ran into the advancing Japanese and were captured, and taken to Boei Glodok Prison in Batavia. From there they were marched to Tandjong Priok docks and shipped to Singapore to await hellship transport to Japan.

From their billets in the former barracks of the Royal Engineers at Changi, Cooper and his fellow prisoners were loaded into trucks and taken to the docks at Singapore. There they were boarded on to a small tramp-steamer called *Dai Ichi Maru*. Despite its name Cooper found a small metal plate on its bulkhead, which read 'Built in Glasgow, 1903'.[8] The crew comprised Japanese Merchant Navy sailors, while the guards were all Imperial Japanese Army men.

Cooper remembers well the embarkation horrors. A rain of blows descended on the men as they mounted the gangways; the usual Japanese method to encourage *speedo* (haste). Once on board Cooper received his first glimpse, as hundreds before him had, of their billet in the hold. Men descended to sit back to back in the shelved hold to allow the sick to lie down. Cooper recalls:

> The nauseous stench of bilges, and men with dysentery, was abominable.
> There was not only the normal or abnormal sickness to contend with, but there were also bugs dropping occasionally from the wooden deck above.
> If this was not enough, men who had the misfortune to be pushed to the steel sides of the ship were pestered with rats running over

bodies and outstretched limbs, disappearing through holes and cracks on to another deck to make more men's lives a misery.

As the ship got under way, it seemed that the engines were reverberating through every little part of the ship. Even our bodies appeared to shake in unison, with the clankety clank of machinery.

The rattling and clanging, the labouring of the ship convinced us we would never reach Japan.

Either the ship would founder or sink, or we would never be able to withstand the terrible torment that we were in . . .

Many prisoners had uncontrollable bowels and it was a daily task to deal with excrement lying on deck . . . A man would shout to a guard on the main deck, who would require ten men to visit the [lavatories]. We staggered up on deck and were beckoned to the stern . . .

Over the side, and lashed to the rails of the ship, was a long box affair, about 10 feet long, and 5 feet high. In the floor was an opening 6 inches wide running the length of the [lavatories]. We had to squat over the opening and do what was necessary. The effluent was washed away into the sea. Accompanied by a guard, snarling obscenities, visiting the [lavatories] was a major feat, as one could fall overboard in a flash . . .[9]

The hellship in which Cooper and his comrades were embarked was to take three weeks to travel the 3,000 miles from Singapore via Saigon and Formosa to Shimonoseki. As slave-labour they were then sent by train via Sendai to Aomori and Hakodate PoW camp – in the northernmost main island of Japan – to work in the coke plants and cement quarries. Of the 600 who embarked, 250 survived. The dead had been unceremoniously dumped in the sea.[10]

The 5,000-ton Japanese supply ship *674 King Kong Maru* was another slave-labour hellship. Testimony of its infamy comes from Rohan D. Rivett (1917–77), who was working as a war correspondent in Singapore when Lieutenant-General Arthur Percival, GOC Malaya, capitulated the British forces to *Taisho* Tomoyuki Yamashita's 25th Army on 15 February 1942.

Rivett had been released from the Australian Imperial Forces in late 1941 to allow him to work as the news editor of the Malayan

Broadcasting Corporation. He escaped from Singapore on a patrol boat and made a hazardous journey in a rowing boat down the west coast of Sumatra, only to be captured in western Java.[11]

From prison camp in Batavia, one of several under the control of *Chujo* Masatoshi Saito, Rivett and the other 1,500 prisoners, mainly from the AIF 7th Division and Corps troops, were marched into Batavia's main port of Tandjong Priok, northern Java, on 8 October 1942. They were bound for work on the infamous Burma Railway. After a *tenko* of prisoners in front of their waiting hellship, 189 men were placed in no. 1 Hold, already packed with Bren guns, 744 in no. 2 Hold, and 567 in no. 3 Hold. Not all prisoners had enough space to sit and most had no room to sleep unless lying on other bodies. All were to remain in the holds for a stretch of 96 hours. There was a liquid allowance of 1½ pints of *o-cha* (Japanese green tea) per man per day. Three times a day buckets of *gohan* (cooked rice) and soya soup with *oka-daikon* (common radish) were lowered into each hold. The 1,500 PoWs shared the small box latrines located on the starboard side of the vessel.[12]

King Kong Maru wove its way through shipping crippled by bombing and sabotage to arrive at Rhea Archipelago. Here, after several hours at anchor, the vessel moved into Keppel Harbour, Singapore, on 11 October. The prisoners were allowed on deck to look across to the nearby Blakangmati Island and the beaches where hundreds of Chinese nationals had been massacred after the fall of Singapore. The prisoners were then taken off the vessel and transported to a holding camp until 14 October, when they went back to Singapore Harbour for their first sight of their new hellship, the Japanese supply vessel *722 Maebashi Maru*.

This time Rivett was one of 650 prisoners crammed into a hold 75ft by 40ft. They climbed down a 40ft ladder into a hold already full of the gear of the Japanese troops occupying the upper decks. In this sweat-box the prisoners languished for the following 54 hours as the *Maebashi Maru* lay at anchor in Keppel Harbour. Soon all the PoWs stripped to the skin because of the infernal heat. At last, on 16 October 1942, the vessel weighed anchor and turned northwards up the Molucca Strait. Those who had a good sense of direction knew they were bound for Burma.

The Japanese vessel's captain allowed a group of prisoners on deck for 20 to 30 minutes at dawn and dusk. Any who tried to seek water for washing were beaten by Japanese guards. Once in ten days a deck hose was turned on for the 650 men to wash. Latrines were basic and inadequate. The meat supplied to augment the Japanese rice and fish-soup diet consisted of Australian mutton carcasses looted from Singapore Cold Stores. Stamped with the dates 1931 and 1935 the carcasses were soon rotten in the vessel's unrefrigerated conditions.

From time to time the Japanese crew and guards indulged in orgies of PoW beating; reasons for these 'punishments' were deemed unnecessary. Psychologically the PoWs suffered too, as they were travelling through waters in which British submarines were known to be operating; their unmarked vessel was a sitting duck.

As labourers were unloading the Japanese gear on arrival at Burma, Rivett noticed Japanese taskmasters using Burmese and Tamil work-gangs. Lines of them, manacled together, were moving railway rails from the *Yingata Maru*. The workers were continually beaten as they toiled; it was a scene out of the worst torture nightmare. The *Yingata Maru* was to be the PoWs' next hellship. This time they were crowded on to a cargo of gravel. Each man was issued with six half-biscuits and all were allowed on deck as the vessel upped anchor and floated down the Irrawaddy River, out into the Bay of Matoban on a course for Moulmein. The next afternoon they entered the mouth of the Salween River to drop anchor off Moulmein.

Through ranks of screaming and ranting Japanese guards flailing sticks, the prisoners were marched to Moulmein gaol. Half the PoWs now suffered from dysentery, and parties of their number were selected to bury the 200 dead men still on board. Some 450 men were incapacitated with illness, and out of the 1,500 PoWs who left Singapore, only 650 marched off to work on the 'Death Railway'.

Similar experiences were related by Private R.H. Whitecross of the 6th Division AIF. He recounts how, on 14 May 1942, his brigade of 3,000 men was shipped aboard the 7,031-ton cargo ship *Toyohashi Maru* and the 5,824-ton freighter *Celebes Maru*. He calculated that in the holds each men had a space 9 inches wide by 6 feet long in which to exist.[13] He describes the PoWs' kitchen on board:

The 'kitchen' was situated on deck, with a flapping piece of canvas strung overhead to protect it from the weather. It consisted of three steam-heated cauldron-like cooking utensils, rather like huge inverted steel helmets, with a capacity of about 20 gallons each. Every day we were issued with a spoonful of dry tea leaves, and as there was always plenty of hot water and a little sugar, we considered ourselves well off.[14]

Toyohashi Maru continued to Victoria Point, Burma, where the PoWs were unloaded alongside the 1920 ex-Canadian 5,493-ton *Kyokusei Maru*, which disgorged Dutch PoWs. On the return trip to Singapore *Toyohashi Maru* was sunk by Lieutenant-Commander Balston's submarine HMS *Trusty*. Empty of PoWs, the NYK vessel's Japanese crew were picked up by *Kyokusei Maru*.

Thus were treated the PoWs whose great *koei* (honour) it was to serve the Divine *Nippon-koku Tenno Heika* (His Majesty the Emperor of Japan) in participating in the *Dai Shigoto* project of the Burma–Thailand Railway.

CHAPTER THREE

KWAI POWS SURVIVE HELL AT SEA

For the Japanese a far-flung but coveted prize was *Indo* – India. Their gateway was Burma, and this they secured on 8 March 1942 when *Shosho* Shojiro Iida's 15th Army captured Rangoon.[1] Yet to service their vast army in Burma they needed a steady flow of supplies and reinforcements, all of which had to make the long journey across the South China Sea to Singapore, thence through the Strait of Malacca, and past western coastal Malaya to the Burmese port of Rangoon. All the way they were exposed to attack by air and sea. After the extraordinary US victory at Midway, where the hopelessly outclassed US Task Forces 16 and 17 of Rear-Admiral Raymond A. Spruance and Rear-Admiral Frank Jack Fletcher defeated the mighty Imperial Combined Fleet of *Taisho* Isoroku Yamamoto, *Chujo* Chuichi Nagumo and *Shosho* Nobutake Kondo on 4 June 1942, sea passage to Burma became more hazardous. If they could dock supplies at the port of Bangkok in Siam, a safer and shorter sea passage could be achieved. As there was no railway connection from Bangkok to Rangoon 250 miles away, they would have to build one.

Back in Tokyo, railway engineers told the *Sanbo hombu* that such a construction would take up to five years to complete. Nonsense, came the reply; it must be built in less than eighteen months – hence by the end of 1943. How would it be done? The *Sanbo hombu* were clear on that point. When the cowardly Allies surrendered, they would supply thousands of workers.

The building of the Japanese railway through the jungles of Burma and Thailand by Allied PoWs and native captives is well documented and frequently written about. That part from Bampong in Siam to Thanbyuzayat in Burma, along part of the River Kwae Noi (Kwai) remains in memory as the notorious 'Railway of Death'. Around half the workers here were UK citizens, with some 18,000 Dutch (or Indonesian-Dutch), around 13,000 Australians and approximately 650 Americans, many of them from the 131st Field Artillery and survivors of the USS *Houston*.[2] Along with 250,000 impressed Asian nationals, these PoWs constructed the 265-mile-long railway under brutal Japanese and sadistic Korean guards. Some 12,568 white PoWs and some 84,000 Asians died during the construction.

In March 1944 orders came from the *Rikugunsho* that they required around 10,000 PoWs, after the railway construction had been completed, to be shipped to Japan as slave-labour. At the *furyo shuyojo* of Tamarkan in Siam, 900 PoWs were selected for this trip. Only about 5 per cent of the men were anywhere near fit to travel. Orders for the transhipment of the PoWs were processed through the GHQ staff at Rangoon, commanded by *Shosho* Masakazu Kawabe. The tactical PoW leader for the group was a 29-year-old Australian infantry officer, Captain Arthur B. Sumner. On Japanese HQ orders the 900 PoWs were to be grouped into six *kumi*, each led by an Australian officer as *kumicho*. They were to answer to Japanese leader *Chu-i* Yamada.[3] The PoWs were divided into two train-loads of 450 men each, and they left Tamarkan on 27 March 1944, after listening to a sickening homily from the camp commandant:

All men should be honoured to know they are going to a land of peace and tranquillity, where even the birds can nestle on the hunter's hand and will not be harmed. Where the snow covers the land in winter and the warm sun of spring melts it, leaving the country clean. A land of milk and honey. In Japan, it is a sin to eat and not work, so to prevent all men from becoming sinners we shall put you to work.[4]

At the railway yard at Kanchanaburi the prisoners were loaded on to open flatcars, to travel to Nan Pladuk junction and thence by connecting train to Bangkok. There they were reloaded on dung-encrusted steel cattle-wagons for the 400-mile journey to Phnom Penh, the capital of Japanese-occupied Cambodia. Here the PoWs caught their first glimpse of their new transport, the 300-ton river steamer *Lang Ho*,

FATE OF THE CREWS OF HMAS *PERTH* AND USS *HOUSTON*

HMAS *Perth* was a light cruiser of 6,980 tons. She carried 680 crew and was armed with eight 6-inch guns. She was built in 1934. She was commanded by Captain H.M.L. Waller, who went down with his ship.

USS *Houston* was a heavy cruiser of 9,050 tons. She carried 1,000 crew and was armed with nine 8-inch guns. She was built in 1930. She was commanded by Captain A.H. Rooks, killed by shrapnel.

On 26 February 1942 HMAS *Perth* joined an Allied fleet under the command of the Dutch Rear-Admiral Karel W.F.M. Doorman aboard the cruiser HMNS *De Ruyter* at Surabaya. The fleet also included the 8-inch gun cruiser HMS *Exeter*, 5.9-inch gun Dutch cruiser *Java*, as well as the British destroyers *Electra*, *Encounter* and *Jupiter*, and four US and two Dutch destroyers. Their task was to intercept a Japanese convoy heading for north-east Java. Japanese aircraft shadowed the fleet and on 27 February the Japanese convoy was sighted. The coming encounter was to be called the 'Battle of the Java Sea'.

The encounter was a disaster for the Allies. *De Ruyter* sank in a sea of flames, as did *Java*; *Electra* was shelled to destruction and *Jupiter* succumbed to a torpedo or mine. In the early hours of 1 March 1942 the remnants of the Allied fleet, with a refuelled *Perth* and *Houston*, attempted to penetrate the Sunda Strait, that 20-mile wide stretch of ocean between Sumatra and south-west Java, heading for Tjilatap, south Java.

The two vessels were quickly engaged by the Imperial Japanese Navy Support Forces and 3rd Escort Force of the Western Java Invasion Force. After only 20 minutes *Perth* was hit, and thereafter both vessels were continually hit, with a torpedo striking *Perth* around midnight. On the strike of a second torpedo Captain Waller ordered 'Abandon ship'; following a fourth torpedo strike the vessel sank in the early minutes of 1 March. The enemy now concentrated on *Houston*. About 20 minutes later *Houston* sank, having been shelled by the 8,500-ton Magomi Class light cruiser *Mikuma* from *Chujo* Kondo's 7th Cruiser Squadron (2nd Fleet or Scouting Force).

A large number of officers and men went down with their ships; some perished in the water by drowning or enemy action, while others were incinerated by the blazing fuel in the sea. Some survivors in liferafts reached the shore only to be captured, a few being handed over to the Japanese by Sundanese natives. Others were murdered by the natives. Around 200 were picked up by Japanese destroyers and transferred to the transport vessel *Somdong Maru*. In time PoWs from both vessels went to a former Dutch barracks known as the 'Bicycle Camp' on Java and were then transported to Sumatra and thence on hellships.

which plied the Mekon River. On 4 April they arrived at their transhipment port of Saigon.

Saigon – modern Ho Chi Minh City in Vietnam – was the French colonial capital. It lies in a rich plain, some 30 miles from the southern coast, and was the principal naval and merchant marine terminus of the Imperial Japanese Navy in the area. Saigon had fallen to the Southern Army and on 6 November 1941 HQ Saigon, Indo-China, was activated by *Shireichoken Taisho Hakushaku* Hisaichi Terauchi. The PoWs were now housed in a former French Foreign Legion barracks, where for the first time in years they enjoyed such luxuries as free-flowing water and toothpaste.

On 9 April the first of the PoWs, under naval guard, were loaded on to motorised barges for the trip down river to Cap St Jacques on the coast, where a Japanese convoy was assembling. To the consternation of the PoWs the ship's captain of the navy vessel they were about to board refused to take them to Japan. It was a remarkable turnaround: the Japanese captain knew that the Allies now had a huge submarine blockade stretching from Cam Ranh Bay, right across the South China Sea to Formosa, and up through the East China Sea. He did not want hundreds of PoWs clogging up his vessel, and acting as fifth columnists if his ship were torpedoed. In the event the Allied bombing of the

Japanese shipping and warehouses at Cap St Jacques saw the PoWs transported back to Bampong to be rerouted to Singapore and the transit camp of River Valley Road.

At Bampong the rerouted PoWs were joined by British PoWs who had also toiled on the 'Railway of Death'. Of the 6,000 British PoWs from two units, 2,742 had died on the railway. The PoWs arrived at River Valley Road on 4 July 1944. They spent the next five weeks in miserable accommodation while the Japanese authorities assembled PoWs from various parts of Malaya and Siam. On 4 September the PoWs received the order: 'All men go Nippon.'

In all, 2,218 PoWs – 1,500 of them British, the rest Australians – assembled for *tenko*, and marched to the dock for embarkation at Keppel Harbour, Singapore. Few were 'fit' and many, ravaged by malaria, dysentery, beri-beri and pellagra, tottered and stumbled on their way, goaded by Korean guards.

The men were loaded aboard two 1921-vintage passenger-cargo vessels. The first was the Mitsubishi Shipping Company's 9,500-ton *Rakuyo Maru*, the second the New Yokohama Shipbuilding Company's 10,500-ton *Kachidoki Maru*. The Japanese had salvaged the second vessel, which was the former United States Lines vessel *Wolverine State* and American President Lines *President Harrison*. The vessels were both painted grey, flew the Japanese merchant marine *hi-no-maru no hata* ('Round of the Sun') flag – a red circle on a white background – but had no markings to show they carried PoWs or the sick. Incidentally, monitors at the US Fleet Radio Unit, Pacific, based at Pearl Harbor, knew every movement of this and other convoys as Japan's naval codes had been cracked early in the war – but they had no intelligence on what cargo the ships carried.

Once the vessels were loaded with their cargoes of rubber, copra, tin, scrap iron and passengers including groups of Japanese wounded, nurses and civilians, the PoWs were ordered aboard.[5] Many of the civilian women were bound for the army whore-houses. Although menaced by their guards, PoWs aboard *Rakuyo Maru* refused to be battened down in the stinking holds.[6] As the guards prodded them with bayonets the PoWs deliberately formed a log jam. The ship's senior officer *Sencho* Yamada parleyed with the senior officer representing the PoWs, Brigadier Arthur L. Varley, and eventually the sick, plus 400 other

PoWs of the 1,318 aboard, were allowed to stay on deck as long as they kept the walkways clear for the crew.

The two vessels, with two more passenger-cargo ships, one of which was identified as the 1920s-built 8,400-ton *Nankai Maru*, were joined by three 800-ton frigates, including *Hirato*, to make a convoy. The leader was the 2,090-ton Fubiki Class destroyer *Shikinami* which had been built at Kosakubu in 1929. Two Kawasaki H6K 'Mavis' flying-boats of the Imperial Japanese Navy's airforce circled overhead.

The convoy set course for Formosa Strait as the PoWs languished in their horrific holds or, in the case of *Rakuyo Maru*, sprawled topside. Hunger and thirst were acute. Drinking water was rationed and food scanty – rice with occasional fish-soup. Water for washing was available at topside saltwater pumps. Extra drinking water could be bartered from the guards. Alfred Allbury remembers:

> In the [guards'] cubby hole was a tap. Regimental badges, woollen hose tops, foreign coins: all the trifling items that had never up to now had a market were suddenly produced and brought . . . a gurgling animation from the tap . . . For a photograph of an English girl, especially a pretty one in a bathing costume, you could fill a dozen bottles . . .[7]

Yards away from the sick and dying, Japanese passengers ate off spotless napery in an immaculate dining room, its tables decorated with flowers and sporting jugs of water.[8] A rain storm brought relief to the filthy, parched PoWs.

By 11 September 1944 the convoy had reached the centre of the South China Sea, where air-cover ceased. Here three freighters and three frigates from Manila joined the convoy. At this point too, the convoy was approaching the most dangerous part of the journey, because the 'wolf-packs' of the Pacific Fleet, commanded by Vice-Admiral Charles A. Lockwood Jnr, US Commander Submarines, were known to be operating in the Luzon Strait. Among the PoWs there was more talk of shipwreck survival procedures. Those who had served aboard HMAS *Perth* were the best trained to survive, and one of their number, Victor R. Duncan, advised them all on abandon-ship routines.

At Pearl Harbor Vice-Admiral Lockwood's Operations Officer, Commander Richard G. Voge, decided to intercept the convoy. There was no information on record that two of the convoy vessels contained PoWs. So on the night of 9 September the submarines *Growler* (Commander Thomas Benjamin Oakley Jr), *Pampanito* (Commander Paul E. Summers) and *Sealion II* (Commander Eli T. Reich) were redeployed to engage, supported by *Barb* (Commander Eugene B. Fluckery) and *Queenfish* (Commander Charles Elliot Loughlin). Once rendezvoused, the three lead submarines formed a scouting line to search for the convoy. The two support submarines maintained a surface patrol east of the main force.

Radar contact was made and aboard *Growler*, Commander Oakley ordered battle stations. The convoy's fleet destroyers picked up *Growler* on radar, and peeled off to engage. *Growler* achieved a torpedo hit amidships of her target, sinking *Shikinami*. The whole convoy was now alerted to enemy action. Two frigates turned to pursue *Growler*. Others changed course to pinpoint other submarines which manoeuvred away.

PoWs on the deck of the *Rakuyo Maru* witnessed the demise of *Shikinami* with curiosity rather than anxiety, while most of the PoWs on *Kachidoki Maru* were in the hold. There was a certain amount of panic among the Japanese on the latter, and the ship was involved in a minor collision with one of the convoy tankers. No PoWs were injured.

The three submarines continued to shadow the convoy. *Sealion II* closed on the formation, selecting *Rakuyo Maru* as her target. She fired her torpedo, and hit the *Rakuyo Maru*, then fired again at a tanker and then at an unidentified vessel, later revealed as the passenger-cargo ship *Nankai Maru*. All three were hit by three Mark XIV steam torpedoes.[9] The Japanese convoy vessels were now totally alerted.

Aboard the *Rakuyo Maru* the PoWs watched events unfold in horrified fascination and with no little terror. For now *Sealion II* set her sights on their ship. Two of the three torpedoes fired hit home, in the bow and the engine room amidships. The vessel rocked violently and hundreds of tons of seawater engulfed crew and PoWs alike. Panic broke out in the holds, but a sort of calm returned when prisoners realised the *Rakuyo Maru* was not sinking. Miraculously no PoWs had died in the explosions, although Japanese engine room personnel, gun crews and others had been killed. *Rakuyo Maru* settled a further 12ft down in the water. All around her the convoy was in disarray, scattering from *Sealion II*'s plotted position. The submarine was largely unscathed by depth-charge attacks. Elsewhere *Pampanito* and *Growler* moved into attack positions.

Issuing no orders to the PoWs the Japanese aboard *Rakuyo Maru* quickly abandoned ship. There were lifeboats for passengers and crew only; no provision at all had been made for the PoWs' safety.[10] Some Japanese with light-machine guns kept the PoWs away from the lifeboats; others jabbed at the ragged band with bayonets. In minutes none but a handful of Japanese remained on board, and the sea was a jumble of jumping bodies and corpses. PoWs who survived the leap into the sea swam to the lifeboats and rafts. Some of the PoWs targeted ship's officers aboard the smaller boats; attacking them with fists, debris or strangulation they drowned as many as they could and requisitioned their craft.

In a strange tribal grouping the Japanese clustered their lifeboats at a distance from the stricken *Rakuyo Maru*. Some way off another group of PoWs formed, bewildered by their sudden freedom, to face a new and unknown plight. The seasoned sailors from such vessels as HMAS *Perth* helped to evacuate the PoW holds. Liferafts abandoned by the Japanese in their flight were pressed into service, and soon one-third of the PoWs were safely aboard around sixty rafts; another quarter of the PoWs were in the sea without life-preservers, clinging to hatch-boards, tables, chairs and assorted floating debris. Those remaining on board foraged into Japanese quarters, feasting on food they found in the galleys and cabins. Some thirty minutes after *Rakuyo Maru* had been hit, some 90 per cent of PoWs had left the vessel.

On 12 September the submarine *Growler* had the 860-ton frigate *Hirato* in its sights. Built in 1943 by Hitachi, the Etorofu Class (Type A) *Hirato*'s doom was witnessed by the PoWs and Japanese. Many of those still in the water suffered from the aftermath of the frigate's disintegration. *Growler* now took up a watching brief. Records show that none of the attacking submarines was aware at any time that there were PoWs in the sea.

All around in the oily ocean and debris, some 1,200 PoWs bobbed in the waves. *Rakuyo Maru* had not sunk and several PoWs slowly paddled back to the vessel. Was there still water and food aboard, clean clothes and weapons? Could better liferafts be fashioned from whatever was left? At least, for those still in the water the ship could give a little respite from the waves. Men scrambled aboard to forage. A serviceable lifeboat was found and launched; soon it was filled with 135 PoWs, with dozens more clinging to its sides in the water. There were many such incidents as the PoWs returned to the *Rakuyo Maru* in search of sustenance and medicines.

By now all of *Rakuyo Maru*'s lifeboats were launched. One lifeboat crammed with PoWs set off in the direction of the Philippines; it vanished, with its passengers, from historical records. Now in two divided groups of around 900 and 300, the PoWs floated in the South China Sea, hungry, sunburnt, salt-stung and exhausted. In their centre *Rakuyo Maru* also clung doggedly to existence.

At last *Rakuyo Maru* sank; the PoWs watched with indifference, the Japanese observed respectfully with a round of *Banzais*.[11] There was more to interest the PoWs, as two Japanese freighters and a merchant vessel came into view, slowly steaming among the dead and debris in the water. Was rescue nigh? Men cheered. Lifeboats, survivors in the water and the Japanese all made for the vessels. The Japanese scrambled aboard but the PoWs were repelled if they tried to climb on; some were sent flying by blows. Aboard one frigate a Japanese officer shouted that he would open fire on any PoWs who tried to board.[12] PoWs in the water now made for the lifeboats vacated by the Japanese. As soon as the Japanese vessels had rescued all the Japanese and Koreans to be seen, they departed.

Pampanito now moved into position to attack the remaining convoy, which had regained air-cover by fighters from the 2nd Fleet (Scouting) on Hainan Island. *Pampanito* had to keep crash-diving to avoid detection. The submarine monitored the convoy's zig-zag course towards Hainan, and plans were made to launch the sub's ten torpedoes at the four larger ships in the convoy. Alas, a torpedo in one of the tubes jammed; as these torpedoes were unpredictable *Pampanito* herself now became vulnerable. However, an experienced torpedoman managed to fire five of the tubes in an attempt to clear the problem. Three hit *Kachidoki Maru*, which quickly sank.

As two of the torpedoes hit *Kachidoki Maru* her 900 British PoWs were in Hold no. 2, with another 100 scattered on deck avoiding the captain's eye. He had forbidden PoWs to leave the hold following enemy action. Realising what had happened PoWs started to scramble out of the hold, while panic-stricken Japanese proceeded to launch lifeboats and liferafts for their own personnel. No order to abandon ship was given; on the bridge the ship's captain shot himself.[13] A Japanese officer, meanwhile, roamed the decks shooting badly wounded Japanese.[14] PoWs were still struggling out of the hold as the *Kachidoki Maru* sank: around a third of the PoWs drowned, along with most of the Japanese wounded who had evaded their officer's bullets. The dreadful tally of some 700 drowned including nurses, women, children and other civilians.[15] *Pampanito* disengaged.

In the water surviving PoWs and Japanese sought debris and rafts to cling to; one raft of Japanese kept PoWs at bay with rifles, while others fought off the PoWs with knives, oars and fists. Both PoWs and Japanese killed one another for spaces on rafts as they struggled to get away from their mutual seaborne enemy – a thick layer of oil which had seeped from *Kachidoki Maru*'s fuel tanks.

From being Japanese PoWs the two groups of survivors from *Rakuyo Maru*'s hellish holds, surviving in a flotilla of lifeboats and a matting of rafts, were now at the mercy of the South China Sea. What food had been salvaged was scarce and fresh water only stretched to about a quarter of a pint per person per day. On the boats led by HMAS *Perth* sailors, a regular watch was mounted, but all the craft floated aimlessly.

By 13 September morale was low; more men in the water were suffering from eye troubles and ear pain because of the spilled oil topping the waves; others were being slowly tortured by thirst and hunger. Those who in their desperation had drunk seawater were descending into a state of madness, which made them a danger to themselves and others. Tempers flared and some of the irredeemably demented were deliberately killed.[16] Others died from exposure.

To the west, some 150 miles away, survivors of the *Kachidoki Maru* were similarly suffering, sharing their fate with Japanese servicemen, nurses and civilians. The PoWs kept their distance from the Japanese after one PoW had been knifed to death by a Japanese while trying to clamber aboard a raft.[17] At length two frigates appeared and began picking up Japanese survivors. Aboard one was *Tai-i* Tanaka, known to many as a scourge of PoWs back in camp. He had been leading a group of them to slavery in Japan. On his orders PoWs were picked up, ostensibly to continue their journey to Japanese work-camps. Others were picked up by a Japanese trawler, but some 200 PoWs were left in the water; many of them swam to the lifeboats vacated by the Japanese. Luckily some boats still contained meagre supplies of food and water. Later the Japanese 'rescue vessels' reached tropical Hainan Island, off the Chinese mainland between the South China Sea and the Gulf of Tongking. The PoWs were greeted with the usual running-the-gauntlet beatings as they disembarked. No medical treatment was offered to the sick, only the knowledge that they were back in the slave-labour transportation roundabout.

By 14 September the two groups from the *Rakuyo Maru* were still floating above the site of the vessel's sinking. Then a trio of Japanese corvettes appeared, steaming towards one of the PoW groups. These PoWs were picked up by one of the vessels. What happened to the other PoW group no one ever knew; all the survivors feared that their comrades had been massacred by the other two corvette crews. The newly rescued PoWs were taken by the corvettes to Sangai Harbour, Hainan Island. There they joined the *Kachidoki Maru* survivors on a Japanese tanker.

On 16 September all the PoWs were transferred to this new hellship, the 20,000-ton whaler *Kibibi Maru*, now converted to carry fuel oil. Those who knew about the transportation of combustible fuel in wartime realised how vulnerable they now were: if the vessel were to be bombed or torpedoed they would all be incinerated. There would be no chance of rescue then. By now the Japanese had discontinued their sweep of the sea around the *Kachidoki Maru* and *Rakuyo Maru* sinkings. The PoWs did a tally. Only 136 men remained out of *Rakuyo Maru's* PoW cargo, and only 520 from the *Kachidoki Maru*. Over a thousand PoWs had vanished.

Out of the sea the submarines *Pampanito* and *Sealion II* were continuing their surface patrol when *Pampanito* came across debris and a lifeboat. Cautiously, lest it was a Japanese booby trap, the submarine approached; the boat was empty. Nearby, though, was a cluster of rafts with a forest of waving arms. The PoWs had been sighted at last. Soon identified as survivors of the *Rakuyo Maru*, this was the submarine's first intelligence that the convoy they had attacked had contained over two thousand PoWs. In all *Pampanito* picked up around seventy-three PoWs.[18]

Pampanito set course for the nearest Allied controlled landfall at Saipan in the Northern Marianas, which US Forces had secured on 9 July 1944 after fierce suicide attacks by *Taisho* Yoshitsugu Saito's 136th Infantry Regiment, the 9th Tank Regiment and the 47th Independent Mixed Brigade. Both Saito and the naval back-up commander *Chujo* Chichi Nagumo committed ritual *seppuku*.

Aboard *Pampanito* Commander Paul Summers requested Commander Eli Reich's *Sealion II* to render assistance in rescuing the PoWs. In all, the submarine rescued fifty-four PoWs.[19] Alas, Reich had to leave many dying PoWs in the water. Messages indicating that PoWs were still adrift were radioed to Pearl Harbor, and the submarines *Barb* and *Queenfish* were sent to their aid after an engagement with Japanese 'hunter-killer' vessels in the Luzon Strait. Both submarines engaged an enemy convoy en route and *Barb* won credit for sinking the Taiyo Class 17,870-ton aircraft carrier *Unyo* (formerly the NYK liner *Yawata Maru*).

On 16 September 1944 the *Kibibi Maru* upped anchor at Hainan bound for Japan. Her passenger load was a strange mixture of survivors of several nations. The PoWs and Japanese survivors of *Rakuyo Maru* and *Kachidoki Maru* shared the vessel with Japanese survivors of the *Nankai Maru*, the destroyer *Shikinami* and the frigate *Hirato*. PoWs were housed in the former whale-butchering area below decks, while the Japanese remained topside; the prisoners were allowed to go topside for rations and *benjo* needs. The captain's manifest recorded 656 PoWs and 1,000 Japanese nationals.

Many of the 520 British survivors from *Kachidoki Maru* were ill or injured, but no medical care or pharmaceuticals were offered. Dysentery was widespread. Again the PoWs' clothing was scanty and all their personal possessions had been lost at sea.

After a short stop at Keelung in Formosa, and delays because of submarine scares, *Kibibi Maru* set a course for the four-day journey to Moji in Japan, staying close to the Chinese mainland wherever possible. They arrived on 28 September. The PoWs had been in transit for six months. Of the 716 Australians who had left Singapore aboard the *Rakuyo Maru*, only 80 docked at Moji. The whole complement of

PoWs was now split into groups and sent by train to labour-camps such as Sakara on Honshu, Kawasaki near Yokohama, and Fukuoka near Nagasaki. There they were to face new deprivations and hardships: 1944 was the worst winter ever recorded in Japanese meteorological history.

What of the immediate fate of the survivors of *Rakuyo Maru* and *Kachidoki Maru*? Many died of malnutrition and cold in the camps. Allied incendiary bombs killed at least thirty PoWs; others were murdered or died from their injuries and hardships in the camps.[20] All who survived – around 540 British and 66 Australians – were liberated by US Forces in August 1945.[21]

Meanwhile *Pampanito* and *Sealion II* rendezvoused with USS *Care* off Saipan, to transfer their 157 and 136 PoWs respectively into medical care. *Barb* and *Queenfish* were also busy in the survivor search area.[22]

Painstakingly the two submarines patrolled the debris- and corpse-strewn search area. At last *Barb* located three survivors, and the *Queenfish* found more. They were all in a dreadful condition, soaked in oil, dehydrated, starving, blistered by the sun, running with sores and too weak to climb aboard the submarines unaided. Some were on the verge of madness. In all, 22 Australians and 10 British PoWs were rescued and taken to Tanapaq Harbour, Saipan, for treatment at the US Army 148th General Hospital.

In the aftermath of the Second World War the Australian PoWs went back home, first aboard *Alcoa Polaris* to Guadalcanal, there to await onward transportation to Brisbane by the Australian minelayer *Monadnock*. The British boarded the liberty ship *Cape Douglas* bound for Pearl Harbor in Hawaii, then by the troopship *Orizaba* to San Francisco. After travelling crosscountry to New York they embarked on the *Queen Mary* to Greenock.

By this time the governments of Britain and Australia had assessed the atrocities suffered by the PoWs at sea and King George VI sent this message to be read out to the survivors by welcoming officials:

The Queen and I bid you a very warm welcome home. Through all the great trials and sufferings which you have endured while in the hands of the Japanese, you and your comrades have been constantly in our thoughts.

I realise from the accounts that you have already given how heavy those sufferings have been. I know too that you have endured them with the highest courage. We mourn with you the deaths of so many of your comrades. We hope with all our hearts that your return from captivity may bring you and your families a full measure of happiness.[23]

Both in Australia and Britain the PoWs went through lengthy debriefing sessions. In Britain in particular the public began to learn about the Japanese atrocities at sea, with newspapers paraphrasing the basic headline 'Japanese Left Prisoners to Drown'.[24] In the House of Commons Sir Percy James Grigg (1890–1964), Secretary of State for War, reviewed the history of the 'Railway of Death' for MPs and detailed the sinking of the *Rakuyo Maru* and the rescue of survivors by the US Forces. He ended his statement:

It is a matter of profound regret to me that these disclosures have to be made; but we are convinced that it is necessary that the Japanese should know that we know how they have been behaving, and that we intend to hold them responsible.[25]

For decades the surviving PoWs felt betrayed by the Allied governments for failing, as they saw it, to exact proper retribution on the Imperial Japanese Forces and their Emperor, in whose name they had murdered, raped and pillaged.

CHAPTER FOUR

A QUARTET OF NAVAL MASSACRES

The deliberate, brutal and gratuitous murder of PoWs by the Japanese Imperial Forces in the Second World War was commonplace. Murder with attendant cruelty and carnage on a large scale at individual locations, and even deliberate massacres, are known to have taken place on around fourteen occasions between April 1942 and August 1945.[1] Several were the responsibility of the Imperial Japanese Navy.

One such is known as the Amboina Massacre. Amboina Island lies south of Ceram and east of Buru in the Molucca Archipelago, facing the Banda Sea. On 3 February 1942 it fell to the Japanese and some 800 Australians and 300 Dutch were taken prisoner. The captives taken on the Ambon side of the island were dispatched to Tan Toey Barracks, just outside the town of Ambon. The rest, captured on the Laha side of the island, were the subjects of the massacre. *Shosho* Hatakiyama, Commander of the Amboina Invasion Force (1st Kure Special Landing Party and two platoons of the Sasebo Special Marines Landing Party), had already issued orders for the execution of ten Australians at his HQ at Soewakoda.[2] So a precedent for the murder of Allied PoWs in this theatre of the war was firmly established.

The growing number of prisoners in his hands caused *Shosho* Hatakiyama some administrative problems. They were a nuisance, and he had no naval guards to spare to monitor them. So he ordered the massacre of around fifty of them following the securing of Laha airfield. Their execution was left in the hands of *Tai-i* Nakagawa, who left this record of the massacre:

[4 February 1942]. In compliance with [*Shosho* Hatakiyama's confirmed] order, I took about thirty petty officers and men to Soewakoda. In a coconut tree plantation, about two hundred metres from the airfield, we dug holes and killed the prisoners of war with swords or bayonets. It took about two hours. The way in which the murder was carried out was as follows: I divided my men into three groups, the first for leading the prisoners of war out of a house where we had temporarily confined them, the second for preventing disorder on their way from the house to the plantation, the third for beheading or stabbing the victims.

They were taken one by one to the spot where they were to die, and made to kneel down with a bandage over their eyes. The members of the third troop stepped out of the ranks, one by one as his turn came, to behead a prisoner of war with a sword or stab him through the breast with a bayonet.

The prisoners were all Australian and their number included four or five officers, one of whom I am sure was a major. All the corpses were buried in holes we had dug. I was the only Japanese officer present . . . When it was all over I reported its completion to my adjutant [*Shosa* Hayashi].[3]

On 5 February thirty Dutch prisoners were executed in the same way for refusing to work. On 17 February *Shosa* Hayashi relayed the order to *Tai-i* Nakagawa to kill all the remaining PoWs. Nakagawa reported the incident in this way.

I divided my men into nine parties, two for bloody killings, three for guarding the prisoners on their way to the place of execution, two for escorting the prisoners out of the barracks, one to be on guard at the spot where the prisoners were to be killed, and one in reserve for emergency.

The prisoners of war were brought by truck from the barracks to the detachment headquarters, and marched from there to the plantation. The same way of killing was adopted as before . . . The poor victims numbered about two hundred and twenty in all, including some Australian officers.

The whole affair took from 6pm to 9.30pm. Most of the corpses were buried in one hole, but because the hole turned out not to be big enough to accommodate all the bodies an adjacent dug-out was also used as a grave.[4]

By 1945 *Shosa* Hatakiyama was dead, thus escaping trial and retribution. But many clearly guilty Imperial Japanese Forces officers, NCOs and other ranks, who survived the war, were to face this destiny.

During the investigations conducted by the Australian War Crimes Tribunal, sitting at Hong Kong from 24 November to 17 December 1947, a massacre inspired and enacted by the Imperial Japanese Navy was brought to light. It remains a further example of how Japanese Navy flag officers endeavoured to cover their tracks. The massacre story begins with an event known as the 'Kavieng Killings'. Kavieng, by the by, is the main port and town of New Ireland, in modern Papua New Guinea, and is a mountainous island in the Bismarck Archipelago to the north-east of New Britain. This was still in Australian possession at the outbreak of the war.

Japanese forces began their attack on New Britain on 4 January 1942 in a combined manoeuvre by the Japanese South Seas Army and the Imperial Japanese Navy's 'R. Operation Unit'. By 21 January Kavieng was secured with little resistance, as the bulk of the 1st Independent Company of the Australian Army had retreated south. Around twenty Australian troops had remained at Kavieng to sabotage military equipment and facilities; a few were captured and sent as PoWs to Rabaul. Nevertheless there remained a scattering of civilians still in New Britain, mostly Australian copra plantation owners and agricultural employees. When the Japanese secured the island there were some forty Australian civilians and around ten German missionaries on New Britain. They were soon to vanish. In this theatre of war the Japanese command was as shown in the panel on p. 72.[5]

When *Shosho* Ryukichi Tamura arrived at Kavieng on 20 October 1943, replacing *Shosho* Miroru Ota, the *Tokkeitai* had already rounded up a dozen Allied civilians on charges of anti-Japanese subversion and they had been executed at Nago Island, off Kavieng, under the supervision of *Tokkeitai*/Security Detachment *Chu-i* Shichitaro Mochizuke. But what had happened to the other civilians, estimated at twenty-three souls? The Australian War Crimes Section investigated. It was to prove a very tortuous inquiry, fraught with obfuscation, twisted testimony and mysterious actions, but the results shed light not only on the fate of the Kavieng PoWs but also on the soon-to-be-discovered '*Akikaze* Massacre'.[6]

On the afternoon of 19 September 1945 *Shosho* Tamura surrendered his command to Lieutenant-General Eather, GOC 11th Division AIF, aboard HMS *Swan* at Frangelawa Bay, New Ireland. Soon afterwards he was interviewed by Australian intelligence officers at Kavieng regarding the missing civilians.[7]

He averred that he dispatched thirty-two civilians to safety at Rabaul, after Allied bombing raids on 16 February. They travelled aboard the 1,106-ton converted merchant vessel *Kowa Maru*. Subsequent investigation showed that a vessel called *Kowa Maru* was sunk while in convoy from Truk by B-25 Mitchell bombers some 30 miles west of New Hanover Island on 21 February 1944. There were no survivors. Staff Officer *Taisa* Tsuyoshi Sanagai, South-east Area Fleet HQ, Rabaul, confirmed that he had authorised the dispatch of the civilian internees to Rabaul aboard *Kowa Maru*. As there was no definite evidence that *Shosho* Tamura had executed the civilians he was released, returning to Japan on 6 November 1946 on the surrendered 2,701-ton Fleet Escort destroyer *Hanatsuki*.

However, the Australian investigators were not happy with Tamura's testimony and continued their investigations into shipping activities between Kavieng and Rabaul. In January 1947 *Shosho* Tamura was arrested at Kamakura and taken to Tokyo; from his bed at the 31st US Occupation Hospital in Tokyo he was further interviewed. At this point he admitted that his command had executed the Kavieng civilians.[8] *Shosho* Tamura was found guilty of war crimes on 17 December 1947 and sentenced to death by hanging.

As they sifted through the testimony records of Imperial Japanese Navy personnel the Australian investigators noted that an unidentified group of Caucasians were mentioned as having been executed on the vessel *Akikaze* in or around March 1943. Were these the missing New Ireland civilians dispatched to an uncertain fate on the orders of *Shosho* Tamura?

To answer this question a group of former *Akikaze* crew members were interviewed in Japan during the period January–April 1947.[9] Piece by piece the following story was put together. The vessel was the 1,215-ton *Akikaze*, a First Class Destroyer of the Minekaze Class. Built by Mitsubishi at their Nagasaki Yard in 1920, the vessel was reported lost in the South China Sea to a US submarine on 3 November 1944. During March 1943 *Akikaze* visited the headquarters of the 2nd Special Naval

JAPANESE NAVAL OCCUPATION COMMAND

I: Kavieng and Namatani

The 83rd Naval Garrison Unit and the 89th Garrison Unit (some 4,699 personnel in March 1944)
Commander of the 14th Naval Base Force was *Shosho* Ryukichi Tamura. The Acting Commander was *Tai-i* Kyoji Mori and the Senior Staff Officer *Chusa* Shozo Yoshino.
Kavieng (Chinatown) Detention Camp was controlled by Commander *Tokumu socho* Funayama, and the *Tokkeitai*/Security Detachment was commanded by *Chu-i* Shichitaro Mochizuki.

II: Rabaul

8th Fleet Headquarters
Commander-in-Chief of the 8th Fleet was *Chujo* Gunichi Mikawa, and his Chief of Staff at 8th Fleet Headquarters was *Shosho* Shinzo Onishi.

Other Japanese officers at Rabaul included: Staff Officer (8th Fleet HQ), *Tai-i* Shigetoku Kame; Staff Officer (Signals), *Chusa* Torao Mori; Staff Officer (Civilian Affairs), *Chusa* Norisaka Ando; and Staff Officer (Ciphers), *Chu-i* Minoru Maeda.

Imperial Japanese Navy Signature Procedure for Orders Concerning the Execution of PoWs, or Other Secret Matters

The order was signed by the issuing officer, and if relevant was countersigned by a staff officer. It was then countersigned by the Chief of Staff, and the Commander-in-Chief. (These signatures were mandatory for the order to be valid. No officer would have proceeded to carry them out without his superiors' signatures or *han* – seals.)

The order was then processed by Staff Officer (Signals) and sent to Staff Officer (Ciphers). The encoded order was sent to ships' captains, with a copy to the commander of the nearest local naval base and naval garrison unit, and where relevant to a *Tokkeitai* commander.

No known executions took place under Imperial Japanese Navy command without this order procedure being carried out.

Base Force at Wewak, New Guinea, to load food and medicines. Under sealed orders the vessel sailed to Kairiru, an islet off Wewak roads, and on 17 May some forty civilians were delivered to the *Akikaze* by personnel thought to have been *Tokkeitai*.

The civilians were mostly German clergy and nuns, relics of the colony on north-east New Guinea, which had been German territory until the Australians assumed possession in 1918. The Germans, nationals of Japan's Co-Axis partners, had been moved from Wewak to Kairiru at the outbreak of the war. Germans in Japanese-occupied territory were deemed neutral and they were able to move about Kairiru freely. Yet Allied airmen had been shot down while attacking Wewak and the *Tokkeitai* believed that the survivors were being helped by certain of the German clergy; other Germans were believed to be fomenting anti-Japanese attitudes among the ethnic population. Thus the *Tokkeitai* at 2nd Special Naval Base Force had requested 8th Fleet HQ to move the Germans and their staff to Rabaul, the headquarters of *Chujo* Junichi Kusaka's South-east Area Fleet.

Along with their Chinese servants, and two orphan children being cared for by the nuns, the Germans left Kairiru aboard the *Akikaze* which made passage towards Manus Island. The ship's captain, *Shosa* Tsurukichi Sabe, seems to have accorded his passengers respect, treating them as neutral civilians in transit rather than as hostile PoWs.

Meanwhile *Kashikan* Harukichi Ichinose, commander of a small naval unit at Lorengau, in the north-east of Manus Island, had gathered a further group of around twenty westerners, including more German clergy, a Hungarian missionary and a few Chinese, for transportation to Rabaul. His orders had come from 8th Fleet HQ. These new passengers were boarded on the evening of 17 March 1943 and the *Akikaze* departed Manus towards Kavieng. Mysteriously *Akikaze* did not dock at Kavieng; instead, a dispatch was delivered by boat from the dock to *Shosa* Sabe and the vessel set off once more.

Shortly after *Akikaze* sailed, *Shosa* Sabe summoned his senior officers to a conference. Present was *Chu-i* Yajiro Kai, who had joined *Akikaze* at Wewak as official *tsuyaku*.[10] *Shosa* Sabe informed the assembled company that he had received an order from 8th Fleet HQ to execute the civilians he had collected at Wewak and Lorengau. He added: '*Fuko-na dekigoto desu*' – ('It is an unfortunate case').

Unfortunate or not, *Shosa* Sabe carried out the orders with speed and efficiency. All the civilians were moved calmly to the front of the ship by the forward bridge, while a curious construction was built at the rear. Planks were placed over the stern of the vessel with mats on top. Above this two posts were strapped together, triangular fashion, with their bases on deck. On this primitive gallows each victim was to be hung by the wrists and shot. Each execution was to take place with the ship travelling at high speed so that when released the corpses would be forced back by the momentum of the vessel into the sea; thus bloodstains on the deck would be lessened and the bodies neatly disposed of. White sheeting was erected between the gallows and the other parts of the ship to shield the executions from view, and nothing was to be heard. The noise of the ship's engines and the rushing of the wind muffled the sound of gunshots.

With studied thoroughness and calmness each victim was separated from the assembled group for'ard, asked for their personal details to give the impression of a normal ship's passenger list check, then led away out of sight of the others behind the sheets. Then they were blindfolded, hoisted on the scaffold and shot. Any screams of terror when the victims realised what was about to happen were carried away on the wind. The firing squad – four riflemen and a machine-gunner – was directed by *Chu-i* Takeo Terada. It took some three hours to execute the sixty victims; the orphans were thrown overboard alive. *Shosa* Sabe led funeral prayers for the victims and swore his officers and crew to secrecy.

Scoured of blood and the execution scaffold dismantled, *Akikaze* docked at Rabaul during the mid-morning of 18 March. *Chosa* Sabe reported to *Tai-i* Shigetoku Kami, Staff Officer at 8th Fleet HQ, that the executions had been duly carried out. The testimony of *Chu-i* Kai, who was present at the meeting between Sabe and Kami, claims the latter ordered all reports on the executions to be kept secret and the civilians' personal effects to be disposed of.

Commander-in-Chief *Chujo* Mikawa and Chief of Staff *Shosho* Onishi denied all knowledge of the *Akikaze* massacre and averred that it was entirely *Tai-i* Kame's responsibility, implying that he had acted alone in issuing the executive order. In an interview with Australian War Crimes Section officers Mikawa suggested that the Staff Officer

(Civilian Affairs), *Chusa* Norisaka Ando, might well have acted in collusion with Kame. That Mikawa and Onishi were clearly lying is made evident by a study of the rigid procedure of the issuing of orders (see panel, p. 72). Yet there was insufficient proof in 1947 to proceed with a prosecution as both the *Akikaze* executioner *Chu-i* Takeo Terada and ship's master *Shosa* Sabe were killed in the war.

Another massacre was carried out at Wake Island during October 1943. Serving at Wake at that time was *Shosa* Soichi Tachibana, adjutant to *Shosho* Shigemitsu Sakaibara, Commander of the 65th Guard Force (4th Base Force) at Wake Island from December 1941. Tachibana had in his remit custody of around one hundred US civilian employees of Pan-American Airways. Of the events he left this record:

> On the 7th [October 1943], just after sundown, I don't remember the time, the Commanding Officer [*Shosho* Sakaibara] and I were at the command post. Then, all of a sudden, he gave this order: 'The headquarters company leader is to use his men and shoot to death the prisoners of war on the northern shore.'
>
> It was so sudden that I was startled but I knew that the CO was a careful man and that he wouldn't come to a conclusion unless he had given it plenty of consideration. When I was a cadet at the Naval Academy [Etajima] he had been my instructor. I didn't, therefore, have any doubt and thought it was justifiable to execute all the prisoners of war according to the situation that night.[11]

The murder of the Allied PoWs was delegated to *Tai-i* Ito, the new commander of HQ Company. The PoWs were lined up at the beach in a single row, sitting side-by-side with their backs to the sea. All were blindfolded, and their hands tied behind their backs. A firing squad was assembled between the PoWs and the sea. Once the platoon commander had reported all in order, Ito gave the command and the Americans were shot. The event was dismissed as an ordinary incident of war by the *Kaigun Gunreibu*.

On the night of 15 August 1945 the duty radio officer on Wake Island reported to *Shosa* Tachibana that Japan had surrendered. No confirming telegram was received from the *Kaigun Gunreibu*, so *Shosho*

Sakaibara dismissed the news as false. But by 18 August Sakaibara realised that the surrender news was true. Assembling his senior officers, he made a grave statement, in which he announced that he had listened to a broadcast from Melbourne which stated that 'all criminals of war whether they were ordered, or were the officers who gave the orders, will be punished'.[12] The officers were then dismissed.

On 20 August *Shosho* Sakaibara addressed his officers once more:

> The case concerning the prisoners of war will be like this. I have thought up a good story. [We'll confirm] half of [the PoWs] were killed in the bombardment on 6 October 1943. The remainder escaped the following night and resisted recapture with rifle fire. A fight ensued and they were all killed.[13]

On 22 August Sakaibara ordered the exhumation of the American cadavers, and had them reburied on the eastern shore of Wake Island, better to substantiate the dissembling he was to record.

Shosho Sakaibara was tried for war crimes at Guam in June 1947. His defence was *Kyoku no tsukemasu*. He was confident of exoneration, for *Shosho* Hiroaki Abe, Commander of the 8th Cruiser Squadron, made it clear that 'superior orders' had to be obeyed, because:

> The Japanese Military Forces are under a strict discipline, by a rigorous chain of command which originates in the supreme prerogative of command of *Tenno Heika*, and penetrates from him at the top down to a private at the bottom, the primary and supreme duty of a military man is absolute submission to an order . . . among hundreds and thousands of Japanese military men, there has never been one person who thought that he could be charged with his own acts which he had committed pursuant of an order. It is beyond the understanding of the Japanese that such things could be penalised.[14]

The prosecuting authority dismissed Sakaibara's defence as invalid and a contravention of the rules of warfare. He was found guilty and hanged for his war crimes on 19 June 1947, as was his adjutant *Tai-i* Tachibana.

This was not the end of the naval massacres. Records show that right up to the last days of the war massacres occurred in such places as Sumatra, Java and the Sumba Islands of Indonesia, with the beheadings of Allied merchant navy personnel at Truk. Details of other massacre stories still surface from time to time.

CHAPTER FIVE

SENSUIKAN TARGETS:
THE KILLER SUBMARINES

On 3 January 1942 the Japanese Ambassador to Germany, Hiroshi Oshima, had an important meeting with Adolf Hitler at the Reichschancellery, Berlin. With the rank of *Chujo*, Oshima was a pro-National Socialist and a leading member of that group within Japan promoting national expansion in the Far East. Ambassador since 1938, Oshima had negotiated the Tripartite Alliance between Germany, Italy and Japan in 1940 and was keen to win Hitler's support for Japan against the United States.[1] This meeting was to explore an important mutual problem.

The United States had entered the European war following Prime Minister Winston Churchill's Washington conference with President Franklin D. Roosevelt in December 1941. It was clear to Hitler that the United States would be able to add 'an almost inexhaustible ship-building capacity' to the Allied war effort. Thus he was issuing orders to his U-boat commanders to adopt a shoot-to-kill policy regarding merchant ships and merchant seamen. Hitler further explained to Oshima that it was vital to cause a manpower shortage in the Allied merchant navy by exterminating all personnel on ships attacked. According to the notes taken at the meeting by the Japanese Military Attaché *Taisa* Ito Seiichi: '*Taishi* Oshima heartily agreed with the Führer's observations and said that the Japanese too would have to adopt these methods.'[2]

Consequently, on 20 March 1943, the *Kaigunsho* issued this order to *Chujo* Teruhisa Komatsu, Commander of the 6th Fleet Submarines, at Truk:

All submarines will act together in order to concentrate their attacks against enemy convoys and totally destroy them. Do not stop at the

INTERNATIONAL PROVISIONS FORBIDDING WARSHIPS AND SUBMARINES ATTACKING PASSENGERS AND CREW OF NON-COMBATANT MERCHANT VESSELS

In action against merchant ships submarines must conform to the rules of International Law to which surface vessels are subject.

In particular, except in the case of persistent refusal to stop on being duly summoned, or of active resistance to visit and search, warships, whether surface vessel or submarine, may not sink or render incapable of navigation a merchant vessel without having first placed passengers, crew and ship's papers in a place of safety. For this purpose the ship's boats are *not* regarded as a place of safety, unless the safety of the passengers and crew is assured in the existing sea and weather conditions, by the proximity of land, or the presence of another vessel which is in a position to take them on board.

Article 22, sections I and II, London Naval Treaty, 1930.
Signatories: USA, UK, France, Italy and Japan.

Note: The Treaty expired on 31 December 1936. However, the Protocol of 6 November 1936 had been signed by the parties represented in London agreeing *without time limit* to uphold sections I and II. The Japanese Government was bound by this Protocol to observe the provisions; in reality, they ignored them totally.

sinking of enemy ships and cargoes. At the same time carry out the complete destruction of the crews of the enemy's ships; if possible seize part of the crew and endeavour to secure information about the enemy.

By late 1941 the Imperial Japanese Navy was the largest naval force in the Far East, with a total of 235 vessels, including 65 submarines. These *sensuikan* were within the 6th Submarine Fleet, first commanded by *Chujo* Mitsumi Shimizu, whose fleet comprised the 1st, 2nd and 3rd *sensui sentai* (Submarine Flotillas). In March 1941 Shimizu was replaced by *Chujo* Teruhisa Komatsu, a cousin of the Empress Nagako. Komatsu's HQ was at Kwajalein in the Marshall Islands, and he commanded his forces from a light cruiser, the 5,890-ton *Katori*. Komatsu was promoted to *Taisho* by 1942 and moved his HQ to Truk in the Caroline Islands. In November 1943, by which time the Advanced Submarine Force consisted of the 1st, 3rd and 5th *sensui sentai*, Komatsu was replaced by *Shosho* Takeo Takagi. Both Komatsu and Takagi were responsible for the shoot-to-kill policy of Japan's submarine commanders. Tagaki was killed on Saipan on 7 July 1944, but Komatsu survived the war and was promoted to the House of Councillors within the Japanese Government. He was saved from prosecution for war crimes by the blanket pardon given to the Japanese imperial family on General Douglas MacArthur's advice.[3]

During the First World War Japanese naval officers had had many opportunities to see British submarines in action. Japan had entered the First World War in August 1914 on the side of the Allies, at a time within the span of the Anglo-Japanese Alliance. Thus the Japanese Government's first experimental submarine, *I-51*, was based on British designs. This led to the I-51 Class (Type KD1). These 1,390-ton submarines were constructed during the period 1919–24 at the Kure Naval Yard. As the Second World War escalated, the submarine classes I, RO and Ha classes predominated. The various types of I submarines were based on the German 'cruiser'-type submarines, and the RO types on the Vickers design for the British L class submarine. As transport submarines, the Ha types consisted only of the Ha101 (Type SS) and the Ha201 (Type STS).[4]

On 15 May 1940, following the heavy bombing of Rotterdam, the Netherlands High Command capitulated to General Fedor von Bock. Dutch possessions in the Far East, however, remained intact. The Spice Islands (modern Maluku, Indonesia), Java and Sumatra were all rich in cocoa, tea, sugar and an abundance of minerals, and they had made Dutch entrepreneurs prosperous since the heyday of the *Vereenigde Oost-Indische Compagnie* (Dutch East India Company) in 1602–1798. Now all this was a rich target for the Imperial Japanese Forces and a Dutch merchantman was soon to experience the brutal reality of Japanese intentions.

COMMAND CHAIN OF RESPONSIBILITY FOR SUBMARINE WAR CRIMES

As at 1943: Boeicho Boeikenshujo Senshibu – Sensuikan Shi

Commander of the 6th Submarine Fleet

Chujo Takeo Takagi. Killed at Saipan, 7 July 1944.
Replaced by:
Chujo Shigeyoshi Miwa, to March 1945.
Replaced by:
Chujo Tadashige Daigo until end of war.

First Submarine Group: 1st Submarine Squadron

Shosho Takeo Kota.

Third Submarine Group: 3rd Submarine Squadron

Shosho Katsumi Komazawa.

Eighth Submarine Group: 8th Submarine Squadron

Shosho Hisashi Ichioka. Directly responsible for sea atrocities of *I-8* and *I-37*.

South-east District Force: 7th Submarine Squadron

Shosho Kaku Harada. Directly responsible for sea atrocities of *I-177*.

South-west District Force: Submarine Division 30

Taisa Toyojiro Oyama. Directly responsible for sea atrocities of *I-165*.

Northern District Force: Submarine Division 7

Taisa Yusaku Okada.

SUBMARINE PERSONNEL IN THE SECOND WORLD WAR

Before the Second World War the Imperial Japanese Navy neglected to prepare submariners for warfare properly, thus training for regular submariners was essentially on-site aboard actual submarines. The *Kaigun Sensuikanbu* (Bureau of Submarines) was not established until May 1943. The Submarine School at Kure was administered by *Shosho* Shigeaki Yamasaki, who was Commander of the 2nd Submarine Squadron in 1941. The school had started courses in the 1920s.

Recruitment and Education

Officers were all volunteers and graduates of the Naval Academy at Etajima, or the Naval Engineering Academy at the port of Maizuru, Kyoto Prefecture. Recruits entered for one of a quartet of courses:

Sensuikan koshu-in: Basic Submarine Officer Course. Aimed at officers just graduated.

Otsushu gakusei: Submarine Officers Course. For officers above the rank of *Chu-i*. All had to complete the Advanced Torpedo Officer Course at the Torpedo Naval Service School.

Koshu gakusei: Submarine Command Course. Candidates were selected from the ranks of senior *Tai-i* and the rank of *Shosa*.

Kikan gakusei: Submarine Engineering Course. For students passing the Advanced Engineering Course at the Maritime Engineering Naval Service School.

Other ranks were also all volunteers, from the rank of Petty Officer [3rd Class] or leading seamen. They were required to undertake the course known as *Senkojutsu renshusei*, Submarine Operating Technique Training.

As the war went against Japan the recruitment net for submariners was cast wider to include men of poor family backgrounds from the *inaka* (Japanese 'boondocks'). By and large submariners of all ranks were considered an elite force. Their indifferent attitude to PoWs was the same as that of any Japanese service personnel.

Deployments in which submarine war crimes occurred

Ambush and pursuit of enemy naval forces; reconnoitring of enemy ports and anchorages; evacuation operations; and forays against merchant shipping. Submarines were also used to launch midget submarines, suicide torpedoes and aircraft, and sometimes acted as fuel stations for seaplanes.

Overall assessment

Japan lost 127 of her 160 submarines. Although morale was generally high among submariners their performance fell short of expectations. They were victims of unreasonable military planning and preparation. They had no effective strategic or operational plans. As frustration grew, war crimes increased. A typical submarine officer war criminal was *Taisa* Tatsunosuke Ariizumi.

Bound for Haifa on the Mediterranean coast, via Colombo, with a shipment of sugar, the 7,395-ton Rotterdam–Lloyd Company Dutch steamship *Langkoeas* slipped anchor at Surabaya, Java, at sundown on 1 January 1942. Already this was her second career. She was built at the Bremer Vulkan Yard on the Weser River for the Hamburg Amerika Line and named *Stassfurt*. She was seized by the Royal Netherlands Navy in May 1940 at Tjilatjap port, Java, and re-registered at Tandjong Priok as *Langkoeas*.[5] By 2 January, under the command of Captain Jan Kreumer and Chief Officer C.J. van de Boom, the vessel was making good progress; she was some 40 miles west of Bowen Island approaching her final stop at Tandjong Priok. But to starboard lurked the *sensuikan* I-58.[6]

Constructed at Yokosuka Naval Yard in 1925, the 1,635-ton *I-58* was of the I-153 Class, Type *Kaidan* KD3A, and had a radius of action of 10,000 sea miles at a surface cruising speed of 10 knots (or 90 miles at 3 knots submerged) and could dive to a maximum depth of 195ft. The submarine's armaments comprised one 4.7-inch gun and sixteen torpedoes. In late 1944 *I-58* was with the 4th *sensui sentai*, acting as a tracker for *Chujo* Nobutake Kondo's Malay Force countering British Force Z out of Singapore.[7] *I-58* was under the command of *Shosa* S. Kitamura, with a crew of eighty-nine volunteer submariners, all from the submarine school at Yokosuka in Tokyo Bay, the second great base of the Imperial Japanese Navy and the base headquarters of the maritime security forces.

Not long after sunset on 2 January 1942 *I-58* sighted the *Langkoeas* and launched a torpedo; it struck the engine space killing a dozen men. As *Langkoeas* began to settle astern the order was given to abandon ship. The vessel's three remaining lifeboats were launched, but one was waterlogged on impact with the sea. As Captain Kreumer and Chief Officer van de Boom marshalled the lifeboats away from the stricken vessel, they were relieved to see *I-58* bearing down on them. Rescue was nigh, and the men in the boats cheered.

The euphoria was soon obliterated by the rattle of *I-58*'s machine-gun fire. The men in two lifeboats were slaughtered before the Japanese gunners turned their attention to the third lifeboat. Among its passengers was the 4th engineer Jan de Mul, who was to be the chief witness to the atrocity. As his fellow crewmen fell under a hail of fire, de Mul jumped overboard and struck away from the lifeboat. Around him seventy-nine dead men floated in the water or hung grotesquely from the lifeboat. In the confusion de Mul found that he had surfaced near the *I-58* and he was dragged from the water by Japanese seamen.

De Mul was one of three crewmen hauled on to the submarine; the other two were Lajar, a Javanese steward, and Lam Dai, a Chinese deck rating. De Mul tried to resist capture but was rewarded with a sword gash on his leg. The Dutchman was interrogated personally by *Shosa* Kitamura. Eventually it dawned on Kitamura that de Mul was small fry among the *Langkoeas*'s western crew. After being kicked and beaten, the three crewmen were thrown back into the sea. *I-58* departed the scene.

Luckily still in their lifejackets, the trio watched *I-58* disappear into the darkness. At dawn de Mul found he was floating alone in the oily waves. His lifejacket was becoming waterlogged, dragging him lower and lower in the water. Then he sighted an empty liferaft and managed to clamber aboard. Some hours into the day he spotted and rescued the two remaining crew members, Lajar and Lam Dai. A few hours later they were able to transfer to an empty work-boat which had survived the *Langkoeas*'s sinking.

Using a fragment of sail they made their way roughly in the direction of Bawean Island. For four days without food, and with only rainwater to slake their thirst under a blazing sun, they arrived at Bawean. Fishermen carried them to a shelter, from where they were taken to the Bawean capital of Sangkapoera. From there they were evacuated by a Consolidated PBY-1 Catalina to Batavia and hospital treatment.

Once he had recovered from this ordeal, de Mul returned to the merchant service aboard the steamer *Boero*. But luck was on his side, for he fell ill and was hospitalised once more. *Boero* sailed for Australia without him, and on 28 February 1942 was torpedoed and sunk in the Sunda Strait by *I-58*. This time *Shosa* Kitamura left no survivors. De Mul was eventually captured when the Japanese secured Java, and spent the rest of the war in a prison camp.[8]

The submarine *I-58* was scuttled by the US Navy on 1 April 1946. Of the war criminal Kitamura little is known. Records seem to show that he commanded the *I-27*, an I-15 Class (Type BI) 2,198-ton submarine built in Sasebo in 1941. *I-27* is recorded as having sunk fifteen merchant ships.[9] *I-27* was lost on 12 February 1944 after being rammed by the British destroyer *Paladin* and torpedoed by the destroyer *Petard* off Maldive Island. Kitamura disappeared. No list of Japanese war criminals brought to trial bears his name.

Port Moresby lies to the south of Papua New Guinea, west of the Owen Stanley mountain range, lapped by the Gulf of Papua and the Coral Sea. In 1942, despite the setbacks suffered at the battles of the Coral Sea and Midway, the *Rikugunsho* was determined to consolidate the Japanese position in the Solomon Islands and therefore renewed the offensive against Port Moresby. To this end a new formation of the 17th Army under *Chujo* Harukichi Hyokutake assembled at Palau, Rabaul and Truk. The garrison of Port Moresby was strengthened by the 21st Australian Brigade (and the 25th Brigade after September 1942) to thwart the estimated 18,500 Imperial Japanese Army troops under *Shosho* Tomutaro Horii who were targeting the New Guinean capital.

HMA Hospital Ship *Centaur* had sailed from Sydney for Port Moresby on 12 May 1943 to evacuate the casualties of the New Guinea operations. The 3,222-ton *Centaur* was built at Greenock in 1924 for the Australia–Singapore service of the Liverpool–flagged Blue Funnel Line. Recently converted as a hospital ship she was crewed by 76 British officers and ratings under Captain George Murray, and had 283 Australian Army Medical Corps personnel, male and female, aboard.

In the early morning of 14 May 1943 *Centaur*'s position was logged at some 40 miles east of Brisbane, making passage along the Great Barrier Reef. Fine weather had given her a good start to the voyage and she steamed on in a blaze of light. In accordance with the regulations stated in Article 5 of the Hague Convention, she displayed floodlit red crosses on the sides of her hull and funnel, on the stern facing aft and the foreside of her bridge. The regulations also required her to have a well-lit white hull with a green stripe running fore and aft. *Centaur* was unarmed and her presence and actions had been notified to the *Rikugunsho* in February 1943 in strict accordance with the articles of war.[10]

As Captain Richard Salt, the Torres Strait pilot on board, guided *Centaur* along the Great Barrier Reef, the very visible hospital ship was fully monitored by *Shosha* Hajime Nakagawa's *sensuikan I-177*. Ex-*I-77* was an *I-176* Class (Type KD7) submarine constructed in 1942 at Kure Naval Yard during the 1939 Fourth Replenishment Law programme. At 1,630-tons, the *I-177* was at this time a transport submarine with reduced armaments, and she was now patrolling the waters of the east coast of Australia after a patrol off Guadalcanal. One of a pack of four patrolling *sensuikan*, the *I-177* had few battle honours for this trip as the only kill for the entire pack had been the British 8,724-ton MV *Limerick* off Brisbane on 25 April 1943. Such lean pickings in part stimulated *Shosa* Nakagawa to take an interest in *Centaur*.

Soon after Nakagawa had given the order to sink to periscope level, torpedoes were launched. One hit *Centaur* on the port side, just forward of the bridge, setting alight a cargo of fuel oil. In minutes *Centaur* was ablaze, her bridge engulfed in flames. She began to sink from the bow and went down within just five minutes.[11]

Some two hundred survivors were now scattered over the sea, some clinging to wreckage, rafts and a miscellany of small boats. It had been over so quickly that *Centaur*'s radio room had had no time to send an SOS and no lifeboats had been launched. *I-177* made no attempt to rescue the stricken survivors. A few days later Lieutenant-Commander

Corey's USS *Mugford* picked up just 64 survivors of *Centaur's* total complement of 360.[12]

Once *Centaur's* fate was known, the Australian Government of John Curtin wired this communiqué to *Sori-daijin* Hideki Tojo's office:

> His Majesty's Government in the Commonwealth of Australia most emphatically protests to the Japanese Government against this wanton attack in disregard not only of the Hague Convention and the International Law, but also on the principles of common humanity accepted by all civilised nations. The Commonwealth Government demands that those responsible for the attack should be punished immediately and demands assurance from the Japanese Government that there will be no repetition by the Forces under the command of the Japanese Government of such an incident in violation of International Law and practice. The Commonwealth Government reserves the right to claim full indemnification and redress for losses sustained.

The *Gaimusho* did not reply.

After the end of the war documents captured and analysed by the Allied Translation and Intelligence Service included a copy of *Kaigunsho: Himitsu-no-kunrei* no. 442 (10 January 1942), which explains, as far as the *Gaimusho* was concerned, why they did not respond to the Australian Government's protest:

> Naturally the rules of international law dealing with hospital ships will be respected. However, it has become known that the enemy – especially Britain and the Netherlands – had resorted in desperation to utilising the immunity of these ships for the escape of important personages. Upon sighting an enemy hospital ship, therefore, an inspection will be made and, if any suspicious persons are aboard, they will be detained. Every effort will be made to uncover and put a stop to illegal actions of this kind.

The command of *sensuikan I-77* was passed to *Tai-i* Katsuji Watanabe and she was sunk with the loss of all hands by the destroyer USS *Samuel S. Miles* off the Palau Islands on 3 October 1944. *Shosa*

Nakagawa was to appear in another theatre of war to continue his deadly war crimes.

During the morning of 1 February 1944 the 7,118-ton British Tanker Company vessel *British Chivalry* nudged her way out of Melbourne Harbour in South Australia, through Port Philip Bay and into the open sea. Built at Palmer's Yard, Newcastle-upon-Tyne, in 1929, *British Chivalry* had a crew of 59, including 14 gunners, 9 from the Royal Navy and 5 from the Maritime Regiment. Although the vessel was well-armed for a merchantman, with a 4-inch anti-submarine gun, a 12-pounder, a 120mm Bofors, six Oerlikons and two twin .5-inch Colt machine-guns, she had no Asdic or depth-charges. Thus she was vulnerable to a prowling submarine. The vessel was heading for a thirty-day voyage to the Persian Gulf under the command of Irish republican Captain Walter Hill.[13]

For six days *British Chivalry* steamed across the Great Australian Bight. On 15 February, when she was 450 miles south-west of the Cocos and Keeling Islands, Captain Hill received orders to alter route because enemy craft were operating in the area of the planned route. To underline this fact, on 21 February they monitored the distress call of the Norwegian tanker *Ferris*, under torpedo attack some 600 miles to the north.

Curiously, on 22 February Captain Hill, against the advice of his senior officers, ceased *British Chivalry*'s zig-zag course, intended to avoid detection, and steamed a straight course. Just before this the radio operator had received a request purporting to be from the Colombo call-sign asking for the ship's position. Asked to repeat it a number of times, the radio officer became suspicious that it was not Colombo calling but an enemy decoy trying to latch on to the vessel's exact position.

This supposedly false call was plausible to maritime historians for 5 miles away lurked the *sensuikan I-37*. This 2,198-ton I-15 Class (Type BI) submarine, built at the Kure Naval Yard in 1941, was the new command of *Shosa* Hajime Nakagawa. He was proud of his vessel's armaments: one 5.5-inch and two 25mm AA guns; six 21m (bow) TT; 17 torpedoes; and one reconnaissance aeroplane. All this with a radius of action of 16,000 surface sea miles at 16 knots. Nakagawa was bursting with confidence, which would help continue his toll of successful strikes.

British Chivalry now offered Nakagawa a classic target. He gave the order for two torpedoes to be launched. One caught the tanker squarely in the engine room, on the starboard side. The second torpedo also hit. Captain Hill immediately gave the order to abandon ship. One lifeboat had been smashed beyond use in the attack, but the two remaining boats were launched, along with four liferafts. As the lifeboats rendezvoused away from the stricken vessel a quick roll-call was conducted. Out of the fifty-nine crew, six had died.

About a mile from the floundering *British Chivalry* I-37 surfaced. Another torpedo was launched and the tanker sank. Then *I-37* opened fire on the lifeboats. In desperation Captain Hill ordered Chief Officer Pierre Payne to semaphore a request to cease fire and a white flag was raised. No one really expected the Japanese commander to comply but, to their great surprise, *I-37*'s machine-guns fell silent.

Captain Hill was ordered to board the submarine, and as he did so the Japanese ratings saluted. The lifeboats were then ordered to move away from the submarine. *I-37* began to manoeuvre, and then, moving back towards the lifeboats, she opened fire once more. One by one the seamen were slaughtered – and on the submarine's deck a Japanese rating calmly filmed the scene. The *I-37* circled the stricken men for some 90 minutes, picking off all the seamen who were visible. When Nakagawa was sure the slaughter was complete he ordered *I-37* away towards the east.

Once the *I-37* had disappeared over the horizon, the survivors were called together by Chief Officer Payne in the one lifeboat still afloat. Nakagawa's tally was surprisingly low: 13 killed and 5 wounded. That was horrific enough, and among those who survived there was a certain sense of relief. The thirty-nine men set off in the general direction of the Seychelles, calculated at 750 miles – or thirty days – away. An extract from the surviving ship's log records a typical poignant moment:

At 11.30 on 23 February Able Seaman Morris lost his life by drowning. His wounds were of such a character that he had been rendered insane and efforts were made by the survivors on the raft to restrain him. He proved to be too violent to hold, and during the struggling he managed to jump overboard and disappeared from view before rescue could be effected.[14]

On 1 March the seamen entered an area of tropical rainstorms which augmented their meagre water supplies; skilful catching of fish helped expand their dwindling rations. By 29 March the seamen's sufferings were intolerable, tempers flared, fists flew, hope ebbed away. By chance they were spotted and rescued by the British MV *Dulane* bound for Cape Town from Calcutta. It took days for the fact of rescue to sink in.

What happened to Captain Walter Hill? Bernard Edwards attests that Hill was made to watch his seamen being slaughtered. On *I-37*'s journey to her base at Penang, Hill was subjected to the mental torture of threatened execution if he did not reveal what he knew about Allied merchant shipping. Exactly what happened to Hill while in Japanese captivity is vague, but he was released when Japan surrendered. Edwards avers that Hill refused to give evidence against the Japanese to representatives of the War Crimes Commission.[15]

On 15 February 1944 the well-armed 5,189-ton MV *Sutlej* of the James Nourse & Co. line[16] steamed out of Aden in convoy bound for Fremantle, Western Australia. Aboard Captain Dennis Jones had a number of reasons to fear for the safety of his ship and his crew of seventy-three. The waters were being patrolled by both German and Japanese submarines and his cargo of 9,700 tons of phosphates would act as a deadweight if the *Sutlej* was struck by torpedoes. By 20 February *Sutlej* had split from the convoy as planned and set off from the waters of Diego Garcia on the 3,000 mile journey to Australia. On the evening of 26 February Chief Engineer Richard Rees was taking the air along the port side of the boat deck when he noted with horror a torpedo approaching the vessel. Within seconds it had crashed into the port side between holds no. 1 and no. 2. The *Sutlej*'s hull was ripped open by *Shosa* Nakagawa's latest gift to the enemy from *I-37*.[17]

Sutlej took only four minutes to sink. It was pitch dark. The survivors had difficulty in locating any wreckage to cling on to. Out of the darkness *I-37*'s searchlight scanned the wreckage. From the conning tower a voice shouted down to Third Engineer Arthur Bennett, who had secured his liferaft to the submarine's hull: 'Where is the ship's captain?' Bennett didn't know. Captain Jones had probably gone down with his ship. A few more questions followed on the *Sutlej*'s details and the enquiring voice fell silent. *I-37* pulled away and the seamen in the water were raked with machine-gun fire.

For a full sixty minutes *I-37* passed and repassed the scene, firing at any target that might shelter survivors. As the submarine finally pulled away there were twelve men left who had somehow avoided the murderous harrowing. In pelting rain the men hauled themselves aboard two rafts. Daylight revealed more survivors; the new tally reached twenty-two. A conference produced the reckoning that they were just under 200 miles from Diego Garcia, and the chances of making landfall seemed thin. Still they tried; as the wind had dropped they were dependent on tidal drift. An assessment of their provisions – biscuits, pemmican, malted milk tablets, and 50 gallons of drinking water – suggested they could last for around sixty days. Rainwater supplemented their fresh water and sea fish their rations.

On 17 March land was sighted. It looked uninhabited, but strong equatorial counter-currents kept them from landing and took them once more out to sea. Two more weeks passed. A ship was sighted on the horizon but flares brought no rescue. Despair deepened when circling sharks were spotted. Then, suddenly and unexpectedly, a PBY Catalina appeared, circled, and dropped a package of provisions. A few hours later HMS *Flamingo* arrived. The survivors had travelled a distance of 650 miles in seven weeks from the spot where *I-37* had sunk the *Sutlej*. The seamen learned, too, that more of their comrades had been picked up by HMS *Solvra*. *Shosa* Nakagawa had slaughtered forty-three men, with two others dying later; yet still his war crimes were not at an end.

The 7,005 British cargo steamer *Ascot*, built at Dundee in 1942 for the London-based trading company of Watts, Watts & Co., set sail from Colombo on 19 February 1944 bound for Fremantle via Diego Suarez, under the command of Captain James Fawcett Travis.[18] With a crew of fifty-six *Ascot* had recently been more heavily armed and carried a cargo of vital food and minerals for the war effort. By 29 February *Shosa* Nakagawa, fresh from his sinking of the *Sutlej*, had locked on to the *Ascot*. Before any alarm could be given, *I-37*'s first torpedo struck the forefront of the engine-room; four crew died instantly. No distress message could be sent as the radio aerials were destroyed.

Soon thirty-four men boarded the fourth of *Ascot*'s lifeboats: two lifeboats had been destroyed in the blast and a third damaged at launch. Other seamen clambered aboard a liferaft. Out to starboard *I-37* surfaced and her machine-guns opened fire. This time the aim was poor and *I-37* edged closer. A shouted exchange took place in which one of the survivors shouted in reply to the usual questions of identification that their captain, chief officer and radio operator were all dead. As the submarine edged even closer to the second group of survivors, a warning rake of gunfire prompted Captain Travis to identify himself in an attempt to prevent further slaughter.

Travis was taken aboard *I-37* with his chief officer Claude Blackett, although Blackett was soon dismissed and sent back to his lifecraft. Curiously Nakagawa erupted in temper, slashing at Travis's hands with his sword and nudging him overboard. There followed two hours of terror and carnage. *Ascot* was shelled to a blazing wreck. When *I-37* at last moved away only eight survivors remained, clinging to a liferaft. The seamen were picked up by the Dutch MV *Straat Soenda* on 3 March and taken to Aden.

After destroying the *Ascot* and murdering most of her crew, *Shosa* Nakagawa returned *I-37* to Penang. Records show that the *sensuikan* was lost in action with the US destroyer escorts *Conklin* and *McCroy Reynolds* on 19 November 1944. *Shosa* Nakagawa was not in command at the time. As with so many Japanese war criminals *Shosa* Nakagawa disappeared from records. Yet in other waters the submarine atrocities went on in parallel.

On 27 November 1943 the 4,087-ton *Daisy Moller* weighed anchor at Bombay and set sail on a 2,300-mile voyage via Colombo to Chittagong (modern Bangladesh). The British cargo steamer had no escort, as Admiral Sir James Fownes Somerville, Commander-in-Chief of the British Eastern Fleet within the Far Eastern Fleet, was hard pressed from his base at Colombo to make a presence with his motley fleet of creaking cruisers and armed merchant ships. At this date the Imperial Japanese Army still held Burma and the sea routes to Chittagong, on the north-east coast of the Bay of Bengal, were within range of Japanese submarines. British Naval Intelligence reported that up to eight Japanese submarines were operating in the area.

Daisy Moller's log showed her lively history.[19] Constructed in 1911 at the German Bremer Vulkan Yard on the Weser River, she had been named *Pindos* for the Deutsche Levant Line. She had become a British prize for the Royal Navy in 1917 and was given to the Glasgow-based

Gem Line with the name *Huntscape*. Re-born as *Wilfred* in 1934, the vessel was bought by the Shanghai-based Moller & Co. Ltd for Far East trading. As the elderly *Daisy Moller*, the Second World War saved her from the breaker's yard.[20]

When *Daisy Moller* set off from Bombay with her cargo of munitions she was commanded by Captain Reginald Weeks and her crew of seventy-one represented various nationalities. Her armaments were served by Royal Navy gunners, and some from the Royal Artillery Maritime Regiment. *Daisy Moller*'s presence in these waters was no secret; Japanese Naval Intelligence had many willing informers among disaffected Indians and the old steamer was a fine target.

On 8 December *Daisy Moller* prepared to leave Colombo for the 1,250-mile journey over the Bay of Bengal to Chittagong, the old port of the Mogul Empire of India, which had been in British hands since 1760. Just before setting sail, Captain Weeks received an order from the Admiralty to stay close to the Indian coastline; this would add some 200 miles to his journey.

Exactly where the 525-ton *sensuikan RO-110* picked up *Daisy Moller* is unclear, but she was still about 650 miles from Chittagong when *Tai-i* Kazuro Ebato moved towards his prey. *RO-110* was of the RO 100 Class (Type KS) and was a product of the 1940–1 construction programme. Built at the Kawasaki Yard in Kobe, the submarine was designed as a coastal vessel to be used mainly in the waters of the outposts of the Japanese Empire. She had an operational duration of 21 days and a radius of action of 3,500 sea miles at 12 knots cruising speed on the surface (60 miles at 3 knots submerged). Able to dive to a maximum depth of 245ft, *RO-110* carried a complement of seventy-five.

Daisy Moller was hit on the starboard side by one of *RO-110*'s torpedoes and soon began to list. As the radio room was not damaged the emergency signal SSS ('I am being attacked by a submarine') was broadcast, to be picked up at the radio station at Vizagapatnam. Because of the ship's volatile cargo, the order to abandon ship was given. Three of the *Daisy Moller*'s four lifeboats were safely lowered but the fourth was smashed when it was released too soon. Only a few minutes after the lifeboats and liferafts pulled away *Daisy Moller* sank. No one had gone down with her.

RO-110 surfaced about 100 yds away. As Japanese ratings began to clamber out on deck the submarine took up position and rammed the lifeboat in which Captain Weeks was now a survivor. The lifeboat was destroyed and *Tai-i* Ebato ordered the men in the water to be machine-gunned. Each of the lifeboats in turn was rammed and machine-gunned. The same treatment was given to the liferafts. *RO-110* then submerged.

The tug *Zerang*, commanded by Lieutenant Lewis Maxwell-Clarkson RINVR, steamed towards Sacramento Shore from where *Daisy Moller's* SSS had been received. On arrival they found fifty-five cadavers floating in the sea. There was no sign of boats or rafts, nor any survivors. Captain Maxwell-Clarkson presumed that the others had made it to land. He pursued a likely course and three days later he found Captain Weeks and fifteen crewmen in the care of the district magistrate at Masulipatam.

The story of what happened then began to unfold. Captain Weeks recounted that when the *RO-110* rammed their lifeboat he was thrown into the water and dodged the machine-gun fire by ducking behind the lifeboat wreckage. Once *RO-110* had gone Weeks and eleven others made their way to a raft. Within hours four more crewmen were found alive. In sight of land the men propelled the available waterlogged rafts as best they could. At midday on 17 December 1943 they made landfall at the Krishna River delta and were rescued by fishermen.[21]

The fate of the *Daisy Moller* was one of the sea atrocities cited in a protest communiqué sent to *Gaimu-daijin* Mamoru Shigemitsu (1887–1957) by the British Government on 5 June 1944, via Monsieur Camille Gorgé, the Minister at Tokyo of the neutral Swiss Confederation. Shigemitsu made no reply. On 15 September M. Gorgé sent a reminder and two months later he received this communication:

[28 November 1944]
I have the honour to acknowledge the receipt of Your Excellency's letter . . . concerning a protest by the British Government which pretends that in the Indian Ocean some Japanese submarines torpedoed British merchant vessels and unlawfully attacked the survivors of the vessels.

Concerning this matter I have caused the competent authorities to make a strict investigation in each case indicated, and it is clear that Japanese submarines had nothing to do with the facts alleged in the protest.

I have the honour to ask Your Excellency to forward this reply to the British Government . . .[22]

On 11 February 1944 *Tai-i* Kazuro Ebato and *RO-110* were patrolling off Vizagapatnam when they sighted a convoy. An initial torpedo damaged the British steamer *Asphalia*. Later *RO-110* and her crew were sent to the bottom with depth-charges.

At Admiral Somerville's headquarters the tally of losses to Japanese submarines was growing as file was added to file. Here's a sample. On 3 March 1944 *Tai-i* Y. Doi's 1,635-ton *I-162* (ex-*I-62*; I-64 Class, Type KD4) sank the British steamer *Fort McLeod*, some 300 miles south-south-east of Ceylon (modern Sri Lanka). On 7 March *Shosa* T. Kusaka's 2,198-ton *I-26* (I-15 Class, Type B5) torpedoed the 8,298-ton US tanker *H.D. Collier* in the Arabian Ocean, and on the same day the 525-ton *RO-111* (RO-100 Class, Type KS), commanded by *Tai-i* Naozu Nakamura, sank the British troopship *El Madina*.[23]

Captain James Hansen and Chief Officer Neil Morris were unaware of any such alarms when the 1907 Sunderland-built but newly armed 3,916-ton British cargo steamer *Nancy Moller* (ex-*Rowena*, ex-*Norfolk*) left Durban bound for Colombo on 28 February 1944 with a cargo of coal. Her voyage, too, was lengthened by some 200 miles south of Madagascar to cut down the risk of submarine attack. Then on 3 March Captain Hansen received a message from the Admiralty revealing that *Fort McLeod* had been sunk along their intended route. At the time *Nancy Moller* was battling through adverse weather and Hansen considered his vessel safe from immediate danger.

By 5 March *Nancy Moller* was bowling along in fine weather following a zig-zag pattern during the daylight hours. On 17 March she was close to the spot where *Fort McLeod* went down, only a day and a half from Colombo. On the promptings of the Admiralty Captain Hansen ordered a new set of co-ordinates, away from the stricken vessel's site.

Alas, this brought *Nancy Moller* into the range of *Tai-i* Tsuruzo Shimizu's 1,635-ton *I-165* (I-165 Class, Type KD5) *sensuikan*. The submarine was well blooded; only months before she had sunk the 10,286-ton British steamer *Perseus* in the Bay of Biscay. *Tai-i* Shimizu and his crew of seventy-five were thirsting for more.

I-165's initial torpedo penetrated *Nancy Moller*'s thin plates on the port side; the second struck below the bridge. Very rapidly the vessel sank. *I-165* surfaced some 50 yards from the survivors struggling in the water. *Tai-i* Shimizu shouted the usual questions for identification and the whereabouts of the ship's senior officers as the dark grey hull of the *sensuikan* nudged alongside two lifeboats. Shimizu repeated his questions, only to receive the stock supply that the ship's master and chief officer were dead. The Japanese commander ordered the six men in one of the lifeboats to climb aboard. Only one of the party was noticeably British, and he was ordered below at gunpoint. The others, two Chinese and three Lascars, were forced to kneel down, facing the bow. Watched in horror by their compatriots in the other liferafts, the two Chinese were shot in the back and kicked into the sea. The three Lascars, not deemed important enough to warrant a bullet, were elbowed into the waves.

For some ten minutes *I-165* circled the wreckage of the *Nancy Moller*, her machine-gunners firing at will. Soon the sea was dotted with cadavers and *I-165* withdrew. Once the submarine was out of sight the remaining seamen emerged from their hiding places in the wreckage. A total of thirty-three of the crew mustered at that place of death, out of a company of sixty-five; Captain Hansen and Chief Officer Morris were among the dead.

Ceylon lay some 250 miles away, but it seemed the survivors' only hope. On the morning of 19 March they set out in a motley collection of rafts into deteriorating weather. Morale was badly dented by the elements. Most of the survivors were Lascars who soon became rebellious at the restricted food and drink; they refused to cooperate in the common goal of survival. Fighting broke out and the rafts drifted away from one another; their hope of reaching Ceylon faded. The weather continued to impede their progress and the ragged armada drifted haphazardly away from their set course. Hopes rose when aircraft were seen – perhaps they had been sighted and a message would be radioed back to base. On 22 March HMS *Emerald* duly appeared on the scene, and four days later the survivors were landed at Port Louis, Mauritius.

The survivors of the *Nancy Moller* atrocity were safe. But what happened to the British citizen who had been taken aboard *I-165*? He can be identified as Mancunian Able Seaman Gunlayer Dennis Fryer. Once aboard *I-165* he was subjected to a rigorous interrogation that was of no use to *Tai-i* Shimizu or naval intelligence. When the submarine arrived at Penang base, Fryer was handed over to the *Tokkeitai* and endured further interrogations and beatings. At last his tormentors realised that he wasn't going to talk and he was transported to Changi Jail, Singapore. There he existed as a slave-labourer until released in 1945.

Nancy Moller was *I-165's* last success. On 27 June 1945 the submarine was lost east of Saipan, sunk by a bombing patrol of US Navy aircraft from Tinian. *Tai-i* Shimizu had by this time transferred to the 1,635-ton *I-153*, which was scrapped in 1946. In peacetime he rose to the rank of *Shosho*. Remaining unpunished for his war crimes, he served in the Japanese Maritime Self-Defence Force which officially replaced the Imperial Japanese Navy after 1950.[24]

Another submarine commander was to win notoriety as a war criminal. *Shosa* Tatsunosuke Ariizumi had graduated from Etajima in 1924, and was variously Staff Operations Officer (submarines) at Naval General HQ, and Staff Operations Officer (Subron 8 and 11). In 1944 he was in command of the celebrated *I-8*. Of the *I-7* Class (Type J3), the 2,231-ton *I-8*, with a complement of 100 and carrying a reconnaissance aircraft, was built at the Kawasaki Yard at Kobe in 1936. In 1943 she completed a record-breaking 30,000-mile round trip from Penang to National Socialist Germany to fetch war materials. The voyage took five months. Yet so far she had not been blooded with an Allied vessel 'kill'.

On 7 March 1944 the 1917 Amsterdam-built steamer *Tjisalak* of the Royal Interocean Lines set sail from Melbourne for Colombo with a cargo of flour. Under the command of Captain C. Hen and Chief Officer Frits de Jong, the vessel had a complement of sixty-five plus ten British DEMS gunners from the Royal Navy and Maritime Regiment. Some twenty-eight passengers occupied the state rooms and cabins. From the start they battled through rough weather at a reduced speed of 10 knots to conserve fuel on the long journey.

Unfortunately, a message was received from the British Admiralty advising a change of course deeper into the Indian Ocean, adding 400 miles to the journey to Colombo. This exacerbated *Tjisalak's* fuel problems, but it was advice that had to be heeded to avoid *Chujo* Naomasa Sakonju's 16th Cruiser Squadron which was harassing Allied shipping from its lair in Banka Straits.[25]

By 26 March *Tjisalak* had sailed into the submarine killer zone south of Ceylon. The weather had improved and the vessel started its zig-zag deployment pattern at dawn. As the sky lightened two torpedoes struck the vessel abaft the bridge; power ceased immediately and the radio went dead. *Tjisalak* settled down in the water with a 15–degree list. Her rudder was locked in a position to drive her round in a circle, and she was sinking.

As the ship was abandoned the periscope of a submarine was seen off the quarter; *Tjisalak's* guns opened fire and the submarine submerged. Nevertheless as the vessel began to sink more rapidly Captain Hen ordered a complete abandonment. The last man swam away from the vessel as it slipped beneath the waves. Three Chinese engine room ratings had been killed. As the liferafts mustered with crew and civilians the attacking submarine surfaced. Her markings showed her to be the *I-8*.

At the second request from the submarine's deck group Captain Hen identified himself and was directed, at gunpoint, to bring his lifeboat alongside. The group of seven in the boat with Hen, including two civilians, were ushered below deck. The next boat, containing eight survivors, was also ushered forward and on to the deck. They were assembled and relieved of their valuables. Then, one by one, they were shot. Second Officer Jan Dekker managed to roll overboard after he had fallen under a rain of blows. Miraculously, none of the hail of bullets that followed his escape hit him and he swam away from the *I-8*. Galvanised by fear, he swam as far away as he could from the now retreating submarine and pulled himself on to a piece of wreckage.

Back on board Second Radio Officer James Blears watched in horror as the crew were shot and the Lascars beheaded. From the conning tower a Japanese rating filmed the carnage. Just as he was about to be assaulted for the second time, Blears jumped overboard, taking *Tjisalak's* crew apprentice Peter Bronger with him. Again, by some miracle Blears avoided the machine-gun and rifle fire, the bullets hissing into the sea around him. Apprentice Bronger was shot in the back and Blears stayed with him until he died. At last Blears reached a group of rafts and found temporary safety with a small group of other survivors including Second Officer Dekker.

Slowly the five survivors collected as many supplies from the wreckage as they could. As they rested they talked about what they had seen. One of their number confirmed that he had seen the execution of Captain Hen. Some twenty survivors had been shot, while a few others had been trussed up and towed behind the submarine to their deaths as the vessel submerged. The Japanese ratings showed great satisfaction at this.

On the afternoon of 28 December the group saw a US Liberty-type merchantman approaching. Incredibly, it opened fire on the raft. The survivors dived into the sea, thinking that the ship was perhaps a war prize captured by the Japanese. The firing ceased as the vessel came nearer. Dekker was helped aboard the ship, now identified as the *James A. Wilder*. Taken to the bridge Dekker was admonished by US Captain Lunt for not firing distress rockets; he had at first mistaken the raft with its mast for a Japanese submarine. On 30 March 1944 the survivors were landed at Colombo. Yet their sufferings were not over. As merchant seamen they were given no succour by agents of the Royal Navy nor the Royal Netherlands Navy.

Following the testimony of the Dutch survivors, the Royal Netherlands Government complained to the *Gaimusho* through the Swiss consular channels. The Japanese authorities dismissed the protest as lies.[26] Admiral Somerville wrote this in his diary following the *Tjisalak* atrocity:

> I hear with grave concern that shocking atrocities were committed by the Japanese submarine [*I-8*] . . . I sent a signal to the Admiralty giving a list of the atrocities which had been committed in this Theatre by the Japanese on the crews of torpedoed ships; in every case these were independently sailed ships . . . [in the future] there might be a reluctance on the part of crews to sail in unescorted ships.[27]

Another unescorted vessel was to give *Shosa* Ariizumi further satisfaction.

Built for the US War Shipping Administration, the 7,176-ton Liberty vessel *Jean Nicolet* was given over to the management of the Oliver J. Olsen Steamship Company, San Francisco, in October 1943.[28] Under the command of Captain David Nilsson, the vessel carried a crew of sixty-nine, including some two dozen US Armed Guard gunners under Lieutenant Gerald V. Deal. Within a year *Jean Nicolet* had undertaken voyages to Honolulu and New Guinea, and by 12 May 1944 was loaded at San Pedro, California, for a trip to Calcutta. Captain Nilsson expected an alarm-free trip; by mid-1944 the Imperial Japanese Navy was on the run to home waters and the Allies had sunk twenty-six Japanese submarines. Once in the Indian Ocean *Jean Nicolet* would have the protection of British Consolidated PBY-5 Catalinas. Nevertheless in the Australian-Indian sea lanes lurked at least two *sensuikan*, including *Shosa* Ariizumi's *I-8*.

Jean Nicolet set off on the 13,000-mile voyage unescorted. The first stop was at Fremantle, thence to Colombo. Aboard was a valuable cargo of heavy machinery from the US Army and some thirty US Army personnel to bring the ship's roster to one hundred souls. It took five weeks and four days to arrive at Fremantle, and she set off again on 21 June for Colombo, 3,122 miles away. Fine weather and a following wind kept the crew in good spirits, and they welcomed the news that the US Army had been successful at the Battle of the Marianas and in the two battles in the Philippine Sea. As the details of the sinking of the Imperial Japanese Navy aircraft carriers *Taiho, Shikoku* and *Hijo* were read out, the sea seemed a safer place. By 27 June the euphoria aboard *Jean Nicolet* had faded a little with the news that a Japanese submarine had sunk the British liner *Nellone* and the 6,589-ton *City of Adelaide*. *Shosa* Ariizumi had made his presence felt again and *Jean Nicolet* was forced to change course out of the suspected danger area.

On the clear, balmy morning of 2 July, Captain Nilsson was expecting to see the patrolling British Catalinas from Diego Garcia. He considered a zig-zagging pattern unnecessary but had doubled the look-outs. On the horizon black smoke was seen, and interpreted as a US cargo ship which would soon join them on the last leg. In reality the smoke came from the *I-8*, by now in need of repairs and maintenance. As the *Jean Nicolet*'s look-outs watched the black smoke disperse, two of *I-8*'s triple salvo of torpedoes hit the ship's starboard side. Bridge, forecastle and no. 5 hold were badly damaged. A distress call was keyed and a response recorded from Bombay Radio.

The four lifeboats and two liferafts were launched and men leapt into the sea; all one hundred personnel were evacuated as *I-8* opened fire on the stricken vessel. The submarine hove to, and a megaphoned enquiry as to the ship's identity echoed across the sea. Captain Nilsson's lifeboat was ordered to the submarine's hull and its passengers taken on board. As a gratuitous warning a junior deck boy was shot, his cadaver kicked overboard, and the lifeboat from which the group came was riddled with machine-gun fire. The dazed Americans were relieved of their valuables; their arms tied behind their backs, they were pushed into a sitting position on the deck.

The men in the water were ordered to clamber aboard one by one; they too were robbed, assaulted and trussed until there were more than ninety men on the deck, including Captain Nilsson and Chief Officer Clem Carlin. Five had managed to hide among the wreckage. Her guns raking the floating debris as she left, *I-8* edged away from the scene. Captain Nilsson and the Chief Officer were taken below with the Radio Officer; none of these men was to be seen again. For sport, some of the prisoners were forced to run the gauntlet abaft through a double line of jeering Japanese submariners carrying baseball bats, swords and bayonets. Some prisoners fell, still trussed, into the sea.[29] Orders were given for the *I-8* to submerge. Panic raged through the prisoners still on her deck. One seaman had worked his hands loose and desperately began to untie as many of his comrades as possible; in this way he managed to save six lives.

Not long after *I-8* had disappeared a Royal Canadian Air Force Catalina flew over the site, but went away again. The men swam to some wreckage and watched the *Jean Nicolet* sink. Again Allied aircraft were seen in the distance, but none showed any sign of having spotted the stricken seamen. At length, on 4 July 1944, a Catalina appeared and dropped an inflatable raft, and soon afterwards HMIS *Hoxa* arrived at the scene to effect a rescue of the twenty-three survivors. The bulk of the crew and passengers on *Jean Nicolet* had been either shot, bayoneted to death or drowned. *Shosa* Ariizuma had made a magnificent kill.

Records show that *I-8* was sunk south of Okinawa on 31 March 1945 by the US destroyers *Stockton* and *Morrison*. *Shosa* Ariizumi was not

aboard, as by then he had taken up a new command. His reward for his
kills was promotion to *Taisa* and mastership of the new 3,530-ton I-400
Class (Type Sto) submarine *I-401*. After the Japanese surrender
Ariizumi took his squadron back to Yokohama and en route shot
himself. *I-401* was taken over by the US Navy and scuttled in 1946.

Two further cases of Japanese submarine atrocities are worthy of
mention. Owned by the US War Shipping Administration and operated
by the Sprague Steamship Company of Boston, Massachusetts, the
7,176-ton Liberty vessel *Richard Hovey* left Bombay in the late
afternoon of 27 March 1944 en route to America via Aden. Under the
command of Captain Hans Thorsen, her roster listed seventy-one crew
including twenty-eight US Armed Guards and a handful of passengers.
A day out of Bombay the ship's radio picked up an SSS message that a
US merchant ship was being attacked in the Arabian Sea; this was
followed by a general all-ships message advising vessels to put in place
their anti-torpedo nets.

It was good advice. Just north of the *Richard Hovey* lurked the
celebrated *I-26* of *Shosa* T. Kusaka. Built at Kure Naval Yard in 1941,
this 2,198-ton I-15 Class (Type BI) submarine had won fame in Japan
as the first Japanese ship to sink an Allied vessel, within hours of the
Pearl Harbor raid. By March 1944 *I-26* had sunk 50,000 tons of Allied
shipping, including the 8,117-ton Norwegian tanker *Grena* off the coast
of Oman only days before she took up position to dog the *Richard
Hovey*.

Just before sundown, as the *Richard Hovey*, her large steel mesh anti-
torpedo nets in place, was about halfway across the Arabian Sea, the
starboard look-out saw three torpedo tracks approaching the ship. One
torpedo slid past, while the other two struck amidships. The anti-
torpedo nets had failed. Huge damage was done to the engine room
and the ship began to settle at the stern. No SSS message was possible as
the radio aerials were destroyed. Abandon ship was ordered, just before
a fourth torpedo broke the *Richard Hovey*'s back.

Once into the three lifeboats and two rafts, the survivors assessed
casualties; three engine room crew were presumed dead and there were
a handful of injured. For a while *I-26* circled the listing *Richard Hovey*,
firing into its stricken hulk. Then the submarine's gunners opened fire
on the survivors. At last, after random but inaccurate fire, Captain

Thorsen thought it best to give himself up. He and three other crewmen disappeared below decks on the *I-26*.

As dusk fell the survivors gathered on or near the remaining lifecraft and a tally of thirty-nine men was recorded; a second lifeboat containing twenty-four men was then added to the roster. The survivors were estimated to be some 400 miles from the Kalthiawar Coast of India, and their drinking water was restricted. Unenthusiastically they set off in the direction where they thought India lay. For days they drifted but then managed to rig a sail which gave them some propulsion. Others experimented with distilling drinking-water from sea water using driftwood as fuel.

After long days of despair and constant fear that the submarine would return to complete the massacre, the two lifeboats, which had lost touch with each other, were picked up by the British vessels *Samuta* and *Samcalia* respectively during early April. The men testified to the murderous fire from *I-26* and another atrocity was logged. *I-26* was deemed lost off the Philippines in 1944; *Shosa* Kusaka was not in command.[30]

Sensuikan I-12 (Type A2) had a very short active life. The 2,930-ton vessel was built at the Kawasaki Naval Yard at Kobe in 1943 as a part of the 1941 Additional Programme and was classed as a 'Headquarters submarine' with a radius of action of 22,000 sea miles at 16 knots surface cruising. In 1944 the vessel was in the command of *Chusa* Kameo Kudo.

I-12's prey in October 1944 was the 7,176-ton Liberty ship *John A. Johnson* of the American Mail Line out of San Francisco bound for Honolulu, with a cargo of foodstuffs and ammunition. Her master, Captain Arnold Beeken, was anxious to make a rapid passage although the prevailing weather was foul. As the storms raged the ship lost a liferaft; the radio message reporting the missing craft was picked up by *I-12* a few miles away cruising the surface to recharge batteries.

Chusa Kudo waited until dark to strike; just after 21.00 hrs on 28 October he ordered the firing of one of his eighteen torpedoes. It struck *John A. Johnson* to starboard and the ship's back was broken. Abandon ship was signalled to all hands and an SSS message radioed. All seventy men aboard escaped without injury and had safely reached the lifecraft amid the wreckage.

But *I-12* deliberately rammed the lifecraft as she circled the scene, and wave after wave of machine-gun fire raked the area. For some 45 minutes the fusillade continued, until *I-12* moved away to finish off the still-floating Liberty ship. Then in the darkness *I-12* came to a stop some distance from the survivors. The guns fell silent, the Japanese crew clambered on deck and victory shouts of *Banzai* echoed over the scene of devastation.

During the night a Pan-American Airlines flying boat civilian flight out of San Francisco spotted the survivors and the submarine in the moonlight and saw the glow of the burning wreckage. A message was radioed to San Francisco and sixty seamen were later picked up by the American vessel USS *Argus*. *Shosa* Kudo's unnecessary slaughter of ten US seamen may have been small compared with other Imperial Japanese Navy atrocities but it was still brutal murder. It seems that the *John A. Johnson* was *I-12*'s only kill. Records further show that *I-12* was sunk during the afternoon of 13 November 1944 in action with the US Coastguard cutter *Rockford* and the minesweeper USS *Ardent* north-east of Kauai. *Chusa* Kudo lived to command other *sensuikan*, including the *I-20*, *I-158* and *RO-65*; he was reported killed in action.

CHAPTER SIX

DEATH BY SURFACE RAIDER

On 19 February 1942 planes from *Chujo* Chuichi Nagumo's Carrier Strike Force launched an attack on Australia's sole northern port of Darwin, capital of the Northern Territories. Some 240 Japanese bombers sank 3 destroyers, 8 merchant vessels and a sub-chaser. Of the 170 Allied seamen killed and in excess of 300 injured, many had been machine-gunned in lifeboats. One of the vessels attacked was an Australian hospital ship distinctively marked with white crosses. As Second Officer Pierre Payne of the tanker *British Monarch* commented: 'That was not war – that was sheer murder.'[1] But the Japanese were only beginning their career of murderous retribution.

On 7 March 1942 the island of Java fell, following the grievous defeat suffered by the Allied Fleet in the Java Sea campaign. While the Allies battled with *Shosho* Raizo Tanaka and *Shosho* Shoji Nishimura in the Java Sea the Dutch tanker *Augustina* weighed anchor and slipped out of Tandjong Priok on north-west Java; her captain's intention was to escape to Australia. Fresh from victory in the Java Sea, the Kamikaze Class 1,270-ton destroyer *Harukaze* caught up with *Augustina* some 300 miles south of Christmas Island. Attacked and outclassed, the thirty-man crew of the *Augustina* abandoned ship after setting scuttling charges. They waited as the *Harukaze* circled the area where the ship had sunk, expecting to be picked up. Instead marksmen on the *Harukaze* raked the lifeboats with machine-guns; only one man survived to tell of the *Augustina*'s fate and of an early naval atrocity by a Japanese surface raider.

Chujo Nagumo's Strike Force moved quickly to capitalise on success. On 5 April 1942 'Operation C' attacked C.-in-C. Ceylon Sir Geoffrey Layton's force at Colombo, wreaking great damage on the British-held port; the cruisers HMS *Dorsetshire* and HMS *Cornwall*, along with 424 dead mariners, were added prizes. By 9 April Nagumo's force was attacking the naval base of Trincomalee, sinking the carrier HMS

Hermes, along with the destroyers HMS *Vampire* and HMS *Athelstan*, and the corvette HMS *Hollyhock*. The Eastern Fleet commanded by Admiral Sir James Somerville was now moved to Mombasa, and the Indian Ocean became 'an Axis lake'. Between 1 and 10 April Japanese submarines sank 145,000 tons of Allied merchant ships, but a new batch of surface raiders was also to appear in the region.

During the Second World War some eighty-seven merchant vessels were taken over by the Imperial Japanese Navy; converted and armed, they were used as gunboats; some thirty-one were also used as minelayers.[2] Another fourteen were designated armed merchant raiders.[3] Two such were the sister-vessels *Aikoku Maru* and *Hokoku Maru*. Built at the Tama Yard in Osaka in 1939, both vessels began their careers for the Osaka Shozen Kaisha line. Both vessels were of 10,439 tons, and were well armed with 6-inch guns, anti-aircraft guns, torpedoes and two catapult-launch spotter aircraft. As they moved into the Indian Ocean to act as raiders and supply vessels for the 8th Submarine Flotilla of *Chujo* Noburo Ishizaki's fleet, they were commanded by *Chusa* Hirishi Imatsato and *Chusa* Tamatso Oishi respectively.

At first, prize returns for the two vessels were few. On 9 May they captured the 7,987-ton Dutch tanker *Genota* bound from Australia to the Persian Gulf, and escorted her to Singapore.[4] With the Imperial Japanese Navy's dominance of the Indian Ocean it was decided to move Ishizaki's force to Madagascar, where Allied merchant vessels were reported on passage from India to Europe via the Cape of Good Hope. This was to be the background for a deadly kill by *Hokoku Maru* and *Aikoku Maru*.

Early on the morning of 5 June 1942 the 6,757-ton UK cargo-passenger liner *Elysia*, belonging to the Glasgow-based Anchor Line, was making passage between Madagascar and the African coast, out of Cape Town bound for Bombay, when she was intercepted by the deadly duo. Captain Morrison decided to try to outrun the hostile vessels although his 1908-built craft, brought out of retirement for the war, was clearly not up to the task. For more than an hour *Elysia* ploughed on at 13 knots amid a hail of shells and shrapnel until her superstructure suffered severe damage. At last Captain Morrison ordered his Anglo-Indian crew and his seventeen civilian and service passengers to abandon ship.

Hokoku Maru and *Aikoku Maru* circled the stricken *Elysia*. A heavy bombardment of shells and a direct hit from a seaplane bomber launched from *Hokoku Maru* failed to sink her. At last the vessel was torpedoed, and she sank some four hours later. By this time the Japanese vessels had left the scene, abandoning their victims to their fate. Fifteen hours later Captain Morrison and his party were picked up by the British hospital ship *Dorsetshire*.

Records show that *Hokoku Maru* and *Aikoku Maru* sailed further into the Indian Ocean. Another victim was the 7,113-ton British MV *Hauraki* off Diego Garcia, sunk just before the sea-raiders docked at Penang for a refit. As war prizes go *Chusas* Imatsato and Oishi had little to boast, but their day would come, and their names would rank high in the history of Japanese naval infamy.

The 6,341-ton Dutch tanker *Ondina* was built at Amsterdam for the Royal Dutch Shell Company in 1939. By 1942, still flying the Netherlands flag, she was a part of the British Ministry of War Transport merchant fleet and was now chartered to carry grain on the 11,000-mile round trip from Australia to the Persian Gulf. Under the captaincy of Willem Horsman and escorted by Acting Lieutenant-Commander William J. Wilson's minesweeper HMIS *Bengal* (as far as Diego Garcia), the *Ondina* set sail with her crew of fifty-six for what was supposed to be an uneventful voyage. Captain Horsman did not anticipate having to use his 4-inch anti-submarine guns, the twin Marlin or the Lewis machine-guns.

Ondina set sail on 5 November from Fremantle, led by *Bengal*, just as *Hokoku Maru* and *Aikoku Maru* were leaving Penang. They steamed steadily in fine weather for six days. Then, some 500 miles south-south-west of the Cocos Islands, Third Officer C.C. Hederick sighted the two Japanese vessels to port at a distance of 8 miles. *Bengal* confirmed the sighting by signal lamp. Action stations were called just in time as the Japanese ships opened fire. Lieutenant-Commander Wilson ordered *Ondina* to escape while his vessel confronted the Japanese raiders with a direct attack on the *Hokoku Maru*. Both Japanese vessels continued a ferocious fusillade as *Bengal* zig-zagged without being hit. Aboard the *Ondina* Captain Horsman decided to abort his escape course and turned to face the Japanese raiders.

The initial fire from *Ondina* fell harmlessly out of range of *Hokoku Maru*, but a direct hit was scored with the third shot. *Chusa* Imatsato manoeuvred his vessel broadside to *Ondina* but he was too late and *Hokoku Maru* sustained several precision hits. As *Aikoku Maru* moved into position *Bengal* also took a direct hit. On fire, *Hokoku Maru* stopped and concentrated her firepower on *Ondina*. She sustained hit after hit, with topmast and wireless aerial damage, a serious foredeck fire and the loss of one lifeboat. Although her guns were still blazing, *Hokoku Maru* was clearly sinking. By now *Bengal* was incapacitated, but even so she was able to draw off *Aikoku Maru* and *Ondina* made her escape.

Hokoku Maru was further disabled by a huge on-board explosion; her part in the action was over. *Aikoku Maru*, however, continued firing on the fleeing *Ondina*. Some 40 minutes after first opening fire *Ondina* ran out of ammunition and Captain Horsman prepared to surrender. His crew began to abandon ship. *Aikoku Maru* did not cease firing. Captain Horsman was mortally wounded in the fire and died minutes after being hit.

In the three remaining lifeboats and two rafts the fifty-six crewmen abandoned ship under the direction of Chief Officer Maarten Rehwinkel, who had assumed temporary command. As the boats pulled away from *Ondina* the survivors cheered loudly as they watched *Hokoku Maru* sink.

Aikoku Maru now closed in on *Ondina* and two torpedoes were launched. Both struck home and the vessel began to list. *Chusa* Oishi then ordered his vessel towards the survivors and the Japanese gunners opened fire on the lifeboats and rafts. The *Ondina*'s crewmen jumped into the water, or ducked into the boats. The gunners raked the lifecraft until they were sure no one was left alive; *Aikoku Maru* then sheered off and steamed away. Slowly survivors began to emerge from the wreckage. Although there were several wounded, only two Chinese stokers were found dead. Terror swept through the survivors once more when *Aikoku Maru* reappeared, but this time she was searching for survivors from the *Hokoku Maru*. A total of 278 Japanese seamen were rescued from the ship's complement of 354, and *Aikoku Maru* steamed away once more.[5]

Ondina's survivors were now drifting some 500 miles north-east of the Cocos Islands without either sufficient drinking water or edible supplies. Obviously they could not make land alive. It was decided that they should return to the listing *Ondina* to scavenge what they could.

An examination of the vessel revealed that despite the damage the ship was still seaworthy. Could she be sailed to a safe harbour? It was worth taking the risk.

Slowly the vessel was pumped out to correct her list and the remaining survivors were hauled aboard. Miraculously Maarten Rehwinkel and his battered crew set sail on the 1,400-mile journey to Fremantle on 12 November. They arrived on 18 November and learned that *Bengal* had reached Diego Garcia safely on the 16th. *Ondina's* crew had, for the most part, survived a Japanese naval atrocity. *Chusa* Hirishi Imatsato had gone down with the *Hokoku Maru*. Records show that *Aikoku Maru* was lost on 17 February 1944, but nothing further is known of her master, *Chusa* Tamatso Oishi, who was never brought to justice for his murder and attempted murder on the high seas.[6]

The atrocity involving the 16-knot, twin-screw MV *Behar* is one of the classic cases of its type and infamous because she was the last Allied merchantman sunk by a Japanese enemy surface raider. By 17 February 1944 Japan had been struck a mortal blow at Truk, now within the Federated States of Micronesia. To this day Truk Atoll displays sunken hulks as relics of the time when US Task Force 58 destroyed some 200,000 tons of Japanese vessels and 75 per cent of the 365 planes assembled there.

Apprised by Japanese Naval Intelligence of the US Forces approaching Truk, *Taisho* Mineichi Koga, Commander-in-Chief of the combined Fleet, had abandoned Truk as a main naval base in the Pacific and adopted a defensive policy. He moved the 16th Squadron of the Japanese South-West Area Fleet under *Chujo* Shiro Takasu from Penang and made for the Indian Ocean via the Sunda Strait.

Koga's intention was to conduct a vigorous counter-offensive against Allied merchant shipping. With this group were three heavy cruisers, the 9,380-ton *Aoba*, as flagship, the 11,215-ton *Chikuma*, and her sister-vessel, the *Tone*, under *Taisa* Haruo Mayuzumi. These vessels were under the overall command of *Chujo* Naomasa Sakonju, Commander of the 16th Cruiser Squadron, who relayed orders to all senior officers that enemy vessels should be captured if possible, sunk if absolutely necessary and only the most senior of enemy personnel captured were to be interrogated, in a *Saishogen* (minimal) way.[7] Other survivors should be . . . senior officers already knew what to do with them. Sakonju's trio of

vessels rounded south-eastern Sumatra on 28 February 1944 and fanned
out of the Sunda Strait into the Indian Ocean to search for enemy
merchant vessels on the Australia–India run.

Some hours after the Japanese fleet entered the Indian Ocean the
British cargo-passenger vessel *Behar* weighed anchor at Melbourne.
Owned by the Hain Steamship Company, a subsidiary of P&O, the
7,840-ton *Behar* was embarking on an important long-haul voyage amid
much Australian press interest, and she came to the notice of Japanese
Naval Intelligence. Now under Captain Maurice Symonds, with a crew
of 102, *Behar* had been completed at the Scottish Barclay Curle yard on
the Clyde in May 1943 and replaced a vessel of the same name which
had come to grief on a mine at Milford Haven in November 1940. The
new vessel had the latest Asdic and depth-charge equipment and an
armament of one 4-inch and one 3-inch dual purpose guns, several
20mm Oerlikons and .5-inch Browning machine-guns, and a multiple
rocket-launcher, all in the remit of Asdic operators and seventeen
DEMS gunners.

Behar set out for Liverpool on 29 February 1944, twelve hours late,
with a cargo of zinc and foodstuffs. The first leg of the journey was the
5,558 miles to Bombay, via Fremantle and Ceylon; the voyage was
expected to last fifteen days. The vessel's passenger cabins housed a
mixture of nine service personnel and civilians, including two women,
wives of dockyard officials.

By 1 March *Chujo* Sakonju's heavy cruisers were sweeping the sea
lanes some 500 miles south of the Cocos Islands. In line abreast,
scanning an arc of 60 miles, *Aoba, Chikuma* and *Tone* were out of sight
of one another. By 9 March Sakonju's raiders had found nothing, but
just as the Japanese vessels were about to move north, the look-out on
Tone reported smoke on the horizon. *Taisa* Mayuzumi altered course to
investigate. It was a moment of bad luck for *Behar;* if she had left on
time she would not have fallen into the raiders' net.

Around 10.00pm Third Officer James Anderson spotted the *Tone*
approaching. The conditions were misty after clear weather, but
Anderson was sure enough of the enemy sighting to call Captain
Symonds to the bridge. *Tone* flashed a signal lamp message for *Behar* to
stop. Symonds ordered a code RRR (I am being attacked by a surface
raider) call. *Tone's* wireless room intercepted the message and the ship

Emperor Hirohito (1901–89) reviews troops on his imperial grey, accompanied by his aides. All atrocities in the Japanese-occupied Far East were carried out in his name. He was shielded from prosecution as a war criminal largely on the intervention of US Army General Douglas McArthur. (Japan Research Projects)

The Kaigun Heigakko *(Imperial Japanese Naval College) at Etajima, Hiroshima Bay, Japan, 1942. Centre right is the* Daikodo *(Great Hall) and the* Seitokan *(Cadets' Quarters). The college was established at Etajima in 1888. The campus also included accommodation for the Imperial Family. (Japan Research Projects)*

Naval cadets assembled for sword practice. It was the naval officer's boast that he could sever a PoW's head with a single sword stroke. The calligraphy on the wall-mounted kakemono *(scrolls) displays the words of the Russo-Japanese War victor* Gensui Heihachiro Togo: *'Katte kabuto no o wo shimeyo' (When you conquer tighten the chin-straps of your helmets – that is, conquer with resolution and thoroughness). (Japan Research Projects)*

Naval cadets practise judo. For sport, naval personnel on the prison ships would practise this art on weak and emaciated PoWs. (Japan Research Projects)

Naval cadets in field dress practise sharp-shooting at the target ranges on Mount Furutaka. Naval personnel were adept at shooting shipwrecked Allied mariners as they tried to swim to safety. All PoWs attempting to escape from prison ships at sea were shot. (Japan Research Projects)

President of the Naval College, Chujo Koshiro Oikawa (centre), poses with guests from HMS Berwick, under Captain S.G. Sedgwick RN (front row, third from left), May 1934. In the Second World War Oikawa advocated mass suicide attacks (Kamikaze) on military and civilian targets. He was summoned before the International War Crimes Trials in Tokyo, 1946–8. (Japan Research Projects)

HRH Prince Edward, Prince of Wales, escorted by Miya-sama Taisho *Hiroyasu Fushimi (d. 1947), a cousin of Emperor Hirohito, and the Japanese Navy General Staff, after landing at Yokohama. As Chief of the Naval General Staff (1932) and Chairman of the Supreme War Council, Fushimi approved the transportation of PoWs as slave-labour and advocated the use of suicide weapons. Prince Edward made a tour of the East aboard HMS* Renown *between 26 October 1921 and 20 June 1922. (Japan Research Projects)*

Prince Edward is introduced to Hakushaka Gensui *Heihachiro Tōgo (d. 1935) at Kagoshima. Deemed the greatest of all Japan's admirals, Tōgo was the hero of the Russo-Japanese War. His flag battleship* Mikasa *survives as a museum and National Monument. (Japan Research Projects)*

At the conclusion of his visit to Japan, Prince Edward entertained the Japanese staff who had escorted him in Japan aboard HMS Renown. *Many naval officers he met were to connive at atrocities at sea in the Second World War. (Japan Research Projects)*

The Hayashi Cabinet of the Japanese Government, February 1937. Seated, left to right: Okura-daijin *Toyatoro Yuki;* Sori-daijin *Senjuro Hayashi;* Norin-daijin *Iatsunosuki Yamazaki. Standing:* Shoko-daijin *Takuo Godo;* Kaigun-daijin *Mitsumasa Yonai;* Rikugun-daijin *Kotaro Nakamura;* Naimu-daijin *Kakichi Kawarada;* Homu-daijin *Suchiko Shiono. Mitsumasa Yonai (d. 1948) gave evidence at the International Tribunal for the Far East War Crimes Trial. (Japan Research Projects)*

Taisho *Jiro Minami (d. 1957), left,*
talks with Taisho *Kenkichi Ueda,*
Shireichokan *Kwantung Army,*
Manchuria. Both sanctioned the
transportation of slave-labour from
their areas of command.
(Japan Research Projects)

Hideki Tojo (1884–1948), when a
General Staff Officer. As a Taisho
and Sori-daijin *he supported harsh*
treatment for PoWs and promoted
their transhipment for slave-labour.
His callousness and indifference to
PoW suffering was honed while
serving as Commander of the
Kwantung Army Kempeitai *in*
Manchuria in 1935. He was
executed as a war criminal at
Sugamo Prison, Tokyo.
(Japan Research Projects)

Nine of the eleven, now rare, stamps issued in May 1943 by the Japanese Naval Administration in the Moluccas and Lesser Sundas; they were also used by the Imperial Japanese Navy administration areas in the Celebes and South Borneo. The calligraphy on mail and stamps usually read: Gunseibu Yuseiyaku, for Post Office of the (Naval) Government; and Dai Nippon Teikoku, for Great Japanese Empire.
(Author's Collection)

Survivors of the Dai Nichi Maru *hellship, which left Singapore on 28 October and arrived at Shimonoseki on 23 November 1942. They were transferred as slave-labour to Hiroshima Camp no. 5. Back row, left to right: AC1 A.E. Seaton; AC1 G.W.G. Spink; LAC H.C. Harris; Sgt C.G. Broadis. Front row: LAC F.A. Squires; Cpl A. Hodson; LAC R.J. Bray; Cpl R.W. Harper. (Terence Kelly)*

The Supreme Court Buildings, Singapore. Here, on 21 January 1946, commenced the first War Crimes Trial to be held in the Far East. It was the first to study evidence of war crimes at sea in the fate of the Thames Maru. (William Hodge)

The ten defendants in the Gozowa Trial of 1946, wherein testimony was introduced regarding war crimes aboard the Thames Maru. (William Hodge)

Tai-i *Sadaichi Gozawa (b. 1900), Commander of the* Gozawa Buntai *and custodian of the PoWs aboard the* Thames Maru. *Charged with maltreating PoWs in transit and condoning murder at the final destination of Yamato Camp, Babelthuap Island, where he was Garrison Commander. Found guilty, he was sentenced to twelve years' imprisonment at Outram Road Jail, Singapore. (William Hodge)*

Chu-i *Kaniyuki Nakamura (b. 1897).
Platoon commander. Charged with
violating the laws and usages of war
aboard* Thames Maru, *and the murder
of a PoW by beheading. Found guilty,
he was hanged at Changi Jail,
Singapore, on 14 March 1946.
(William Hodge)*

Tai-i *Ken Okusawa (b. 1915).
Medical officer. Charged with
maltreating PoWs in transit. Found
guilty; sentenced to two years'
imprisonment at Jurong Camp,
Singapore. (William Hodge)*

Chu-i *Ruyichi Kajino (b. c. 1915).*
Platoon commander. Charged with
maltreating PoWs in transit and at
Yamato Camp. No prima facie case
against him could be proved and former
PoWs failed to substantiate the charges.
Discharged on 24 January 1946;
repatriated to Japan in February 1947.
(William Hodge)

Shosho *Sueyoshi Kusaba,*
Commander of the FUGO *project*
between November 1944 and
March 1945. This project was the
Imperial Japanese Navy's
'Kamikaze' balloon bombs which
transported explosives (and was
scheduled to carry loads of
biological weapons) to the
US mainland.
(Japan Research Projects)

A Japanese naval officer supervises navy personnel during a trial launch of a Type B 'Kamikaze' balloon. (Japan Research Projects)

opened fire. The initial shells ricocheted off the ocean surface and hit the foredeck. Now firing at point-blank range *Tone* launched salvo after salvo in *Behar*. Huge holes were blasted below the waterline and *Behar's* decks were ablaze. Under this devastating fire the vessel's four lifeboats were launched safely, and the ship was abandoned.

Behar sank some 20 minutes after the Japanese had opened fire. Captain Symonds ordered the lifeboats to cluster together while a head count was taken; 108 of the 111 on board were accounted for, with three seamen dead. As the captain discussed what to do next with his Chief Officer, *Tone* edged towards the lifeboats out of the mist. A loud-hailer, in an echoing flurry of words promising that all would be well, with fine treatment for all who surrendered, directed the lifeboats to come alongside as Japanese ratings trained rifles and machine-guns on the survivors. Boarding ladders snaked down the side of *Tone* and the survivors were hauled aboard. Using extracts from the diary of Lieutenant J.G. Godwin, author James MacKay notes what happened next:

> Rings, watches, wallets, handkerchiefs, money, lighters and cigarettes, everything and anything of value or for personal use was seized. The survivors were then lined up and had their hands bound behind their backs, with a piece of rope leading from their tied wrists that was looped around their necks and retied to their wrists but only after the arms had been yanked upwards. Eyes bulged and breathing became laboured as the weight of trussed arms forced the looped rope around each survivor's neck to cut off air to the windpipe. Only by raising their arms further up their backs, an agonising procedure, could breathing be assisted.[8]

Chief Officer Phillips complained that brutally securing civilians in such a way was a direct contravention of the Geneva Convention. He was beaten for his audacity, but a Japanese officer ordered that the women survivors be released.

Hours passed while the trussed survivors sat on the deck in the blistering sun that had broken through the mist; eventually they were bundled below decks into a small storeroom. The *Tone* took on the role of a hellship. Here the Japanese ratings set about the survivors with bamboo canes, beating the writhing, screaming bodies until their blood-lust was quenched. Bleeding and battered from this brutal assault the survivors, now clearly PoWs, were untied and moved to a larger room; even so, the oven-like conditions soon produced feelings of suffocation as 108 bodies bled and sweated in the darkness.

For six days the survivors suffered these terrible conditions, relieved by scant food and water. Some of the Indian crewmen from the *Behar* were tricked into drinking seawater, which added to the torture of their thirst. Two periods of exercise were allowed every twenty-four hours and latrines were crude devices rigged over the ship's side. On 15 May *Tone* reached the anchorage off Tandjong Priok in Java.

Meanwhile *Taisa* Mayuzumi had signalled his success to *Chujo* Sakonju. A stinging reply was returned. Why had Mayuzumi not captured *Behar* and her cargo? Why had he lumbered himself and the 16th Cruiser Squadron with 108 useless prisoners? *Shobun suru* – dispose of them, reiterated the order.

Usually such an order would have caused an Imperial Japanese Navy officer no difficulties. But Mayuzumi was different from most Japanese officers in that he was a *Kirishitan* (Christian). The murder of dehumanised enemies was not his way. He conveyed his anguish to his second-in-command, *Chusa* Mii, who was not a Christian but agreed with his superior. Mayuzumi signalled Sakonju personally aboard his flagship *Aoba*, with a plea for his captives to be put ashore unharmed. Sakonju repeated his order. Mayuzumi still demurred and even crossed in his launch to *Aoba* to press his plea 'on his knees', as he testified in the subsequent war crimes trial. Sakonju dismissed his captain with the words *Watashi no iitsuke ni shitagai nasai* ('Obey my orders'). Against his conscience Mayuzumi capitulated.

For reasons not entirely clear the *Behar* prisoners were divided into two groups of 72 and 36. The smaller party included: Captain Symonds, Chief Officer Phillips, Chief Engineer Weir, Second Engineer McGinnes, First Radio Officer Walker, Petty Officer Griffiths, the two Asdic ratings and twenty-one Indian ratings, along with seven of the nine passengers including the two women, Captain Green and Dr Li.[9] They were transferred to the flagship *Aoba*.

The remaining prisoners left the scene when *Tone* weighed anchor. As *Taisa* Mayuzumi observed from the bridge, the seventy-two men

KNOWN SERVICE AND CIVILIAN PERSONNEL ABOARD THE MV *BEHAR* WHO SUFFERED SEVERE ILL-TREATMENT AT THE HANDS OF THE IMPERIAL JAPANESE NAVY

Captain Maurice Symonds
Chief Officer William Phillips
Chief Engineer James MacWeir
Second Engineer E. McGinnes
Bosun A.B. Macleod
Second Officer Gordon Rowlandson
Third Officer James Anderson
Fourth Officer John Robertson
Officer Cadet Denys Matthews
Officer Cadet Alan Moore
First Radio Officer Arthur Walker
Second Radio Officer James Smyth
Third Radio Officer Henry Cummings
Petty Officer W.L. Griffiths
Duncan MacGregor, retired Australian banker
Captain Percy J. Green of the Indo-China Steam Navigation
Dr Lai Yung Li, a Chinese physician
RAF Flight Sergeant Allen Barr
Australian Lieutenant S.C. Parker
Australian Sub-Lieutenant R. Benge
New Zealand Fleet Air Arm Sergeant J.G. Godwin
Mrs Shaw
Mrs Pascovey

Total crew: 102. Three died in action and Mr MacGregor was reported to have died at sea. Seventy-two were murdered.

from the *Behar* were beheaded in groups. At the subsequent war crimes trial *Chusa* Mii described what happened:

On the evening of 18 March I was told by *Taisa* Mayuzumi that the execution of the prisoners still remaining on board must be carried out that night at sea. I refused to be associated with the execution, so the captain issued orders direct to *Tai-i* Ishihara. I cannot now remember the names of the members of the execution party, but learnt that most of them were gunroom officers, though *Tai-i* Tani and a few other wardroom officers were in the party. I later heard *Chu-i* Tanaka and *Chu-i* Otsuka boasting of their participation in the execution. As I was not an eyewitness I could not describe the exact method used, but I did hear that the prisoners were knocked down by a jab in the stomach and a kick in the testicles and then beheaded.[10]

Captain Symonds and the other thirty-five survivors were put ashore at Tandjong Priok, to be imprisoned at an office requisitioned by the *Tokkeitai*, which had belonged to the Royal Interocean Lines. On the day their compatriots were murdered they were moved to a PoW camp outside Batavia, and the women taken to a corresponding female camp. To the Japanese Chief Officer Phillips was a continual irritation; he never stopped complaining about the group's ill-treatment. Once at the camp Phillips was placed in solitary confinement, bound hand and foot, with a bamboo cane tied across his throat to silence him. Once the *Tokkeitai* and Japanese Intelligence had completed their interrogations, the survivors of the *Behar* were split up; some went to other camps, others to slave-labour in Japan. They were released at the end of the war.

Of Sakonju's three surface raiders *Aoba* and *Tone* were sunk by US planes at or near the port of Kure in July 1945, and *Chikuma* was sunk at the Battle of Leyte Gulf in October 1944. Sakonju was found guilty of capital war crimes and was hanged, while Mayuzumi received seven years' imprisonment.[11]

CHAPTER SEVEN

THE LAST HELLSHIP TRANSPORTS, 1944–5[1]

As the first rays of the sun flooded the courtyards of the Imperial Palace, Tokyo, in 1944, the Japanese General Staff officers assembled to tell the Emperor the grave news. The tide of Japanese domination and occupation of the Far East was ebbing ever faster. Day after day the *Kaigunsho* recorded more and more losses. By February Truk had been abandoned as a main naval base, and at the close of the year the navy had suffered shipping losses of around 3,825,000 tons. Morale was dealt blow after blow with such events as the death of the Commander-in-Chief of the Combined Fleet, *Taisho* Mineichi Koga, in a plane crash off Cebu on 31 March 1944. This loss was kept secret for a month.

While the Imperial Japanese Forces were being relentlessly driven from the Admiralty and Marshall Islands in January and February 1944, the hellships sailed on. More and more they came under attack and sank, taking with them hundreds of PoWs. On 21 January, for instance, the 3,156-ton NYK Line transporter *Ikoma Maru*, in convoy from Palau to New Guinea, was sunk by Commander Slade D. Cutter's submarine USS *Seahorse*; 43 crewmen and 418 Indian PoWs were listed drowned, killed or missing. On 25 February the 6,200-ton *Tango Maru*, which the Japanese had raised from scuttling at Priok harbour, was in convoy to Surabaya when she fell foul of Lieutenant-Commander Willard R. Laughan's submarine USS *Rasher*. Herein in excess of three thousand Javanese labourers and PoWs perished.

Another hellship salvaged by the Japanese was the *Harugiku Maru*, under the command of *Sencho* Miyosaki. On 25 June the 3,040-ton vessel left Belawan port, Medan, with 730 Australian, Dutch and British PoWs, bound for railway construction slave-labour on Sumatra. So cramped were the prisoner holds that the PoWs could only stand, and a single bucket latrine served all. On 26 June the convoy in which *Harugiku Maru* was travelling was spotted by Lieutenant-Commander R.L. Alexander's submarine HMS *Truculent*. Alexander attacked, but his submarine became grounded in the shallow water in that area; release was effected with the help of depth-charges from the sub-chasers guarding the convoy. The submarine moved away from the scene. Meanwhile two torpedoes fired by HMS *Truculent* had hit *Harugiku Maru*, and the explosions split her in two. PoWs spilled into the water largely unmolested by the Japanese. Nevertheless it ranked as a war atrocity as the Japanese captain had condoned the harsh conditions on board and rendered little assistance as the vessel sank; 180 PoWs died. Three days later the rest were saved and sent to the River Valley Road PoW Camp, Singapore.

Back in Japan, the prison camps were registering hundreds of sick and debilitated PoWs. The *Eiseibu* (Army/Navy Medical Dept) and the co-opted civilian *igakushi* (medical licentiates) could not cope. As the Imperial HQ staff ranted that ill and dying PoWs were no use to the Emperor's mission, the camps in the Philippines were scoured for Allied PoW medics for shipment to Japan. By March 1944 two hundred assorted medical personnel were assembled at Manila for boarding into the stinking holds of the merchantman *Kenwa Maru*. They were accompanied by four hundred Japanese nationals, and safe passage was made.

Among the records of the last hellship voyages the final hours of three vessels are of particular interest, namely *Arisan Maru, Brazil Maru* and *Enoura Maru*.[2]

The 6,886-ton *Arisan Maru* made passage from Manila on 10 October 1944 bound for Japan with around 1,800 American PoWs. On 24 October the vessel was sunk east of Hong Kong after being struck by three torpedoes from the USS *Snook*. About 1,782 PoWs died or were missing. Three survivors were later recaptured by the Japanese from the waters of the Bashi Straits and were interned in Formosa. Five others had a remarkable story to tell when they returned to the USA.

In their testimony, preserved by the Office of the US Provost Marshal General, they explained what happened.[3] The five survivors floated in the sea for some time and eventually clambered on to a liferaft. A mast and sails were rigged and scavenging in the sea produced a keg of drinking water and a tin box of biscuits. Through a typhoon and raging seas they made the 300 miles to landfall on the China coast, where luckily there were no Japanese. Their story remains a celebrated case in the history of the hellships.

The fate of the 5,860-ton *Brazil Maru* and the *Enoura Maru* are intertwined. Both vessels set off for Japan from the Philippines on 27 December 1944, the former from Lingayen Gulf and the latter from San Fernando. Each vessel carried survivors from the *Oryoku Maru* which had been bombed and torpedoed by US planes off Bataan Peninsula on 15 December. When she sank, around 236 survivors boarded the *Enoura Maru* with a further 1,105 on the *Brazil Maru*.

The vessels arrived at Takao, Formosa, on 31 December 1944. On 8 January 1945 US Navy aircraft attacked Takao Harbour. The *Enoura Maru* was hit several times and the casualties were recorded as 'heavy'.[4] The Japanese authorities in Takao would not allow the dead to be removed, nor the wounded to be treated. Several days later squads of PoWs were impressed to gather up their dead compatriots, who were stacked on pyres and burned.

An unknown number of survivors were herded aboard the *Brazil Maru* for onward transportation. On 14 January *Brazil Maru* sailed for Japan and two weeks later around 450 PoWs disembarked at Moji. This was to be the last hellship voyage from the Philippines. Incidentally, at Takao the *Brazil Maru* was joined in convoy by the *Melbourne Maru*, carrying survivors of *Arisan Maru*, and the smaller *Hokusen Maru*, making up one of the last shipments of PoWs from Takao.

In September 1944 the Japanese evacuated PoWs from Indo-China, with such vessels as the 11,249-ton passenger-cargo vessel/hospital ship *Awa Maru* being a prominent sailing. Under a naval guard this vessel made safe haven at Moji, her PoW passengers being transhipped to camps in the Nagasaki area. In due course *Awa Maru* was sunk by Commander Elliot Loughlin's USS *Queenfish* in 1945.

During June 1944 the *Kaigunsho* ordered that all Allied PoWs in the East Indies territories be moved to Surabaya. A fleet of assorted vessels ferried the PoWs to Java; during the voyages there were PoW casualties and deaths through 'friendly' strafing and sinkings.

THE RECKONING

Still today the recorded numbers of hellships, PoW transhipments and deaths, for whatever reason, remain controversial. Each year's research brings to light more instances of hellship voyages and war crimes. Few Japanese historians have tackled the subject, nor have they been encouraged to do so by such institutions as the *Gaimusho* or the *Mombusho*.

Because both the Japanese and the Allies destroyed records immediately before and after Japan's surrender, the exact number of hellship voyages is not known, and is never likely to be. Fragmentary statistics have appeared from time to time. For instance, in 1982 Sumio Adachi, Professor of the National Defence Academy of Japan, published some statistics. He averred that the following shiploads left occupied Japanese territory for Japan:

> 10 shiploads in 1942.
> 12 shiploads in 1943.
> 17 shiploads in 1944.
> 6 shiploads in 1945.

He estimated that 34,000 prisoners were transhipped in total and that the twenty-five vessels sunk were carrying 18,901 PoWs, of whom 8,048 survived.[5]

Twenty years on Professor Adachi's figures were undoubtedly too low. A more up-to-date figure would suggest that some 140 vessels left Japanese-occupied territory and sailed either to Japan or to other occupied territories. Herein some 127,000 PoWs were transhipped, with a death-toll of around 21,000 representing a death rate of 16.5 per cent. *Each* death would be reckoned by many as a war crime in itself.

CHAPTER EIGHT

JAPANESE NAVY INVOLVEMENT IN BIOLOGICAL WARFARE

The *Kempeitai* and *Tokkeitai* called them *maruta*, 'logs'. They were the two thousand or so 'disposable' PoWs, both Asian and Caucasian, who became the victims of the monstrous Japanese biological warfare experiments carried out mostly in Japanese-occupied Manchuquo. Many of the *maruta* were shipped to their horrendous guinea-pig fate by the Imperial Japanese Navy.

In 1999 the Chinese newspaper *People's Daily* reported that some 270,000 Chinese nationals had been killed in the war by the Japanese spreading anthrax, gangrene, tetanus, cholera and typhoid from their germ warfare base in Wuchang county, in the north-east of Heilongjiang province. The report brought to public notice once more the 'bacteriological experimentation units' at Harbin, Changchun, Beijing, Nanjing and Guangzhou[1] and the research programme of human experiments at the notorious Unit 731.

The secret biological warfare unit *Tokushu Butai Nana-San-Ichi* (Unit 731) appears in the wartime records of the *Kaigunsho* as the 'Epidemic Prevention and Water Supply Unit'. It was founded by *Taisho* Shiro Ishii, a distinguished physician who had studied biological weapons in Europe in the 1920s.

By September 1940 biological weapons developed by Ishii's Unit 731 were used by the Japanese at battle areas in central China.[2] In November 1993 papers were discovered which proved that the Japanese planned to use biological weapons in the Pacific War against the Allies.[3] A ship carrying 'a biological warfare battalion' was dispatched to Saipan in 1944, but the routing of the Japanese and the evacuation of the naval base at Truk caused the plans to be aborted. But what exactly was the involvement of the Imperial Japanese Navy in this biological warfare?

Evidence shows that the navy was involved in three areas of research, namely, endurance and stamina tests, medical experiments and bacterial bombs. About the first, testimony comes from Greg Rodriguez Snr, a wartime private in the 59th Coast Artillery Corps, US Army. He was one of the thousand or so US troops marched from the Manila camp to the docks in October 1942 to board the hellship *Tottori Maru*. He remembers:

> From the moment we went aboard that hellship, they were experimenting on us. They threw us on board to see how much we could stand and many of us died. They took us from the tropics to a bitterly cold climate, and that took its toll on us. They gave us a few crackers and a little rice to eat and I feel that it was a systematic way of beginning to test us, to find out how much the Americans – and the British and Australians – could endure.[4]

Others attested to being thrown into the sea for 'survival tests', others to various vaccine tests.

United States Intelligence cadres made a particular examination of data on the Japanese 4th Fleet Naval Hospital, Truk, and the 8th Fleet Naval Hospital, Rabaul.[5] Herein they found evidence from 1943 of Allied PoWs being subjected to experiments on malaria immunisation, diet and poisons. Victims for these experiments were selected at Rabaul, for instance, by the 6th Field *Kempeitai* and the 81st Naval Garrison Unit testified to giving orders for bayonetings and beheadings.[6] Medical observers are known to have been present at such executions to study the effects of bayonet wounds and the results of beheading. A civilian at Matupi also averred that '40 men were anaesthetised, then buried alive' at Matupi.[7]

With regard to bacterial bombs, it is recorded that the Imperial Japanese Navy tested a version of one labelled 'Special Bomb Mark VII' in Tokyo Bay in 1943.[8] The plans for this bomb had been captured by the Americans in the South Pacific in May 1944 from the notebooks of a dead flying trainee. It was not until Saturday 5 May 1945 that the results of initial plans by the Imperial Japanese Navy to bomb east coast

America with incendiary bombs, then bacterial bombs, were apparent. This was the opening phase of Operation FUGO. Although Operation FUGO ('Operation Windborne-weapon') was under the command of Imperial Japanese Army *Shosho* Sueyoshi Kusaba, it had the support of *Rikugun-daijin Taisho* Mitsumasa Yonai and men of the Imperial Japanese Navy were prominent players. The background to Operation FUGO developed in this way.

Gearhart Mountain lies a few miles east of the timber-processing community of Bly in Oregon. Around 10.30am on Saturday 5 May 1945 a huge explosion was heard some 5,000ft up on the southern slopes of the mountain on land belonging to the Weyerhauser Timber Co. The local Sheriff's Office recorded that the wife of the community pastor Revd Archie Mitchell and five children were killed in the explosion while out rambling. By nightfall on that day US Army sources had confirmed that the explosion came from a 15kg anti-personnel high-explosive bomb manufactured by the Imperial Japanese Navy.[9]

American newspapers that covered the story did not reveal that the Japanese had been bombing the west coast of North America since 6 December 1944. The Gearhart Mountain bomb was in fact the 240th logged by the US Army. Fragments of such bombs from an area stretching from Holy Cross in Alaska to Kalispell in Montana had been examined by the US Naval Research Laboratory and identified as of Japanese origin. US Military Intelligence had requested a news blackout.[10]

US Military Intelligence knew that the Japanese had been experimenting with 'upper air current bombing' since the 1930s. Jolted by the raid on Tokyo in 1942 by Major James Doolittle's squadrons of B-25s, by early September 1942 the Imperial Japanese Navy High Command had responded with orders to bomb Oregon. From coastal navigation and land maps captured at Wake Island, the Japanese naval strategists selected targets and dispatched scouting class *I-25 sensuikan* to the southern coast of Oregon. In this vicinity on 9 and 29 September *I-25* catapulted a *Yokosuka* E1 4Y1 reconnaissance aircraft to drop incendiary bombs over the Siskiyou National Forest; a small conflagration was reported on Mount Emily. The Imperial Japanese Navy had more than enough results to show that US mainland cities were vulnerable to their balloon strikes. The next step from explosive bombs to biological weaponry was feasible. However, events took a retrogressive step for the navy.

By 1943 the Japanese were experimenting with unmanned paper balloons with 20ft envelopes. An arsenal of two hundred such balloons, with a range in excess of 600 miles, was in place by August 1943. To carry these balloons, with their deadly payloads, the I-15 Class scouting *sensuikan I-34* and *I-35* were specially modified. Yet as the situation at sea deteriorated for the Japanese, including the loss of both *I-34* and *I-35* in November 1943, the Imperial Japanese Navy dropped their own research. Nevertheless the army persisted. *Shosho* Sueyoshi Kusaba supervised the design of new balloons and by the end of the war an estimated 9,300 balloon launches were logged, yet with only 285 strikes in American territory.[11] Kusaba, by the by, is known to have been involved in the transportation of biological weapons materials from his days as Chief of the Field Railway Administration in Central China.[12]

The six people killed on Gearhart Mountain were the only fatalities from enemy action on mainland USA.[13] Nevertheless in Operation FUGO a new form of naval atrocity was set in motion which could have involved thousands of non-combatant citizens.

Research on the papers relating to Unit 731 in the 1980s confirmed that, with the collusion of Douglas MacArthur, dozens of Unit 731 scientists were given immunity from war crimes prosecution in exchange for releasing research material and information on biological weapons and human guinea-pigs. There is proof, too, that *Taisho* Shiro Ishii travelled to America to deliver 'a series of lectures, that included human testing of infectious organisms'.[14] Imperial Japanese Navy officers who had knowledge of the navy's involvement in researching balloon biological weaponry were recruited under war crimes immunity to MacArthur's *Kaijo Hoan Cho* (Maritime Safety Board), which would develop into the naval branch of the future Japanese Self-Defence Force.

CHAPTER NINE

THE JAPANESE NAVY AND THE COMFORT WOMEN

Historically, women have largely been held in contempt in Japanese society. The exploitation of women for sexual gratification by men was long an accepted tradition. As early as 1613 Captain John Saris, in the service of the Honourable East India Company, aboard the *Clove*, reported how female sex slaves were offered to him and his officers for 'frolicke', when he docked at the island trading centre of Hirado, a few miles north of Nagasaki.[1] Again, commanders of ships were in touch with chandlers and portside hotel keepers for the supply of whores for maritime use.[2] Some women were bought and sold by the pimp-chandlers for transportation by ship to areas elsewhere in Japan. So even before Queen Victoria presented the steam yacht *Hanrio Kan Maru* to *Shogun* Iesada Tokugawa in 1857, the Japanese Navy of the Tokugawa Government was directly involved in the procuring and transportation of prostitutes.

The deployment of women for military and naval service prostitution in the Far East War Theatre had its roots in Shanghai around 1932.[3] During January of that year there occurred what was called the 'Shanghai Incident'. Herein the Japanese attempted to provoke war with China by staging phoney incidents against their nationals. In the subsequent invasion Imperial Japanese Army soldiers raped scores of Chinese women. On the orders of *Shosho* Yasutsugu Okamura, Deputy Chief of Staff to the Kwantung Army in Manchuria, military brothels were set up to counter the wholesale rapes. Okamura was not concerned about the humanitarian aspect of the rape of Chinese women but was anxious lest such behaviour should lead to antagonism among the Chinese populace. After the 'Rape of Nanking' in December 1937, wherein *Taisho* Iwane Matsui, C.-in-C. of the Central China Army, oversaw the slaughter of thousands of Chinese, the *Rikugunsho* adopted Okamura's action as general policy, setting up military brothels in particular sectors of occupied China. These were of three types: those run wholly by the army; privately owned brothels under mandate from the army; and privately owned brothels for civilians which by arrangement with the local army chief supplied 'special services' for soldiers. Thereafter the army occupied itself, with the help of the *Kempeitai*, with 'recruiting' potential whores for the soldiery. The euphemism *ianfu* (comfort women) was coined for the victims.

An examination of the papers of the *Zai Shanghai soryu jikan* (Shanghai Consular Division) shows that following the 'Shanghai Incident', brothels were set up by the *Kaigunsho* for seamen.[4] By 1934 the number of these naval brothels in Shanghai increased to fourteen; much to the disgust of visiting ships' crews they were administered by the military.[5]

It became clear only in the late 1990s to western historians that the Imperial Japanese Navy had been involved in this vile trade of forced prostitution. For instance, in the autobiography of *Tokkeitai Tai-i* Harumichi Nogi, published in 1975, he mentions that he collaborated in the procuring of women for prostitution at Ambon, within the remit of the South-east Area Fleet (4th Southern Expeditionary Force).[6] It is known that the comfort women – also dubbed *kakubu* (staff services) – were transported from the place of 'recruitment' to the front lines by army trucks, railroads and ships. What was the direct naval involvement in what is now called a war crime?

Documents compiled by *Shosho* Takasumi Nagaoka, Head of General Affairs of the *Kaigunsho*, on 30 May 1942 for *Shosho* Toshihisa Nakamura, Chief of Staff of the South-west Area Fleet, testify that the navy dispatched comfort women to naval bases throughout South-east Asia. Sample figures show that 45 women were sent to the Celebes; 40 to Balikpapan, Borneo; 50 to Penan; and 30 to Surabaya. It appears that these were the second batches of such women sent to these areas.[7] The orders for the dispatch of the women was authorised by *Kaigun-daijin Taisho* Shigetaro Shimada.

The main recruitment areas for the comfort women, and therefore the primary transportation ports, were in China, Taiwan and Korea, and a few other South-east Asian and South Pacific locations. Taking

Taiwan (Formosa) as an example, this was the remit area of Commander of the Combined Naval Air Fleet *Chujo* Nishio Tsukahara's 11th Air Fleet, with Takao as its Naval Guard District.

The Japanese had controlled Formosa from 1895, when they annexed the island from the Chinese Empire after the Sino-Japanese War, and were to continue their rule until the island was surrendered in the general capitulation of Japanese forces in the Chinese theatre on 9 September 1945, at the central Military Academy, Nanking, to Chinese General Ho Ying-chin.[8] Comfort women were largely recruited by the agents of *Shosho* Toshio Nomi, Commander of the Formosa Police, and *Chujo* Makoto Tsukamoto, Commander of the Formosa *Kempeitai*, and they were shipped from the Naval Guard District of Takao. Some of the vessels used had seen service in the old OSK (*Osaka Shosen Kaisha*) Line.[9]

The reason why Formosa and other areas of South-east Asia were selected for the recruitment of comfort women was largely racial. Among the nations of the world the Japanese are the most racially prejudiced and the wartime Japanese authorities looked upon all non-Japanese orientals as inferior, and thus available for indiscriminate exploitation. There were, of course, dozens of Japanese native prostitutes working in wartime locations, but they were deemed of higher worth than comfort women from the occupied territories. Japanese women worked mainly in brothels for Japanese officers.

Undoubtedly the most prominent area for recruitment and transportation of comfort women was Korea. For decades the Japanese had cast covetous eyes at Korea, which had come under Chinese suzerainty as early as the T'ang dynasty (618–907). Korea became a tributary state of the Ch'ing Empire during the period 1644–1911 and had been opened to trade with Japan in 1876. After the Sino-Japanese War, Korea was the cockpit of Japanese aggression in mainland Asia, and its influence grew. Following the Russo-Japanese War, Japan effectively controlled the 'Land of Morning Calm' and on 22 August 1910 Japan enacted *Nikkan Heigo* (annexation of Korea) as a colony they called *Chosen*. They inaugurated the *Chosen Sotoku Fu* (Government General of Korea) with a Governor-General. This colonial government was largely military and was the central organ of rule in *Chosen* until 15 August 1945.

From the 1920s the Japanese government used Korean women as cheap labour forces. They were transported in large numbers to mainland Japan for sweatshop work. Thus, among all the comfort women during the Second World War, 80–90 per cent were Korean.

Data about the comfort women began to be gathered properly in July 1990 with the inauguration of the Research Association for Women Drafted for Military Sexual Slavery by Japan.[10] The impetus this engendered led to the forming of the Korean Council for Women Drafted for Military Sexual Slavery by Japan in November 1991. Slowly a horrific picture of sexual exploitation through abuse, fear, blackmail and coercion was built up on the Imperial Japanese Army in general and the Imperial Japanese Navy in particular.

The testimony of the comfort women showed that the Korean port of Pusan was one of the prominent transhipment bases.[11] Developed during Japanese colonial rule, Pusan, on the south-east tip of South Korea, remains the country's leading port. From here Japanese merchant and naval vessels plied mostly to Nagasaki and Osaka with their human cargoes, with some groups of women being shipped on to Shanghai for relocation to the front.

Three women in particular came forward to tell their stories to the Korean Council for Women Drafted for Military Sexual Slavery by Japan. Their testimonies helped to establish the pattern of 'recruitment' and the role played by the Imperial Japanese Navy in their deployment.

Born at Kosong, Taegu City, in 1928 of an impoverished family, Yi Yongsen worked for a while in a Japanese ginnery (where cotton was made). At sixteen she was enticed from her home with a bribe of new clothes by a Japanese male procurer and joined a group of girls being taken by the man to Dalien (Luda). There the group was put aboard one of an eleven-ship naval convoy. The five girls were the only females aboard among hundreds of Imperial Japanese Navy ratings. The ships made their way to Shanghai, but the women were not allowed to disembark. Once out at sea again the convoy was bombed; ten ships sank but the one on which Yi Yongsen travelled only suffered damage to the prow. During the resulting turmoil she was raped by one of the sailors. Rape was now to be a regular occurrence for the girls as the vessel sailed on to Formosa.

On arrival at Formosa, Yi Yongsen was ill; her body was swollen with abuse and she had difficulty in walking. The Japanese procurer who brought the women from Korea was now revealed to them as a comfort station operator at Sinzhu. When Yi Yongsen refused to cooperate in sex slavery she was tortured with electric shocks into submission. Thereafter she and the other women sexually served navy commandos. Yi Yongsen survived bombings, starvation and venereal disease, and remembers being immortalised by a *kamikaze* pilot-client. For her he wrote this song:

> I take off with courage, leaving Sinzhu behind,
> Over the golden and silver clouds.
> There is no one to see me off:
> Only Tosiko grieves for me.[12]

Tosiko was Yi Yongsen's Japanese name. Traumatised by her experiences, Yi Yongsen returned to Korea in 1945. She married in 1989; now divorced, she was still alive in 1992.

Yi Tungnam was born at Koch'ang, South Kyongsang province, in 1918, and left home to avoid her poor farmer father's profligacy and violence. She went from Korea to Manchuria to work in an aunt's café. In 1939 she and other women accepted an offer from a Japanese man who promised them better pay and advancement at another café. It became clear to her that they were to be inducted into prostitution and she tried to leave the group; she was beaten by the Japanese for her trouble. At length the group was taken to Hankou in China, to be handed over to a Korean who ran a whorehouse for the military. After being raped, Yi Tungnam submitted to prostitution. In 1942 she and other girls were transported by ship to Singapore and then in a navy vessel to Medan, Sumatra. There she joined other women sexually serving the military. She too suffered bombings, beatings and venereal disease.[13]

At the end of the war Yi Tungnam was repatriated to Pusan by the Americans. After her life as a comfort women she needed several operations and she suffered years of pain. In the 1990s she was still living in Hapch'on.[14]

Kim T'aeson, born in 1926 at Kangjin, South Cholla province, was brought up by an uncle after her parents divorced. In 1944 a visiting Japanese army pimp duped her uncle by saying he could find Kim well-paid work in a factory. Her uncle released her and the Japanese took her to Seoul, and then to Inch'on. At length she and other women were taken to Pusan and in a convoy of ships left for Osaka, Japan, via Shimonoseki. All the time the women were told they were going to work in Japanese factories.

In October 1944 Kim and around one hundred other women boarded the *Arabiya Maru* bound for Burma. They travelled only at night because of the risk of daylight bombing raids. En route some women were dropped off and taken on at Okinawa and Saigon. At Rangoon, Kim T'aeson began work as a comfort woman. Unable to run away, she submitted. In 1945 she recovered from her trauma and was treated for cholera at a British camp at Rangoon. At the end of the war she returned to Pusan and in the late 1990s received medical treatment for conditions she had contracted as a comfort woman.[15]

At the end of the war the involvement of the Imperial Japanese Navy in the comfort women rape camps and other horrors was buried deep in the general cover-up of Japanese war crimes. A forum to discover the truth about the comfort women was established in December 1991. During 1993 South Korean and Filipino women respectively sued the Japanese Government for monetary reparation in Tokyo District Court. Their petitions failed.

On 31 August 1994, on behalf of the *Gikai* (Japanese parliament), *Sori-daijin* Tomiichi Murayama refused to admit any legal responsibility for the actions of the Imperial Japanese Army and Navy regarding the comfort women, and refused to pay monetary reparation. The *Gikai's* position was publicly criticised by the International Commission of Jurists.[16]

In 1996 the UN Human Rights Commission called on Japan to apologise to the few remaining *jugun ianfu* – but of an estimated 200,000, some of whom had been only eleven years old – and their families, and to accept legal responsibility. Repeatedly the Japanese Government issued – and issues – the same defence. The treaties negotiated with the US, UK and other countries after the war prevent victims from claiming reparation. But the reluctance to apologise, or to make acknowledgement of wrongdoing, lies deep in the Japanese psyche. The fundamental teachings of the nation's Confucian-Shinto philosophy avers that deference to one's ancestors is sacrosant. To apologise, then, for past war crimes, dishonours the dead.

CHAPTER TEN

KENDARI: *TOKKEITAI* KILLING FIELDS

Most of the hundreds of Japanese PoW camps in the home islands and occupied territories were run by the Imperial Japanese Army. As the territory administered by the Imperial Japanese Navy was small by comparison, they had relatively few PoW camps, and mostly these would be better described as PoW compounds administered by the *Tokkeitai*. Again, as material on the *Tokkeitai* is sparse, the records of the prison compound at Kendari, and the subsequent trials of the *Tokkeitai* personnel in the Celebes, provide a rich source of data. The story of the killing fields of Kendari begins with PBY airmen and their last and doomed flight.

The PBY series of Second World War aircraft, known to enthusiasts as Catalinas from its British designation, was renowned for its reliability and endurance. The prototype flying boat made its maiden flight in March 1934 and was manufactured as Consolidated (Aircraft) PBY-1 to PBY-5 and Consolidated PBY-5A and PBY-6A for a period of some ten years. The fate of one Catalina, PBY-5 no. 08233, of patrol squadron 29 (VPB-29) and her eleven-man crew features in the history of the *Tokkeitai*.

This doomed PBY was one of the US Navy seaplanes serviced by USS *Tangier* and the small tender fleet based offshore of the small Pacific island of Morotai.[1] PBY-5 no. 08233 took off from Morotai on the evening of 1 October 1944, under the command of US Naval Reserve officer Lieutenant John Schenck and his second-in-command Lieutenant William Francis Goodwin Jnr. The seaplane's target was the Japanese-held harbour and airfield of Kendari, a coastal mining town on the south-east coast of the Celebes (modern Sulawesi). Easily won by the Japanese from the mixed garrison of Dutch and Indonesian soldiers, the island became the base of the Imperial Japanese Navy's 23rd Air Flotilla and a home for the *Fuhai no Zero-sen* ('The Invisible Zero-Fighters') and Air Group 202.[2] Kendari's garrison was composed of around 1,500 Imperial Japanese Navy personnel under the command of *Taisa* Gosuke Taniguchi.

Before each tour of duty, US airmen were made aware of the *Teki sojushi no gumpo* (Enemy Pilot's Law) which *Sori-daijin* Hideki Tojo had agreed on 13 August 1942. By this time the US Forces had begun to strike the home islands of Japan and B-25 Mitchell bombers had bombed Tokyo, Osaka and Nagoya, as well as the Imperial Japanese Army in China. Thus the law gave the Japanese a flexible pretext to treat any captured Allied airman with severity. Already captured Allied aircrew PoWs had been used for target-practice and beheaded under this law.

Around 1.00am on Monday 2 October 1944, PBY no. 08233 and her crew arrived over Kendari harbour and began looking for enemy shipping to bomb. Back at base the PBY's continuously transmitted code was monitored to follow the events of the attack. Suddenly the transmitted codes stopped, and after a pause came this message: 'One man wounded, control cable shot. Am returning to base from Kendari.' Then there was silence.[3] A subsequent search of the patrol area revealed nothing and the crew of the PBY were posted as 'Missing in Action'.

In fact the PBY crash-landed near the island of Umbele in the Salabangka Islands, around 50 miles north of Kendari and deep within Japanese-occupied territory. Nine of the eleven crew members survived the crash. The PBY sank soon after and the survivors turned the liferaft towards Umbele. Finding the island not conducive to refuge they set off again for nearby Bungkinkela and made landfall at a cove named Tanjung Lepe. As they hid themselves in the jungle they were spotted by natives from the village of Paku. After reviewing their rations, they endeavoured to send an SOS on their short-wave radio. Then they settled down to plan their future. Tragically their SOS was never heard.

Around 4 October the crewmen made contact with a fisherman from Paku; with difficulty they explained that they wanted to be taken to his village. It was important for them to meet any local officials, but *not* the Japanese. They deduced that there were no Japanese on any of the nearby local islands. Meanwhile a local man from Paku, Abdul Rijai,

COMMAND STRUCTURE CELEBES – KENDARI *TOKKEITAI*

Commander 23rd Naval Base Force, Makassar, Celebes

Chujo Morikazu Osugi. b. 1892. Graduate of Etajima, 1910. Command included Kendari Naval Base. Osugi's second-in-command was *Taisa* Minoro Tayama, commander of a *Tokkeitai Buntai*.

Commander Kendari Naval Air Base, Celebes

Shosho Tamotsu Furukawa. b.*c.* 1897. Graduate of Etajima, 1915. Naval aviator. Commanded 23rd Naval Air Flotilla.

Tokkeitai *Structure Levels*

L1: Older, higher ranking, well-educated, usually professional naval officers with previous active service experience.

L2: Junior officers; several former NCOs on rapid promotion.

Known Tokkeitai *personnel at Kendari*

L2. *Tokumu socho* Abe. Involved in several *Tokkeitai* killings; committed suicide on Japan's surrender.

L2. *Sho-i* Sazae Chiuma. b. 1911. In command of 12 *Tokumu socho*, 6 *Kashikan* and 3 *hon-yakusha*. Doubled up as *Shotaicho* of heavy weapon *shotai*.

L2. *Sho-i* Seijiro Dan. Enlisted seaman, 1927. Kendari garrison, 1942.

L1. *Sho-i* Takioka Maeda. b. 1921. 53rd Anti-aircraft Unit.

L1. *Sho-i* Yoshiotsu Moritama. b. 1897. Commander of *gohaku*, 23rd Naval Air Unit, 1,500 men.

L2. *Chu-i* Keiichi Nozaka. b. 1907. Enlisted in 1923. Commander 53rd Anti-aircraft Unit.

L2. *Sho-i* Yoshitaka Ogawa. b. 1912. Ordinary seaman, 1929. Platoon leader motor section.

Tarao Sato. b. 1934. Peacetime police inspector. Counter-intelligence agent for the *Tokkeitai*.

L1. *Taisa* Takao Sonokawa, b. 1900. Chief of Staff to *Shosho* Furukawa.

L2. *Tai-i* Saburo Taketa. Commander *Tokkeitai*.

L2. *Kashikan* Tooru Tanaka. b. 1913. Naval recruit, 1941. Became *Tokkeitai Sho-i* by 1945.

L1. *Taisa* Gosuke Taniguchi. b. 1897. Graduate of Etajima. Commander Kendari Naval Base, and *Tokkeitai* prison compound.

L2. *Sho-i* Isokichi Yamamoto. b. 1911. Entered Imperial Japanese Navy, 1928. Platoon leader Kendari garrison.

had reported the PBY's landing to the headman of Salabangka, one H. Komendangi.

Alas, Komendangi, who was an administrator under Dutch colonial rule, was pro-Japanese and a *Tokkeitai* informer. By subterfuge he lulled the airmen into a false sense of security, before overpowering them with the help of the Paku village headman M. Rivai and fellow Indonesians. The airmen were locked up. Komendangi sent a report of what he had done to *Tai-i* Gosuke Taniguchi at Kendari Naval Base and he dispatched *Tokkeitai Sho-i* Sazae Chiuma to arrest the airmen. Taniguchi then sent word to *Chujo* Morikazu Osugi, Commander of the 23rd Special Naval Base Force at Makassar, Celebes, that the US airmen had been located. Osugi ordered a small float plane to help secure the airmen. Meanwhile *Tokkeitai Sho-i* Seijiro Dan had been patrolling the Salabangka Islands in his motor vessel *Daikeku Maru*. Komendangi, only too pleased to get rid of his prisoners, signalled to *Sho-i* Dan, who headed off with them to Kendari on 8 October. Komendangi received a Japanese 'Judas medal' for his work.[4]

Kendari was to be the scene of a whole series of naval personnel war atrocities. Shortly after the area was secured by the Japanese on 24 January 1942, a dozen Dutch-trained Indonesian soldiers were captured. A prison compound was made for them at the old Dutch Guard House, and here they were joined by thirty-six US Navy PoWs captured from a warship. Their fate was horrific.

One by one these US PoWs were interrogated by *Sokan* Teitje Nakamura. When he had completed his copious notes a *tenko* was called and Nakamura shouted out the names of seventeen US PoWs. The men were trussed, hands behind their backs, and loaded into trucks. The twelve Indonesian PoWs were loaded into another truck. With Nakamura in a *shikisha* (staff car), the convoy drove to the nearby village of Amoito. Here the PoWs were disembarked and the Indonesian prisoners were set to work digging three large pits. When they were finished a Japanese officer was delegated to stand at each pit with drawn sword. *Sokan* Nakamura now ordered the US PoWs to be blindfolded, guided forward and forced to their knees beside the pits. One by one they were beheaded and their bodies kicked into the pits. The Indonesians were then pushed forward to fill the pits in again. For around two weeks the twenty-five remaining US PoWs were held at Kendari, then were transported north to the nickel mines of the Celebes as slave-labour. The *Tokkeitai* had made their first killings in the Celebes.

Within six months the *Tokkeitai* at Kendari received seventeen survivors from a British merchant ship sunk off Tjilatjap, Java. Of various nationalities, they too were slaughtered and buried alongside the US airmen at Amoito. After the war the war crimes investigators assessing events at Kendari recorded early instances of *Tokkeitai* tortures:

Three Allied spies, two natives and an Arab, were caught sending radio messages to Allies. They were tortured to death. First burned by fire on the buttocks, then rolled over glowing embers and finally rolled over barbed wire. We were told about a method of torture practised [by the *Tokkeitai*], and inspected the place where it took place. Victims were strapped on to a bamboo bed, and a fire lighted underneath. The bed was there at the date of writing [some time after the war] with a hole in the centre two feet long by a foot wide . . . and charred and blackened by fire, and beneath on the cement floor was a blackened patch where the fire had obviously been placed.[5]

Evidence collected by investigators clearly showed that Kendari was regularly used by the *Tokkeitai* as a slaughterhouse for British, US and

Dutch merchant seamen and service navy personnel, along with native inhabitants.[6]

When the nine US airmen from PBY-5 no. 08233 arrived at Kendari they were taken to the *Tokkeitai* prison compound. By now they were numbered among the 3,000 or so US, British, Dutch and Australian PoWs held captive in the Celebes. The bulk of the prisoners were at a camp on the outskirts of Makassar City (modern Ujung Pandang), the other side of Bone Bay from Kendari.[7]

On arrival, *Tokkeitai Sho-i* Chiuma handed over the PBY prisoners to *Tokumu socho* Abe, who put each man into a separate cell after relieving them of their belongings. The *Tokkeitai* listed them thus:

> Lieutenant (jg) William Francis Goodwin Jnr, second-in-command of flight. b. 1920.
> Aviation Machinist Mate 1st Class Harvey Harbecke. b. 1924.
> Aviation Radioman 1st Class Joseph Sommer. b. 1923.
> Aviation Radioman 3rd Class Edwin McMaster. b. 1925.
> Aviation Machinist Mate 2nd Class Jake Nilva. b. 1913.
> Aviation Machinist Mate 3rd Class Raymond L. Cart. b. 1925.
> Aviation Ordnanceman 1st Class Paul Schilling. b. 1925.
> Aviation Machinist Mate 1st Class Walter G. Price. b. 1922.
> Aviation Radioman 2nd Class Henry T. Zollinger. b. 1921.

This information was extracted by *Tokumu socho* Abe with the help of a local native civilian, Yohn Tjio, acting as *hon-yakusha*. Next day the interrogation was conducted by the English-speaking *Taisa* Taniguchi. He seems to have been satisfied with the answers he received, and wrote a preliminary report for *Chujo* Osugi and *Shosho* Furukawa. The following day an interrogation party consisting of *Taisa* Taniguchi, *Tai-i* Taketa, *Sho-i* Chiuma, a representative of *Shosho* Furukawa, and a flown-in *hon-yakusha* Rijuitso Nose assembled at the prison compound. Their interrogation was concluded without apparent violence.

As the days passed the nine US prisoners were set to work on maintenance tasks in the *Tokkeitai* compound. Then a new group of staff officers arrived at the compound, led by *Taisa* Takao Sonokawa, *Shosho* Furukawa's Chief of Staff. It seems that Sonokawa was to assess the

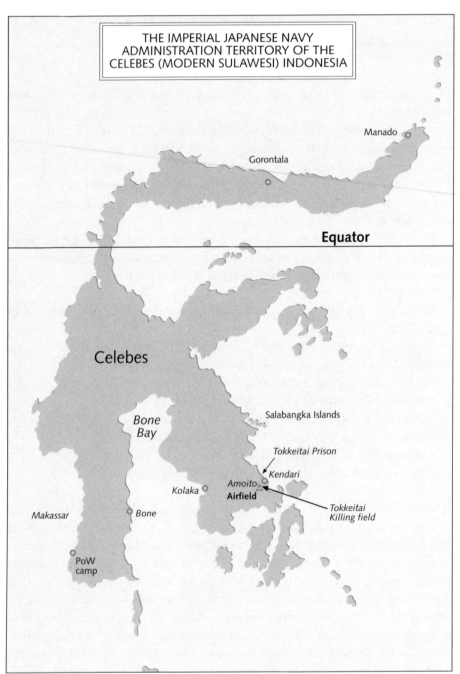

THE IMPERIAL JAPANESE NAVY
ADMINISTRATION TERRITORY OF THE
CELEBES (MODERN SULAWESI) INDONESIA

Manado

Gorontala

Equator

Celebes

*Bone
Bay*

Salabangka Islands

Tokkeitai Prison

Kendari

Amoito
Airfield

Kolaka

*Tokkeitai
Killing field*

Makassar

Bone

PoW
camp

*The Celebes, then part of the Netherlands East Indies, was taken by the Japanese during 12–24 January
1942. Composed of 69,255 square miles of landmass between Borneo and New Guinea, the largely
mountainous island was patrolled by the Tokkeitai who monitored the native population for signs of
insurrection and anti-Japanese activity, and supervised the in-island transportation of PoWs. The native
population was used as forced labour by the occupying forces. Makassar is now called Ujung Pandang.*

situation; his report brought an order some two weeks later that the prisoners were to be taken in groups to the 23rd Naval Air Flotilla airfield at Amoita. Over a period of days the prisoners were all re-interrogated. Despite beatings, nothing further was gleaned from them. Weeks went by for the prisoners with nothing but work in the *Tokkeitai* compound. The Japanese personnel at Kendari were busy with the paperwork that emanated from *Chujo* Osugi's office at Makassar. The interpretation of one message in particular was to have grave consequences for the nine PBY prisoners. On 8 October *Taisa* Taniguchi had reported the Americans' capture to Osugi; in reply a message was eventually received at Kendari. What was to happen to the Americans? *Shobun* was the reply.

Shobun is a Japanese word of Chinese origin which can mean any of four things: to deal with; to dispose of; judgement; punishment. *Shobun suru* is the verb transitive. In the later years of the Second World War *shobun* came to mean 'severe disposal' – that is, execution. It was a policy interpretation that had been formulated by *Chujo* Sanji Okido, Commander of the *Kempeitai* at Kuden HQ, Tokyo. He used it to justify the killing of captured US pilots of Boeing B-29 Superfortress bombers. Some forty-five US pilots were thus executed. It was a policy rubberstamped by both Osugi and Furukawa at Makassar.

As the American PBY prisoners worked on at Kendari *Tokkeitai* compound, *Taisa* Taniguchi acted on orders sent via *Shosho* Furukawa's Chief of Staff *Taisa* Sonokawa on 23 November 1944. Four of the nine Americans were to be selected as a group to be executed first. The selection was left to the *Tokkeitai* and fell to *Tai-i* Taketa, who randomly picked out Edwin McMaster, Walter Price, Joseph Sommer and Henry Zollinger. As the four were loaded by the *Tokkeitai* into a vehicle to travel to the killing field of Amoito, *Shosho* Furukawa sat in his staff car with its yellow admiral's *hata* (pennant).[8]

What passed through the minds of the American airmen as they drove out of the compound is a matter of speculation; but fear must have been one of their emotions, exacerbated when their transport stopped at Mondonga, midway between Kendari and Amoito. Here personnel of the Mondonga aerial torpedo maintenance unit were drawn up with their superior officer *Chu-i* Toshisuke Tanabe. Joe Sommer was dragged out of the transport. Amid *Banzais* and applause from the drawn-up

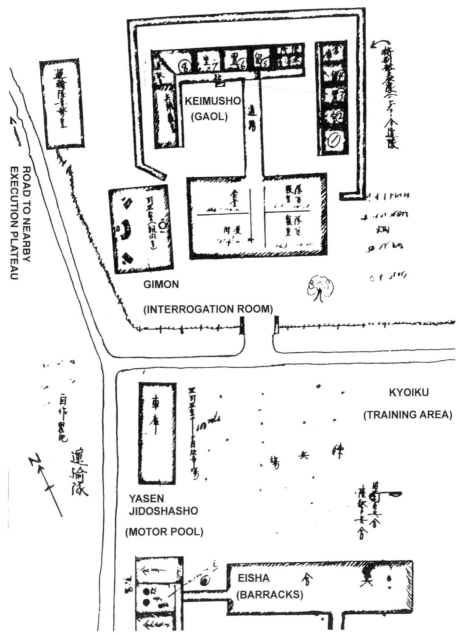

Japanese sketch to illustrate background notes of the trial of Taisa Gosuke Taniguchi.

servicemen, he was pushed to where a pit had been dug with a curious post hammered at the pit head. Sommer was manhandled forward, forced into a kneeling position, blindfolded and lashed with his back against the post. An officer stepped forward, bowed to his superior, and took up position a few feet away from Sommer. Unsheathing his sword the officer decapitated Sommer to the acclaim of the assembled Japanese. Sommer's head bounced into the pit; the post and his body were then kicked into the depths, now a grave, to be filled-in by waiting Indonesian forced labour.

Following the execution the grim motorcade of vehicles drove away to Amoito where the remaining three Americans were beheaded as Sommer had been. The next day, 24 November, *Taisa* Taniguchi gave orders for the execution of the five other Americans.

The ritual execution of the remaining Americans was more bizarre even than that of Sommer. Taketa charged *Sho-i* Chiuma with selecting an execution party of five; and they had to be men who understood the techniques of *kendo*, the martial art swordsmanship taught to all officers at Etajima. With this remit Chiuma chose himself, *Chu-i* Toshio Mitani, *Sho-i* Yoshitaka Ogawa and Isokichi Yamamoto, with *Kashikan* Tooru Tanaka making up the numbers.

In the late afternoon the execution party, in their naval dress uniforms, along with forty or so rankers, assembled at a small plateau near the *Tokkeitai* compound. Indonesian forced labourers had already dug a large pit at the site. Blindfolded, the prisoners were frogmarched to the site, their hands secured behind their backs, by *Tokkeitai* personnel. William Francis Goodwin Jnr was the first to be beheaded, by *Sho-i* Chiuma, and the others soon toppled into the pit, dispatched in turn by each of the assigned executioners.

After Japan's capitulation in August 1945 the British occupied the Celebes, and *Chujo* Osugi surrendered his command and the *Tokkeitai* to Brigadier I.N. Dougherty at Makassar. In the early days of October 1945 Flight-Lieutenant Martin O'Shea, Royal Australian Air Force, was ordered from Makassar to Kendari to investigate reports of the *Tokkeitai* killing fields of Kendari. He filed a report[9] which was passed by the British to the War Crimes Branch of the US Army, who nominated their own investigators. British involvement with the situation, however, was not finished.

Following their occupation of the Celebes the British organised PoW camps outside Makassar and here former *Tokkeitai* personnel and members of the naval garrison were held. Flight-Lieutenant O'Shea began an investigation here of re-examined war crimes data. A key witness was former policeman Tarao Sato, who had conducted counter-intelligence activities among native Indonesians for the *Tokkeitai*. Sato had witnessed the executions of the Americans, and had even loaned his sword to *Kashikan* Tooru Tanaka for one beheading. Sato revealed the name of *Taisa* Taniguchi as senior officer in charge of the executions.

When questioned Taniguchi admitted his involvement, noting that he did so on the *kyoku no tsukemasu* of *Chujo* Osugi. It appeared that Taniguchi considered the following of 'higher orders' was enough to relieve him of any responsibility for the deaths. Taniguchi and Sato also testified to the names of the others who had taken part in the executions. All this material O'Shea passed on to his US opposite number First Lieutenant Sheldon A. Key, who submitted his own report to his superiors.[10]

When the reports had been studied the Allied War Crimes Commissioners concluded that there were cases of war crimes to be answered by Osugi and the staff officers involved in the Kendari events. The British handed over the Japanese war crimes suspects to the US Army and preparations were made for four trials.

TRIAL OF *CHUJO* MORIKAZU OSUGI[11]

Location: Manila, Philippines; 1–31 October 1946.
Charges: 1. Authorising the execution of nine US airmen from PBY no. 08233, 25 November 1944.
        2. Authorising the execution of four US airmen from 13th Air Force B-24 bombers, during July 1945.
Plea: Not guilty; denial of all knowledge of US airmen in the PoW holding areas.

Osugi's denial of all knowledge concerning the US airmen was ludicrous. Because of the structure of the Japanese field orders system all orders *had* to come through him. In any case, *Nihon Hoso Kyokai* (Japan's broadcasting station) had boasted about the capture of the airmen during the Zero House programme of 'Tokyo Rose' (Iva Toguri) beamed to the Allies and the Occupied Territories.

Prosecution witnesses: Sho-i Seijiro Dan confirmed that the execution orders had been given; *Taisa* Gosuke Taniguchi confirmed that the execution orders had been received and the penalties carried out. Several staff officers testified against Osugi.

Verdict: Osugi was found guilty on all counts. He was sentenced to life imprisonment with hard labour.

Because of his high rank Osugi's trial remains an important one in the history of Japanese Naval War Crimes annals. It also proved that, as with the Imperial Japanese Army's *Kempeitai*, *Tokkeitai* activities were known about and promoted by naval officers at the highest level. And Osugi would never have acted without the direct agreement of the *Kaigunsho*.

TRIAL OF *TAISA* GOSUKE TANIGUCHI[12]

Location: Manila, Philippines; 14–28 February 1947.
Charge: Scheduling and supervising the carrying out of the execution of five US airmen.
Plea: Not guilty on account of following superior orders.
Verdict: Guilty. Sentenced to death by firing squad. Sentence later reduced to life imprisonment.

TRIAL OF *SHOSHO* TAMOTSU FURUKAWA[13]

Location: Yokohama, Japan; 24 May–mid-July 1948.
Charges: Unlawfully consenting to the execution of US airmen; failing to prevent unlawful killings; failure to take corrective punishment of perpetrators.
Plea: Not guilty. Denied knowledge of executions or being present at the Amoito and Mondonga executions.
Verdict: Guilty. Sentenced to seven years in prison.

During the trial Furukawa made one statement which is of particular interest when considering the Japanese attitude towards enemy prisoners. He said, '*Kore wa watashi no kangae desu* [This is my opinion]

. . . I think the fliers were killed because of the antagonism of the
Japanese people towards American fliers. When any were captured . . .
[*execution*] was the first thing they thought of.'

TRIAL OF *SHO-I* SAZAE CHIUMA[14]

Location: Yokohama, Japan; 29–30 July 1948.
Charges: 1.   Executing William Francis Goodwin Jnr.
             2.   Directing others to kill four US airmen at Kendari.
Plea: 1st charge, Guilty; 2nd charge, Not Guilty.
Verdict: Guilty on both charges. Sentenced to ten years in prison.

These four trials brought to a wide public the presence and
machinations of the *Tokkeitai* in the Second World War, as well as
illustrating their organisation and command structure. All the convicted
war criminals of Kendari were released in 1958.

BETRAYAL OF THE DAMNED

By means of a special Proclamation by General Douglas MacArthur, the International Military Tribunal for the Far East was established on 19 January 1946. Eleven countries were represented. Its remit was to try the accused on war crimes against peace, conventional war crimes and crimes against humanity. Indictments were heard for incidents between 1 January 1928 and 2 September 1945. The date of 1928 corresponded with the Japanese occupation along the Kiaochow–Tsinan Railroad in Shantung, China.

A war crimes trial began at Tokyo on 3 May 1946.[1] All the accused pleaded 'Not Guilty' and prosecution and defence representation extended the proceedings until November 1948. War criminal suspects were divided into three classes, A, B and C.[2] Twenty-eight defendants came into the first category of 'high policy' crimes, while the others were implicated in serious breaches 'of the customary and conventional laws of war'. Including the trials instigated by the Australian Government (1945–51), there were 2,244 trials in all of 5,700 defendants, 4,405 of whom were convicted.[3] The figure of executions for war criminals is generally accepted as 920.[4] The Emperor and the entire Imperial Family were exempted from prosecution. Hereafter hundreds of suffering ex-PoWs began to feel betrayed by their governments. Retribution was deemed to be too limited.

General Douglas MacArthur's list of potential Class A war criminals included some 300 men, of whom only 28 appeared before the Tokyo Tribunal. Hundreds of Imperial Japanese Army officers had played prominent roles in naval war crimes, but of the infamous Class A '28', there were three 'high policy' marine administrators.

Gensui Osami Nagano (1880–1947) was *Kaigun-daijin* during 1936–7; fleet commander (1937); Navy Chief of Staff (1941); and naval adviser to the Emperor (1944). A former diplomat (*Kaigun bukan* – naval attaché – to the Japanese Embassy in Washington (1920–3), by 1941 Nagano was a key planner in the *Kido Butai* surprise attack on Pearl Harbor, Hong Kong, Manila and South Pacific targets. He was charged with waging an aggressive war. He died of pneumonia during the trial on 5 January 1947.

Shosho Takasume Oka (1890–1973) was Intelligence Chief, Naval General Staff (1939); Chief of the Naval Affairs Bureau (1940–4); and *Jikan Kaigun-daijin* (1944). He was an important participant in the surprise attacks. Oka's naval bureau issued directions for the transport of Allied PoWs on the hellships; through the *Tokkeitai* and Naval Guard Districts he organised POW camps in the Pacific islands. He ordered a shoot-to-kill policy for survivors of torpedoed Allied vessels. He was charged on five counts of war crimes. Oka had covered his tracks well; no satisfactory evidence of his direct involvement in PoW murder was proved. He was sentenced to life imprisonment and paroled in 1954.

Taisho Shigetaro Shimada (1883–1976) was *Kaigun-bukan*, Italy (1916–17); Vice-Chief of Naval Staff (1935–7); Commander, China Fleet (1940); *Kaigun-daijin* (1941–4); member of the Supreme War Council (1944). Authorised naval surprise attacks in 1941. Authorised use of and research into *kamikaze* weaponry. Naval units under his command massacred Allied PoWs, organised hellships and murdered survivors of torpedoed Allied ships. He was charged on five counts. Shimada had also covered his tracks well and it could not be proved he was directly responsible for the murder of PoWs or survivors of seagoing vessels. He was sentenced to life imprisonment in Sugamo prison, Tokyo, and paroled in 1955.

There were six other Class A war criminals who were directly involved in the transhipment of PoWs and civilians in hellships.

Taisho Seishiro Itagaki (1885–1948). *Rikugun-daijin* (1938–9); Commander, Singapore (1945). Ruthless militarist conductor of terror campaigns in occupied territories; brutal PoW camp organiser. Executed.

Okinori Kaya (1889–1977). Financier. Promoted use of slave-labour, especially on the Burma railway. Life imprisonment; paroled 1955.

Taisho Heitaro Kimura (1888–1948). Chief of Staff, Kwantung Army (1940–1); *Jikan-Rikugun-daijin* (1941–3); Army Commander Burma

(1944–5). Approved brutalisation of Allied PoW slave-labour and condoned civilian atrocities. Sentenced to death.

Taisho Akira Muto (1892–1948). Vice-Chief of Staff, China Expeditionary Force (1937); Director Military Affairs Bureau (1939–42); Army Commander Sumatra (1942–3); Army Chief of Staff, Philippines (1944–5). Servicemen under his command played a role in the 'Rape of Nanking' and the 'Rape of Manila'. Muto ruthlessly controlled PoW camps in Sumatra, and recruited native slave-labour. Sentenced to death.

Taisho Teiichi Suzuki (b. 1888–known to be alive in the 1970s). Chief, China Affairs Bureau (1938–41); adviser to the Japanese cabinet (1943–4). Prominent mastermind of the Japanese wartime economy, promoted recruitment and transportation of slave-labour. Sentenced to life imprisonment; paroled 1955.

Taisho Hideki Tojo (1884–1948). Pre-eminent war criminal; honed his talents in *Kempeitai* in Manchuria and rose to be *Sori-daijin* (1941–4). The ultimate authority on brutalisation of PoWs and civilians. Authorised transhipment of any captives relevant to the war effort. Sentenced to death.

Among the *Shokan* – Imperial Japanese Navy flag officers – the following may be added as examples of naval war criminals and suspects.

Shosho Koso Abe. While Naval Commander of Kwajalein, Marshall Islands, he ordered the beheading of US PoWs in 1942. He was hanged at Guam on 19 June 1947.

Shosho Takesue (?) Furuse. Charged with war crimes at trial on Luzon, Philippines. Hanged in 1949.

Shosho Hamanaka. Ordered the execution of Australian PoWs. Shot after trial at an Australian Military Court, Monotai Island, 15 January 1946.

Chujo Kanezo Hara. Commander of the 12th Special Naval Base Force, Andaman and Nicobar Islands, June 1944. Found guilty of slaughtering natives of South Andaman Islands. Death by hanging prescribed at Changi Jail, Singapore, 18 June 1946.

Chujo Ichise. Commander of the Naval Base, Ambon Island (1945). Implicated in the murder of Dutch and Australian PoWs, 1 and 5–6 February 1942. He cited the then dead *Shosho* Hatakeyama,

Commander of the Ambon Island Invasion Force, as a prime mover in the above murders.

Shosho Michiaki Komada. Commander of the 22nd Naval Base Force. Found guilty at a Military Court at Pontianak of ordering the decapitation of 1,500 West Borneo nationals in 1944 and the murder and brutalisation of 2,000 Dutch PoWs on Flores Island. Executed Borneo.

Taisho Seizo Kobayashi. Governor-General of Formosa (1936–40). Suspected of naval atrocities. Arrested 2 December 1945; released 31 August 1947.

Shosho Nisuke Masada. Charged with murder of US airmen on Jaluit Atoll, Marshall Islands. Committed suicide in 1945.

Chujo Kunezo Mori. Held command posts in Kuril Islands (1944) and Bonin Islands (1945). Accused by junior officers of cannibalism of executed US airman at Chichi Jima. No known action taken.

Taisho Taketori Ogata. As a Minister of State he was held as a war criminal suspect. Released without prosecution on 31 August 1947.

Chujo Shigemitsu Sakabara. Commander of the 65th Guard Force, 4th Base Force, Wake Island. Ordered execution of 98 US civilian employees in October 1943. Tried and hanged at Guam, 19 June 1947. His adjutant *Shosa* Soichi Tachibara was hanged for the same crime.

Chujo Naomasa Sakonju. Commander of the 16th Cruiser Squadron, South-west Area Fleet. He ordered the *shobun* (execution) of 72 survivors of MV *Behar* aboard the cruiser *Tone*, 18 March 1944. Sentenced to death for the atrocity at Hong Kong, September 1947.

Chujo Ito Takahashi. Vice-Chief of the Naval General Staff (1932); Commander-in-Chief Combined Fleet (1934–6); Commander of various operations, forces and transports to 1945. Arrested as strong suspect of war crimes in Tokyo on 2 December 1945. No evidence.

Shosho Ryukichi Tamura. Commander of the 14th Naval Base Force and 83rd Naval Garrison, New Ireland. He ordered the execution of PoWs at Kavieng. Tried by an Australian War Crimes Tribunal, Hong Kong, November–December 1947. Found guilty of murder; hanged at Stanley Jail, 16 March 1948.

Chujo Soemu Toyoda. Saw service in China and was Commander of Kure Naval District in 1941. Before he became Commander-in-Chief of the Combined Fleet in 1944, he was (probably) Commander of the Yokosuka Naval Base, where it is rumoured he supervised the selection of candidates for the *Tokkeitai*. Ordered mass *kamikaze* and other suicide operations. By 1945 he was Chief of the Naval General Staff. He was arrested as a war criminal but managed to be cleared of all responsibility for the atrocities enacted by his naval personnel. He is known to have died from cardiac arrest in 1957 at the age of seventy-two.[5]

As this book shows, a very large number of naval commanders directly responsible for the murder of PoWs, the on-board executions in transit of recalcitrant candidates for slave-labour, and the cold-blooded killings of survivors of torpedoed Allied ships were never brought to trial. Many were able to cover their tracks; others simply assumed new identities; still more were helped back into postwar society by the various ex-naval personnel 'friendly societies'; several, too, were aided by the *yakusa*, the Japanese equivalent of the Mafia.[6] Yet from the first months after the Japanese surrender a powerful feeling of betrayal by their home government was engendered in Allied PoWs of all services.

Following the International War Crimes Trials, and the executions of men such as Hideki Tojo, the rehabilitation of key militarists in Japan took place with the help of the occupying US administration. As far as the Americans were concerned, the Japanese had been replaced by Chinese communists as the major threat to peace in Asia. The vast continent was seen as 'going communist'; by March 1948 Chiang Kai-shek's Nationalist forces were losing to the Communists and on 1 September 1948 the Communists proclaimed a North China People's Republic; eight days later the Korean People's Democratic Republic was established under the Communist Kim Il Sung. So on the orders of Democratic Party President Harry S. Truman, MacArthur closed the War Crimes Trials as US long-term naval bases in Japan were planned as a Far Eastern bastion against international communism. As the East turned 'Red', the US Supreme Command for the Allied Powers clandestinely recruited former Japanese service personnel to support the much-needed anti-communist forces. Hellship war criminals like *Chusa* Masanobu Tsuji had their criminal status lifted. Tsuji even won election to the *Gikai* (Japanese parliament). Even those who had been involved in the transhipment of human guinea-pigs to the infamous Unit 731 were employed by the US Government. US hellship PoWs had good reason to feel betrayed.

And what of other Allied troops? In Britain Prime Minister Clement Attlee's socialist government supported the demise of the War Crimes Trials, as did Labour Prime Minister Joseph Benedict Chifley in Australia and National Party Prime Minister (Sir) Sidney George Holland in New Zealand. All had economic and political reasons to maintain a presence in the Far East. In the minds of many PoWs, the Allied betrayal was complete.

KNOWN JAPANESE HELLSHIPS, 1942–5

This is not meant to be, nor should be taken as, a *comprehensive* list of Imperial Japanese Navy and Imperial Japanese Army hellships. Spellings of vessel names are sometimes idiosyncratic, depending upon the recollections of PoWs. Vessels represented herein offer an ongoing compilation by the author to the present day from the following sources: Australian Archives, Melbourne; Australian War Memorial, Canberra; Ex-PoWs' recollections; author interviews and correspondence over many years; Japanese Labour Camp Survivors' Association, and associated groups; Japanse Krygsgevangen-transportshepen, Algemeen Rijksarchif, Amsterdam; Public Record Office, Kew, London; Rijksinstituut voor Oorlogsdocumentatie, Amsterdam; US Office of the Provost Marshal General, Washington, DC; US Naval Historical Centre, Navy Yard, Washington, DC.

Each entry shows the name of the hellship, as recorded in the sources above, the relative date of operation, approximate numbers of PoWs carried, numbers of deaths, and additional notes of interest.

Aki Maru (ex-*Mishima Maru*). 11,409 tons. 1943. 74 PoWs.

Akikaze. 1,715 tons. Destroyer. 1943. 60 PoWs. 60 deaths. Lost 3 November 1944.

Amagi Maru. 3,700 tons. 1943. Troop transport. 1,071 PoWs.

Amaku Maru. 1943.

Argentina Maru. 12,755 tons. Liner. 1942. 800 PoWs.

Arisan Maru. 6,886 tons. 1944. 1,782 PoWs. Torpedoed in Bashi Straits, 24 October 1944. 1,782 dead or missing.

Asaka Maru. 1942. 738 PoWs. 31 deaths. Shipwrecked and sunk, 13 August 1942, south of Formosa.

Asama Maru. 16,975 tons. Liner. 1942. 1,020 PoWs. 1943. 71 PoWs.
Atsuki Maru. 1943.
Awa Maru. 11,249 tons. Passenger-cargo vessel/hospital ship. 1944.
   Sunk. 525 PoWs.

Brazil Maru. 5,860 tons. 1944. 250 PoWs. 5 deaths. 1945. 925 PoWs.
   450 deaths. Torpedoed by aircraft in Bay of Takao, 8 January 1945.
Byoke Maru. 4,000 tons. Cargo ship. 1944. 1,250 PoWs.

Canadian Inventor. Freighter. 1944. 1,100 PoWs. 6 deaths.
Celebes Maru. 5,824 tons. Frigate. 1942. 1,000 PoWs.
Cho Saki Maru. 8,000 tons. 1943. 100 PoWs.
Chukka Maru. 1944. 1,200 PoWs. 5 deaths.
Chuyo (ex-*Nitta Maru*). 17,830 tons. NYK liner. 21 PoWs. 20 deaths.
   Lost 4 December 1943.
Clyde Maru. 5,298 tons. 1943. 500 PoWs.
Coral Maru. 1943. 800 PoWs.

Dai Ichi Maru. 1942. 1,920 tons. 500 PoWs. 1943. 86 PoWs.
De Klerk (later *Imbari Maru*). 1943 (various runs). 1,986 tons. 1,760
   PoWs.

England Maru. 5,068 tons. Cargo ship. 1942 (various runs). 1,000
   PoWs. 1,000 deaths. Sunk.
Enoshima Maru. 1945. 500 PoWs.
Enoura Maru. 1944. 1,070 PoWs. 316 deaths. Torpedoed by aircraft in
   Bay of Takao, 8 January 1945.
Erie Maru. 5,493 tons. 1942. 1,000 PoWs. 2 deaths.

France Maru. 5,828 tons. 1943. 300 PoWs.
Fukkai Maru. 3,829 tons. Cargo ship, ex-British. 1942. 1,100 PoWs.
Fuku Maru. 1944. 1,289 PoWs. 1,226 deaths. Sunk by Allied dive-
   bomber near San Narciso, Subic Bay, 21 September 1944.
Fukuji Maru. 1944. 354 PoWs (including high-ranking military men).

Hakodate Maru. 1943. PoW numbers not known.
Hakusan Maru. 1944. 707 PoWs.

Hakushika Maru. 1944. 609 PoWs.

Haru Maru. 1944. 1,100 PoWs. 60 deaths.

Harugiku Maru (ex-Dutch SS *Van Waerwijck*). 3,040 tons. 1944. 730 PoWs. 178 deaths. Sunk by torpedoes south of Balawan by HMS *Truculent*, 26 June 1944.

Haruyasa Maru. 1945. 2,500 PoWs.

Hawaii Maru. 1943. PoW numbers not known.

Heiyo Maru. 9,816 tons. 1942. 200 PoWs.

Hiyoki Maru. 1944. 315 PoWs.

Hofoku Maru. 1944. 1,287 PoWs. 1,047 deaths. Sunk.

Hokusen Maru. 1944. 1,100 PoWs. 39 deaths.

Hoshi Maru. 1943. 9 PoWs.

Hozan Maru. 1944. 451 PoWs.

Ikoma Maru. 3,156 tons. NYK line. 1944. 611 PoWs. 418 deaths.

Jun'yo Maru. 1944. 6,520 PoWs. 1,047 deaths. Sunk by HMS *Tradewind*, 18 September 1944 off Moaka, Sumatra. Various Allied PoWs but designated vessel for *romusha* (Asian slave-labourers). Logged as the 'largest maritime disaster in world naval history'.

Kachidoki Maru (ex-SS *President Harrison*). 10,509 tons. 1944. 900 PoWs. 400 deaths. Sunk by torpedoes, Hainan, 13 September 1944, by USS *Pampanito*.

Kaishun Maru. 1944. 150 PoWs. 29 known dead. Sunk, 15 September 1944.

Kamakura Maru (ex-*Chichibu Maru*). 17,256 tons. 1942 (various runs). Liner. 2,213 PoWs. 10 deaths.

Kenkon Maru. 4,574 tons. 1942. 1,500 PoWs. 1 death.

Kenwa Maru. Merchantman. 1944. 200 PoWs.

Kenzen Maru. 1944. 300 PoWs. 25 deaths.

Kibibi Maru. 20,000 tons. Whaler. 677 PoWs. 8 deaths.

King Kong Maru. 5,000 tons. 1942. 1,500 PoWs.

Kinta Maru (ex-*Kinta*, British). 1,220 tons. 1944.

Kokusei Maru. 5,494 tons. 456 PoWs.

Koryu Maru. 6,680 tons. 235 PoWs.

Koshu Maru. 2,295 tons. Cargo vessel. 1944. 1,513 PoWs. 1,239 deaths.

Kotobuki Maru. 1944. 400 PoWs.
Kunishima Maru. 1943. 300 PoWs.
Kunitama Maru. 3,127 tons. 1943. 100 PoWs.
Kurimata Maru. 1943. 2,000 PoWs.
Kyokku Maru. 6,738 tons. Cargo vessel. 1943. 1,500 PoWs. 2 deaths.
Kyokusei Maru. 5,493 tons. Ex-Canadian. 1942. 1,200 PoWs.

Lang Ho. 1944. 300 tons. River steamer, Mekong River. 900 PoWs.
Lima Maru. 6,989 tons. NYK vessel. 1942. 300 PoWs. 8 deaths.
Lisbon Maru. 1942. 1,816 PoWs. 834 deaths. Sunk, 27 September 1942,
  by USS *Grouper* 6 miles from Tung Fushan Island, China.

Maebashi Maru. 1942. 7,005 tons. 1,700 PoWs.
Makassar Maru. 4,026 tons. 1943. 3,500 PoWs.
Maros Maru. 1944. 650 PoWs. 325 deaths.
Maru Go. 1942. 100 PoWs.
Maru Hachi. 1944. 150 PoWs.
Maru Ichi. 1942. 32 PoWs. 14 deaths.
Maru Ni. 1942. 500 PoWs.
Maru Roku. 1942. 74 PoWs.
Maru San. 1942. 100 PoWs.
Maru Shi. 1942. 616 PoWs.
Maru Shichi. 1943. 500 PoWs.
Matsue Maru. 1943. Number of PoWs not known.
Matti Matti Maru – see *Canadian Inventor*
Melbourne Maru. 1945. 500 PoWs. 1 death.
Miyo Maru. 1944. 208 PoWs.
Moji Maru. 3,000 tons. 800 PoWs. 25 deaths.
Montevideo Maru. 5,493 tons. Passenger-cargo vessel. 1942. 1,053 PoWs.
  1,053 deaths. Sunk, 1 July 1942, off Bagador, east of Luzon.

Nagara Maru. 7,149 tons. Passenger-cargo ship. 1942 (various runs). 180
  PoWs.
Nagato Maru. 1942. 1,600 PoWs. 20 deaths.
Nankei Maru (ex-*Nora*). 1942. Number of PoWs not known.
Nanshin Maru. 1944. 3 PoWs. 1945. 416 PoWs. 1 death.
Naruto Maru. 7,148 tons. Passenger ship. 79 PoWs.

Natoru Maru. 1942. 60 PoWs and Australian Army Nurses.
Nichimei Maru. 4,693 tons. 1943. 1,000 PoWs. 40 deaths. Sunk, 15 January 1943, by submarine action.
Nichinan Maru. 1943. Number of PoWs not known. 25 deaths.
Nishi Maru (ex-*Kalgan*, British). 2,655 tons. Passenger-cargo ship. 1,974 PoWs.
Nissyo Maru. 6,527 tons. 1944. 1,600 PoWs. 12 deaths.
Nitta Maru. 17,830 tons. Liner. 1942. 1,187 PoWs. 5 deaths.
Noto Maru. 1944. 1,135 PoWs. 1 death.

Op Ten Noort (later *Tenno Maru*). 1942. 900 PoWs.
Orinoco Maru (later *Oryoku Maru*). 7,362 tons. Passenger-cargo vessel. 1944. 1,620 PoWs. 300 deaths. Torpedoed by aircraft, Bay of Takao, 8 January 1945.
Oyo Maru. 5,000 tons. 1942. Number of PoWs not known.

Pacific Maru. 5,872 tons. 1942. Number of PoWs not known.
Panama Maru. 5,289 tons. 1942. 130 PoWs.

Rakuyo Maru. 9,500 tons. 1944. 1,318 PoWs. 1,159 deaths. Sunk East Hainan Island, 12 September 1944.
Rashin Maru. 1944. 1,065 PoWs.
Rio de Janeiro Maru. 9,627 tons. Passenger liner/submarine depot ship. 1943. 200 PoWs. Lost 17 February 1944.
Roko Maru. 3,338 tons. 1943. 500 PoWs.

Saka Maru. 1944. 738 PoWs.
Samdong Maru. 1942. Transported USS *Houston* survivors.
Samurusan Maru (ex-Dutch). 1,871 tons. 1942. 500 PoWs.
Sandakan. 1943. 30 PoWs.
Sanko Maru. 5,461 tons. Steamer. 1942. 346 PoWs.
Seiko Maru. 2,600 tons. 1943. 3 PoWs.
Sekiho Maru. 1944. 1,024 PoWs.
Shinsei Maru. 1942. 1,816 PoWs. 842 deaths.
Shinyo Maru. 1944. 750 PoWs. 667 deaths. Torpedoed near Mindanao, 17 September 1944.
Shinyo Maru. 1942. 4,621 tons. Cargo vessel. 500 PoWs. 100 deaths.

Sibijac (Dutch). 1943. 8 PoWs.

Singapore Maru. 5,800 tons. Cargo vessel. 1942 (various trips). 4,080 PoWs. 60 deaths.

Singoto Maru. 1944. 1,194 PoWs. 1 death.

Soerabaja Maru. 1943. Number of PoWs not known.

Soon Cheong. 1943? 504 PoWs.

Subuk. 1943. 72 PoWs.

Suez Maru. 1943. 546 PoWs. 546 deaths. Torpedoed, 25 November 1943.

Sugi Maru 1944. 200 PoWs. 17 deaths.

Tachibana Maru. 1,772 tons. 1942. 200 PoWs.

Tacoma Maru. 5,772 tons. 1943. Number of PoWs not known.

Taga Maru. 2,868 tons. Cargo vessel. 850 PoWs. 70 deaths.

Taiko Maru. 1945. 700 PoWs.

Taikoku Maru. 2,636 tons. 1944. 308 PoWs.

Taiwan Maru. 1944. 23 deaths.

Taka Maru. 1943. 500 PoWs.

Tamabuko Maru. 1944. 772 PoWs. 560 deaths. Torpedoed off Goto, Nagasaki, 24 June 1944.

Tamahoko Maru (ex-*Yone Maru*). 6,780 tons. 1942. 268 PoWs. 1944. 772 PoWs. 560 deaths.

Tango Maru (ex-German *Rendlsberg*; ex-Dutch *Toendjoek*). 6,200 tons. 1944. 3,500 PoWs. 3,000 deaths.

Tatsuta Maru. 16,975 tons. Liner. 1942. 200 PoWs. 1943. 663 PoWs.

Tatu Maru. 1942. 300 PoWs.

Teia Maru (ex-French *Aramis*). 17,537 tons. 1944. 500 PoWs.

Tencho Maru. 1944. 1 British murder.

Thames Maru. 5,871 tons. 2,022 PoWs. 200 deaths.

Toka Maru. 1944. 6 PoWs.

Toko Maru. 1942. 500 PoWs.

Tone. 11,215 tons. Light cruiser. 1944. 111 PoWs. 72 deaths. Lost 24 July 1945.

Tottori Maru (ex-British). 5,973 tons.1942. 1,961 PoWs. 30 deaths.

Toyama Maru. 1943. 504 PoWs. 1 death.

Toyofuku Maru. 1942. 1,287 PoWs. 907 deaths. Sunk by aircraft, 21 September 1942, Bataan, Philippines.

Toyohashi Maru. 7,031 tons. Cargo ship. 1942. 2,000 PoWs. Sunk.
Treasure. 1943 (various trips). 30 PoWs.

Ubi Maru. 1942. Number of PoWs not known.
Ume Maru. 5,859 tons. Cargo vessel. 1942. 1,494 PoWs.
Umeda Maru. 1942. 1,500 PoWs. Around 15 'casualties' reported.
Unyo. 2,040 tons. Merchant conversion. 1943. 20 PoWs. Lost 14 July 1945.
Uruppu Maru. 1944. 5 PoWs.
Usu Maru. 6,000 tons. 1943. 1,978 PoWs.

Yamagata Maru. 3,807 tons. 1942. 1,000 PoWs.
Yangtze Maru. 1942–3. Number of PoWs not known.
Yashu Maru. Cargo freighter. 1944. 1,250 PoWs. 56 deaths.
Yingata Maru. Dates of operation unknown. 1,799 PoWs. Known to be carrying PoWs from sunk *Maebashi Maru.*
Yoshida Maru. 5,425 tons. 1943–3. 2,700 PoWs. 10 deaths. Known to be carrying PoWs from sunk *Dai Michi Maru.*

Wales Maru (also *Weills* or *Weiles Maru*). 6,586 tons. 1943. 950 PoWs.
Wein (ex-Dutch). 1943. Number of PoWs not known.

Zukara Maru. 1942. Number of PoWs not known.

MEMORIALS TO THE WAR DEAD: JAPANESE NAVAL ATROCITIES ON LAND AND SEA

The *exact* number of Allied war dead who perished while being transported for Japanese slave-labour is not known. Where possible the numbers of known dead aboard specific ships have been mentioned in the text or the appendix. An unrecorded number of Allied service personnel and civilians were murdered as they clung to the wreckage of doomed vessels.

The War Cemetery at the former Japanese treaty port of Yokohama, constructed by the Australian War Graves Group, contains 1,518 graves. In the cemetery stands the Yokohama Cremation Memorial containing the ashes of 335 soldiers, sailors and airmen of the British Commonwealth, USA and the Kingdom of the Netherlands, who died as PoWs in Japan. Most of these two groups were transported to Japan in the hellships. The American Battle Monuments Commission, Washington DC, confirms that there are no specific war graves within their remit for Allied service personnel killed during, or as a consequence of, transportation in hellships. From time to time such people as the US and Australian Graves Registration teams came across graves of those murdered by the *Tokkeitai*. Such remains were flown to Barrackpore, India, for possible identification. Thereafter, following talks with the victims' families, the remains were shipped back for family burials, or to such resting places as the National Cemetery of the Pacific in Honolulu, Hawaii, or the Manila American Cemetery. Names of those executed with no known graves are listed in memorials such as the Courts of the Missing at Honolulu.

NOTES

PROLOGUE

1. Supreme Commander for the Allied Powers (SCAP). 'Trials of Class "B" and "C" War Criminals', *History of the Non-Military Activities of the Occupation of Japan*, SCAP, 1952, pp. 46–9, 67–8.
2. International Military Tribunal for the Far East (IMTFE). *Judgment*, Tokyo, 1948.
3. For a readable overview of the *Bushido* cult, see: Inazo Nitobe, *Bushido: The Soul of Japan*, Charles E. Tuttle, 1969.
4. Cecil Bullock, *Etajima: The Dartmouth of Japan*, pp. 97ff.
5. *Law Reports of the Trials of War Criminals*. Vol. 13, Case no. 79, pp. 138,140.
6. Ibid, pp. 140, 144–5.
7. For details of *Kempeitai* recruitment and duties, see: Raymond Lamont-Brown, *Kempeitai: Japan's Dreaded Military Police*, Ch. 2.
8. Yoji Akashi 'Lai Tenk, Secretary General of the Malaysian Communist Party 1939–47, *Journal of the South Seas*, 1994.
9. For a general overview of codebreaking, see: Michael Smith, *The Emperor's Codes*, Bantam Press, 2000.
10. M.R.D. Foot and J.M. Langley, *MI9*, p. 119.

INTRODUCTION

1. Around 370 of the complement of officers and men aboard the USS *Houston* survived the engagements. Most of them were captured at sea or in the jungles of Java. A roster of only 266 eventually returned to the US.
2. Gavan Daws, *Prisoners of the Japanese*, p. 301.
3. Ray Parkin, *The Sword and the Blossom*, pp. 74ff.
4. Ibid, p. 104.
5. Anthony Cowling, *My Life with the Samurai*, pp. 79–80.
6. Don Peacock, *The Emperor's Guest*, p. 73.
7. Ibid, p. 186.
8. Isogai was found guilty of war crimes by the Chinese Government and sentenced to life imprisonment; he was later pardoned by Chiang Kai-shek. He died in 1967. See: O. Lindsay, *At the Going Down of the Sun*.
9. Lord Russell of Liverpool, *The Knights of Bushido*, pp. 124–5.
10. In October 1946 Nimori was tried by a British military court on eight war crimes charges. Sentenced to fifteen years' imprisonment, he was released in 1958.

CHAPTER ONE

1. For a summary of losses see: Walter Lord, *Day of Infamy*, pp. 219–20.
2. *Yubari* was sunk on 27 April 1944 by the US submarine *Bluegill*.
3. Gavan Daws, *Prisoners of the Japanese*, p. 45.
4. The *Nitta Maru* was converted into the aircraft carrier *Chuyo* during May–November 1942; it was sunk by a US submarine on 4 December 1943.
5. Gavan Daws, *Prisoners of the Japanese*, pp. 47–8.
6. Lord Russell of Liverpool, *The Knights of Bushido*, p. 120.
7. Ibid, pp. 120–1.
8. Gavan Daws, *Prisoners of the Japanese*, p. 49.
9. *Proceedings of a Military Court of Tribunal for the Trials of War Criminals*, Singapore, Monday 21 January 1946.
10. Ibid. Recounted in Colin Sleeman (ed.), *Trial of Gozawa Sadaichi and Nine Others*, pp. 12–13.
11. Ibid, p. xlv.

CHAPTER TWO

1. Lord Russell of Liverpool, *The Knights of Bushido*, p. 128.
2. Ibid, pp. 128–9.
3. James McEwan, *The Remorseless Road*, p. 184.
4. Ibid, pp. 185–6.
5. Lord Russell of Liverpool, *The Knights of Bushido*, pp. 129–30. Blackwood gives a description of the typical latrines for PoWs aboard Imperial Japanese Navy and Merchant Navy vessels.
6. Ibid, p. 132.
7. Ibid, p. 133.
8. Correspondence with the author, 13 April 2000.
9. Eric S. Cooper, *Tomorrow You Die*, pp. 31–2.
10. Ibid, p. 33.
11. Rohan D. Rivett, *Behind Bamboo*, pp. 3ff.
12. Ibid, p. 170.
13. R.H. Whitecross, *Slaves of the Son of Heaven*, p. 21.
14. Ibid, pp. 21–3.

CHAPTER THREE

1. The British Army finally withdrew from Burma on 20 May 1942. For a good overview of the campaign see: Louis Allen, *Burma: The Longest War 1941–1945*.
2. Gavan Daws, *Prisoners of the Japanese*, p. 184.
3. Joan and Clay Blair, *Return from the River Kwai*, p. 18.
4. Ibid, p. 20.
5. A.G. Allbury, *Bamboo and Bushido*, p. 127.

6. Ibid, pp. 13–33.
7. Ibid, p. 130.
8. Joan and Clay Blair, *Return from the River Kwai*, p. 79.
9. Ibid, p. 120.
10. A.G. Allbury, *Bamboo and Bushido*, p. 142.
11. Joan and Clay Blair, *Return from the River Kwai*, p. 160.
12. Ibid, p. 162.
13. Ibid, p. 175.
14. Ibid, p. 176.
15. Ibid, p. 180.
16. Ibid, p. 195.
17. Ibid, p. 203.
18. Ibid, p. 233.
19. Ibid, p. 238.
20. There are no British records of the sinking of the *Rakuyo Maru* and the *Kachidoki Maru*, but oral testimony avers that some thirteen British prisoners died at the Sakata camp as a consequence of the atrocities at sea.
21. Joan and Clay Blair, *Return from the River Kwai*, p. 274.
22. During their passage into medical care, Commanders Paul Summers and Eli Reich encouraged PoWs to make a record of their experiences. These were later to be of use to US Intelligence and the War Crimes Commissions.
23. Royal message, November 1944.
24. *Morning Herald*, Sydney, 18 November 1944.
25. Hansard, 17 November 1944.

CHAPTER FOUR

1. Lord Russell of Liverpool, *The Knights of Bushido*, p. 107.
2. James MacKay, *Betrayal in High Places*, pp. 246–9 for interrogation of survivors of No. 1 Kure SLP personnel (and others) by Captain Jones Gowing Godwin, Australian Army Intelligence, 2nd War Crimes Section.
3. Lord Russell of Liverpool, *The Knights of Bushido*, pp. 100–1.
4. Ibid, pp. 101–2.
5. For reference to the 'Kavieng Killings' see: *Australian National Archives*, 'Attacks on Kavieng, 21 January 1942', MP158/98 and 'Missing Civilians', MP742/1/336/1/160.
6. Their corpses were discovered by Australian investigators. Ibid, MP137/93, 'Nago Island' file.
7. Ibid, MP137/93.
8. Ibid, MP137/3.
9. Ibid, MP742/1/336/1/1444. Ref: '*Akikaze* Massacre'.
10. Ibid, MP742/1/336/1/1444. Ref. 'Testimony of Yajiro Kai'.
11. Lord Russell of Liverpool, *The Knights of Bushido*, pp. 107–8.
12. Ibid, p. 108.
13. Ibid, p. 109.
14. Ibid.

CHAPTER FIVE

1. *Chujo* Hiroshi Oshima (b. 1886). Negotiated Anti-Comintern Pact, 1936. Japanese Ambassador to Germany, 1938–9; 1940–5. Negotiated Tripartite Alliance, 1940. Honoured by Adolf Hitler with Grand Cross of the German Eagle (gold), 1941. Friend of Foreign Minister Joachim von Ribbentrop. Arrested and tried as a Class A war criminal; found guilty and sentenced to life imprisonment; released in 1955.

2. Lord Russell of Liverpool, *The Knights of Bushido*, p. 214. Hitler's Standing Order No. 154, 12 September 1942, read: 'Rescue no one and take no one on board. Do not concern yourselves with the ship's boats. Weather conditions and the proximity of land are of no account. We must be hard in this war.'

3. After *Shosho* Takagi's death he was replaced by *Shosho* Shigeyoshi Miwa, founder of the 'Chrysanthemum Special Attack Force' of suicide *kaiten*; he was replaced in turn by *Shosho* Tadashige Daigo, who remained in command until the end of the war.

4. The Class Yu-I and Yu-1001 submarines were also transport submarines, built by the Imperial Japanese Navy. For data on the suicide submarines, see: Raymond Lamont-Brown, *Kamikaze: Japan's Suicide Samurai*.

5. Bernard Edwards, *Blood and Bushido*, pp. 11–12.

6. On 20 May 1942 *I-58* was renumbered *I-158*.

7. Boeicho Kenshujo, *Senshishitsu*, vol. 21, pp. 435, 450–7 and Track Chart 7.

8. Bernard Edwards, *Blood and Bushido*, p. 22.

9. Anthony J. Watts, *Japanese Warships*, p. 185.

10. The Imperial Japanese Navy converted six merchant vessels as hospital ships. *Takasago Maru* was captured in 1945; *Hikawa Maru* and *Kiku Maru* (British-built) surrendered, while *Asahi Maru* (Italian-built), *Muro Maru* and *Tenno Maru* (ex-Dutch *Op ten Noort*) were sunk in 1944, having been considered to be acting as disguised warships.

11. Bernard Edwards, *Blood and Bushido*, p. 62.

12. Ibid, p. 64.

13. For data on *British Chivalry*, see: Lord Russell of Liverpool, *The Knights of Bushido*, pp. 215, 219; Bernard Edwards, *Blood and Bushido*, pp. 79ff.

14. Lord Russell of Liverpool, *The Knights of Bushido*, p. 219.

15. Bernard Edwards, *Blood and Bushido*, p. 104.

16. A subsidiary of the P&O Line.

17. For additional data on the *Sutlej*, see: Lord Russell of Liverpool, *The Knights of Bushido*, p. 216; Bernard Edwards, *Blood and Bushido*, pp. 107ff.

18. For additional data on *Ascot*, see: Lord Russell of Liverpool, *The Knights of Bushido*, pp. 216, 219ff; Bernard Edwards, *Blood and Bushido*, pp. 124ff.

19. For additional data on the *Daisy Moller*, see: Lord Russell of Liverpool, *The Knights of Bushido*, pp. 215, 218; Bernard Edwards, *Blood and Bushido*, pp. 67ff.

20. Bernard Edwards, *Blood and Bushido*, pp. 68–9.

21. Ibid, p. 77: Testimony of Captain Reginald Weeks.

22. Lord Russell of Liverpool, *The Knights of Bushido*, p. 217. Mamoru Shigemitsu (1887–1957) was a lawyer and diplomat whose posts included *taishi* (ambassador) to Great Britain, 1938–41. *Gaimu-daijin* in Tojo's War Cabinet, he represented Japan at the signing of the surrender aboard the USS *Missouri* in Tokyo Bay. Arrested and tried as a Class A war

criminal, he was found guilty and sentenced to seven years in prison. Released on parole in 1950 he entered Japanese politics. He was *Gaimu-daijin*, 1955–6.

23. *I-162* survived the war, to be scuttled by the Allies on 1 April 1946. *I-26* was presumed sunk by USS *Richard M. Powell*, 25 October 1944. *RO-111* was lost in action, 10 June 1944, with US destroyer *Taylor*, north of the Admiralty Islands.

24. Carl Boyd and Akihiko Yoshida, *The Japanese Submarine Force and World War II*, p. 226.

25. *Chujo* Sakonji was executed at Hong Kong on September 1947 for atrocities at sea. See: MV *Behar* killings.

26. Lord Russell of Liverpool, *The Knights of Bushido*, pp. 216–17.

27. As quoted by Peter Elphick, *Life Line*, pp. 193–4.

28. Liberty Ships: By 1941 the US Maritime Commission realised that their yards would not be able to meet the increasing demand for tonnage. One answer was to look afresh at the British Ocean Class design. Ruthless cuts and changes were made to the design and ships of the new type were laid down. Nine yards got to work on the vessels which were dubbed 'Liberty Ships'. The first of them was the 10,805 tons, 11-knots, dry cargo ship *Patrick Henry*, launched on 27 September 1941. Over 2,700 were to be built in total.

29. Lord Russell of Liverpool, *The Knights of Bushido*, pp. 222ff; testimony of Able-Bodied Seaman McDougall.

30. Claims of *I-26* as an Allied kill are conflicting: Bernard Edwards, *Blood and Bushido*, p. 201, cites the escorts USS *Lawrence C. Taylor* and USS *Anzio* as responsible on 17 November; Carl Boyd and Akihiko Yoshida, *The Japanese Submarine Force*, p. 210, cites USS *Richard M. Powell* east of Leyte, 25 October 1944.

CHAPTER SIX

1. Bernard Edwards, *Blood and Bushido*, p. 24.

2. Anthony J. Watts, *Japanese Warships*, p. 268.

3. Ibid, p. 318.

4. *Genota*, built in Hamburg by Deutsche Werke, became the Imperial Japanese Navy vessel *Ota* and was lost on 30 March 1944.

5. Bernard Edwards, *Blood and Bushido*, p. 51.

6. Anthony J. Watts, *Japanese Warships*, p. 348.

7. Lord Russell of Liverpool, *The Knights of Bushido*, p. 228.

8. James MacKay, *Betrayal in High Places*, p. 10.

9. As identified by Bernard Edwards, *Blood and Bushido*, p. 148.

10. Trial Records, British Military Court, Hong Kong, September 1947.

11. Ibid. Although *Chujo* Sakonju pleaded 'superior orders', the testimony of *Taisa* Shimanuchi, Chief of Staff of the 16th Cruiser Squadron, clearly indicated that the murders were Sakonju's 'own idea'.

CHAPTER SEVEN

1. This chapter should be read in conjunction with the Appendix notes on Hellships.

2. For additional notes see: Van Waterford, *Prisoners of Japan in World War II*, pp. 152ff.

3. Testimony of Calvin Graef, Office of the Provost Marshal General.
4. Van Waterford, *Prisoners of Japan in World War II*, p. 157.
5. Sumio Adachi, *Unprepared Regrettable Events*.

CHAPTER EIGHT

1. See allegations by Guo Chenzhou and Liao Ying-Chang of the Chinese Academy of Medical Sciences. Quoted in *The Times*, 30 November 1999.
2. Yuki Tanaka, *Hidden Horrors*, p. 137.
3. Ibid, p. 139. The papers are the *Gyomo Nisshi* (Record of Military Plans and Operations).
4. Peter Williams and David Wallace, *Unit 731*, p. 52.
5. *Australian National Archives*, MP742/1/336/1/1398–155C.
6. Yuki Tanaka, *Hidden Horrors*, p. 156.
7. Ibid.
8. Lieutenant-Colonel Murray Sanders, *Report on Scientific Intelligence Survey in Japan*, vol. 5, Scientific and Technical Advisory Section GHQ.
9. Raymond Lamont-Brown, *Kamikaze: Japan's Suicide Samurai*, p. 154.
10. Ibid, p. 155.
11. Ibid, p. 157.
12. Peter Williams and David Wallace, *Unit 731*, p. 65.
13. Raymond Lamont-Brown, *Kamikaze: Japan's Suicide Samurai*, p. 154.
14. Peter Williams and David Wallace, *Unit 731*, p. 272.

CHAPTER NINE

1. E.M. Satow (ed.), *The Voyage of Captain John Saris*, pp. 90–1.
2. Fernando Henriques, *Stews and Strumpets*, p. 287.
3. It is difficult to verify the exact date of the start of such transportation as most relevant documents were destroyed by the Japanese and the Allies after the war.
4. *Gaimusho keisatsusuchi, Shina no bu* (Foreign Office Police History, China Section), 1938.
5. Ibid, Reports, 1935–7.
6. Harumichi Nogi, *Kaigun Tokubetsu Keisatsutai: Anbon-to BC-kyu Senpan no Shuki*, ch. 9.
7. Yoshiaki Yoshimi (ed.), *Jugun Ianfu Shiryoshi*, pp. 365–75.
8. *Taisho* Tikichi Ando, C.-in-C. 10th Area Army, officially surrendered Formosa to Chinese General Chen Yi.
9. Alfred Stead, *Japan by the Japanese*, p. 584.
10. Keith Howard (ed.), *True Stories of the Korean Comfort Women*, p. 12.
11. Ibid, p. 43.
12. Ibid, p. 93.
13. Ibid, pp. 88–94.
14. Ibid, pp. 134–42.
15. Ibid, pp. 151–7.
16. Reports in the *Mainichi Shimbun* and *Japan Times*, 6 September 1994.

CHAPTER TEN

1. The background for this chapter is taken from Michael J. Goodwin, *Shobun: A Forgotten War Crime in the Pacific*.
2. Ikuhiko Hata and Yasuho Izawa, *Japanese Naval Aces and Fighter Units in World War II*, pp. 128–31.
3. Michael J. Goodwin, *Shobun: A Forgotten War Crime in the Pacific*, p. 30.
4. The Japanese Government issued many civilian lapel badges, medals and cuff-links, including 'collaboration medals' to be distributed to non-Japanese in the *Dai Toa Sen*.
5. Michael J. Goodwin, *Shobun: A Forgotten War Crime in the Pacific*, pp. 46–7.
6. Ibid, p. 47. After the war a grave registration team from the US Army identified pits containing in excess of a hundred executed bodies.
7. The Imperial Japanese Navy authorities did not inform the Allies, as was usual through the International Red Cross, of the existence of the PoWs. Their whereabouts were only discovered after the war.
8. Naval captains, commanders and lieutenant-commanders sported a red pennant on their cars; naval officers of lesser rank on shore duties flew a blue pennant.
9. US National Archives, Washington, War Crimes Trials. 19 October 1945: Australian case no. 7 – Beheading of Nine Americans at Kendari.
10. US National Archives, Washington, War Crimes Trials. 26 February 1946: File Report – Kendari Executions. During April 1946 all the Japanese witnesses were individually questioned by a US investigation team at Kendari. *Chujo* Osugi was questioned in May 1946 while being transhipped under arrest from Makassar to Manila.
11. US National Archives, Washington, War Crimes Trial Record. 'The United States v. Morikazu Osugi.' Record Group 153. Case 1.
12. US National Archives, Washington, War Crimes Trial Record. 'The United States v. Gosuke Taniguchi.' Record Group 331. Case 307. Also on trial were Toshio Mitani, Yoshitake Ogawa, Tooru Tanaka and Isokichi Yamamoto. Each man was found guilty and sentenced to life imprisonment. All were released in 1947.
13. US National Archives, Washington, War Crimes Trial Record. 'The United States v. Tamotsu Furukawa.' Record Group 331. Case 307. Also tried in this case were ten others.
14. US National Archives, Washington, War Crimes Trial Record. 'The United States v. Sazae Chiuma.' Record Group 331. Case 307 and 336.

EPILOGUE

1. Herein the agreements regarding stern judgment of Japanese war criminals within the Declaration of Potsdam were implemented. The Declaration had been made at Potsdam, near Berlin, by Churchill (thence Attlee), Truman and Stalin in July–August 1945.
2. Broadly speaking, Class A war criminals were arraigned for crimes 'against peace', with the inference that they had planned, started and conducted a war of aggression. Class B criminals were indicted with murder, rape, slave-labour, torture, pillage and allied war crimes; while Class C criminals were accused of 'crimes against humanity', from genocide to terrorism. In some trials there was a certain amount of overlapping of such definitions.

3. Trials of B and C category war criminals:

Australian Trials, 1945–51.	Darwin; New Britain; Moluccas.
British Trials, 1946–9.	Beijing; Manchuria; Nanjing; Shanghai; Taiwan; Canton (Guangzhou).
Dutch Trials, 1946–9.	Sumatra; Borneo; Sulawesi; Timor; Ceram; New Guinea.
French Trials, 1946–50.	Saigon.
Philippine Trials, 1947–9.	Manila.
US Tribunals, 1945–9.	Tokyo; Shanghai; Manila; Guam.

The archives of all these nations contain material on naval atrocities.

4. John W. Dower, *Embracing Defeat*, p. 447.

5. For additional biographical background see: Richard Fuller, *Shokan: Hirohito's Samurai*.

6. James MacKay, *Betrayal in High Places*, p. 189.

GLOSSARY

While nuances of the tortuous Japanese language are explained where relevant in the text, this glossary offers an extra overview of the Japanese terms used. Pronunciation stress-marks have been omitted and the Romanisation of Japanese terms and vocabulary follows the Modified Japanese Language System of the US medical missionary Revd Dr James Curtis Hepburn (1815–1911).

Where Japanese persons are mentioned in the text, their given name then surname is set out as in the western style. All ranks and titles are expressed in Japanese style.

Banzai '[May the Emperor live for] 10,000 years'. Battlecry; salute; exclamation of joy. Often used at the moment of death for executed prisoners.

Bassuru Punishment.

Benjo Latrine.

Bentatsu The everyday striking, punching or beating of soldiers to underline orders given. In Japan's military code it was carried out as *shinsetsu-na-okonai* (an act of kindness). In the Imperial Japanese Navy the bashings were called *tekken/seisai* (the iron fist) delivered as the *ai-no-muchi* (whip of love). Slapping of PoWs was thus a common practice.

Bento Lunch box; in hellship context, prepared meals for PoWs.

Bunkantai Army/Navy detachments.

Buntai Army/Navy sections.

Bushido 'The Way of the Warrior.' A code of honour on which every *samurai* (warrior) was expected to base his conduct.

Chancorro Term used to describe enemies/PoWs, meaning 'sub-human'.

Chian-Iji (Police) maintenance of order, within the *Chian Iji Ho*, Peace Preservation Law.

Chiji Governor.

Chinjufu Navy District.

Chomansai Method of loading PoWs (in hellships).

Chosen Japanese name for Korea; annexed in 1910.

Chu-i Rank: Army, First Lieutenant; Navy, Sub-lieutenant.

Chujo Rank: Army, Lieutenant-General; Navy, Vice-Admiral.

Chusa Rank: Army, Lieutenant-Colonel; Navy, Commander.

Dai ni-ji Sekai Taisen Second World War. By the Japanese it was usually expressed as *Dai Toa Sen* ('Great East Asia War').

Dai Nippon (or **Nihon**) Great Japan.

Dai Nippon Teikoku Empire of Great Japan.

Dai Nippon Teikoku Kaigun Imperial Japanese Navy.

Dai Nippon Teikoku Rikugun Imperial Japanese Army.

Dai Shigoto   Great Work/Mission.

Dai Toa Kyozonken   'Great East Asia Co-existence Sphere'; Japanese euphemism for their occupied territories from Manchuquo to the Dutch East Indies; policy under the guise of a politically and economically integrated Asia 'free from Western domination'.

Daikon   Japanese radish (cf. PoWs' meals).

Danshaku   Title: Baron.

Dorei-seido   Slavery; forced labour.

Eiseitai   Medical unit.

Furyo   PoWs.

Furyo shuyojo   PoW camps.

Gaijin   Foreigner.

Gaimu-daijin   Foreign Minister.

Gaimusho   Foreign Office.

Gensui   Rank: Army, Field Marshal; Navy, Admiral of the Fleet.

Gocho   Rank: Army, Corporal.

Gohan   Cooked rice (cf. PoWs' meals).

Gumi   Families; term used by the Japanese Mafia.

Gunso   Rank: Army, Sergeant.

Hakko Ichiu   'The Whole World Under One Rule'; Japanese national sentiment for occupied territories.

Hakushaku   Title: Count.

Hata   Pennant.

Heimu Kyoku   Military Administration Bureau.

Heisocho   Rank: Warrant Officer.

Heiho   Volunteers (or collaborators).

Hinomaru   'Round of the Sun', the Japanese national flag showing a red circle (the sun) on a white background. In the Second World War the Army and Navy used a flag with the Rising Sun, red rays on a white background. The use of the latter at modern parades and rallies is deemed provocative of nationalism.

Hon-yakusha   Interpreter, translator.

Ianfu   Comfort women; ie, those forced into prostitution for the armed services. Asiatic women forced into prostitution are usually referred to as *Jugun ianfu*.

Ianjo   Comfort House (ie, brothel; usually Army). Navy equivalent, *Kaigun ianjo*.

Igakutaki   Medical (inspection).

Imin   Immigration (inspection).

Indo   India.

Ittohei   Rank: First Class Privates; Navy, Ratings.

Jikan Kaigun-daijin   Vice-Minister of the Navy.

Jikan Rikugun-daijin   Vice-Minister of War.

Jotohei   Rank: Superior Privates; Navy, Ratings.

Junshikan   Rank: Warrant Officer.

Kaigun bukan   Naval attack.

Kaigun-daijin   Navy Minister.

Kaigun Gunreibu   Naval General Staff Office.

Kaigun Heigako   Navy Academy.

Kaigunsho   Navy Ministry; replaced the *Hyobusho* in 1872.

Kaigun-guntia Old name for Imperial Japanese ratings.

Kaigun Sensuikanbu Navy Bureau of Submarines.

Kaigun Shikan Itakutaki Navy Medical Office.

Kaijo Hoan Cho Maritime Safety Board.

Kami Japan's pantheon of gods.

Kamikaze Suicide weapons and pilots.

Kamotsu Freight; euphemism for PoWs.

Kanshi-hei (Camp) guards; usually a rank given to Koreans, Sikhs and Formosans.

Karayuki Travelling prostitutes, usually Japanese nationals.

Kashikan NCOs, Petty Officers.

Katei-Kyoshi no aisatsu Tutor salutation; usually on graduation.

Kempeitai Japanese Military Police.

Kendo Japanese martial (fencing) art.

Kido Butai Attack force.

Kisoku no furyo Regulations for PoWs.

Kodanshugisha 'Japan's Imperial Way' (ie, of doing things).

Kyoku no tsukemasu [A plea] of following 'superior orders'.

Kyokuto Kokusai Gunji Saiban International Military Tribunal for the Far East.

Manchuquo Japanese name for Manchuria; modern Dongbei, China. From 1931 to 1945 the provinces of modern Heilongjiang, Jilin and Liaoning formed a Japanese puppet state.

Manju Rice-paste buns.

Maru Suffix for Japanese merchant ships.

Maruta 'Logs': term for prisoners intended for human experiments programmes.

Miso-shiru Weak rice soup.

Nan'yo-cho South Seas (Occupation) Government; Micronesia.

Nihon Hoso Kyokai (NHK) Japanese broadcasting station.

O-cha Japanese green tea.

Oka-daikon Common radish.

Rikugun-daijin Minister of War.

Rikugunsho Ministry of War.

Sake Rice wine.

Saishogen Interrogation.

Sanbo Hombu Imperial General Staff.

Samurai Medieval Japanese warriors; third level of Japanese social class.

Samurai-no-Umi Samurai of the Sea.

Seibu Kyoku Economics Mobilisation Bureau.

Sencho Ship's captain (Merchant Navy).

Senshi Sosho Japan's official military history record.

Senso Hanzai War crime.

Sensuikan Submarine.

Sensui sentai Submarine flotillas.

Seppuku Ritual disembowelment; the polite term instead of the vulgar *hara-kiri*. Japan's aristocracy was the only one to evolve a highly ritualised method of committing suicide. It underlined the *Bushido* code of 'Victory or Death'.

Seto Naikai 'Inland Sea'; part of the Pacific Ocean between the Japanese main island of Honshu to the north and east, and the southerly main islands of Shikoku and Kyushu.

Shinjuwan Kogeki Assault on Pearl Harbor.

Shikei Death penalty.

Shikisha Staff car.

Shireichokan Commander-in-Chief.

Sho-i Rank: Army, Second Lieutenant; Navy, Sub-lieutenant (Acting).

Shoban Rank: Orderly officer.

Shobun suru To dispose of; euphemism for the execution of PoWs.

Shocho Rank: Army, Sergeant-Major.

Shogun Japanese generalissimos who exerted almost unlimited powers in medieval Japan in the name of puppet emperors. Hereditary *Shogun* ruled Japan from the twelfth century to 1867.

Shokan General Staff Officer.

Shonan 'The radiant South'; Japanese-occupied Singapore.

Shosa Rank: Army, Major; Navy, Lieutenant-Commander.

Shosho Rank: Army, Major-General; Navy, Rear-Admiral.

Shotai Platoon.

Shotaicho Platoon Commander.

Sori-daijin Prime Minister.

Speedo Command: Make haste.

Suifu Mariner.

Tai Sea bream.

Tai-i Rank: Army, Captain; Navy, First Lieutenant.

Taisa Rank: Army, Colonel; Navy, Captain.

Taisho Rank: Army, General; Navy, Admiral.

Tanko Coal mines; the destination of many hellship PoWs.

Tasogare Basic Naval Reporting Codes.

Tatami Straw mat.

Teki Sojushi no gumpo Enemy Pilot's Law (1942).

Tekken seisei The 'Iron Fist'; disciplinary system.

Ten-chi Heaven/Hell.

Tenko (PoW camp) roll call.

Tenno The Emperor. *Tenno-Heika*, His Majesty. *Tenno-Banzai* (colloquial), 'Long Live the Emperor'.

Tokkeitai Imperial Japanese Navy Special Police Force.

Tokumu Socho Rank: Warrant Officer; Special Service transport commander.

Tsukemono Pickled vegetables.

Tsuyaku Interpreter.

Uragirimono Traitor.

Yakusa Japanese Mafia.

Yasukuni-jinja Yasukuni Shrine: Japan's main war memorial.

Bibliography

JAPANESE SOURCES

It is as well to remember that the Supreme Command for Allied Powers (SCAP), under US General Douglas MacArthur, initiated and colluded with the soon-to-be-disbanded Japanese *Rikugunsho* and *Kaigunsho*, in the suppression and destruction of wartime documents. Much of this data was relevant to atrocities. Many remaining documents relating to the Second World War are closed to the public in Japanese national archives.

Senshi sosho is the 102-volume official Japanese War History. It was edited by Boeicho Boei Kenshujo, *Senshishitsu* (Asagumo Shinbunsha, 1966–80). War atrocities are ignored herein.

Gaimusho keisatsu, Shina no bu (Foreign Office Police History, China Section). Various years.
Rengo Kantai Sensaku (Combined Fleet Tactical Index), Tokyo, 1943.
Harumichi, Nogi, *Kaigun Tokubetsu Keisatsutai: Anbon-to BC-kyu* Yoshiaki, Yoshimi (ed.), *Jugun Ianfu Shiryoshi*, Otsuki Shoten, 1992.

WAR CRIMES TRIALS

Pritchard, R. John and Zaide, Sonia Maganua (eds), *The Tokyo War Crimes Trials: The Complete Transcripts of the Proceedings of the International Military Tribunal for the Far East*, Garland, 1981.
Proceedings of a Military Court for the Trials of War Criminals, War Crimes Trial Records, US National Archives, Washington.
Sleeman, Colin (ed.), *The Trial of Gozawa Sadaichi and Nine Others*, vol. III, War Crimes Trials, William Hodge, 1948.

LAW

Lauterpacht, H.L. (ed.), *Oppenheim's International Law*, London, 1952.

GENERAL WORKS

Allbury, A.G., *Bamboo and Bushido*, Robert Hale, 1955.
Allen, Louis, *Burma: The Longest War 1941–1945*, J.M. Dent, 1984.
Audus, Leslie J., *Spice Islands Slaves: A History of Japanese Prisoner of War Camps in Eastern Indonesia, May 1943–August 1945*, Alma Publishers, 1996.
Beets, N., *De Verre Oorlog*, Amsterdam, 1981.
Blair, Joan and Blair, Clay, *Return from the River Kwai*, Futura, 1980.
Boyd, C. and Yoshida, A., *The Japanese Submarine Force and World War II*, Airlife, 1996.
Brown, Lieutenant-Colonel Charles M., *The Oryoku Maru Story*, Magalia, California, 1983.
Brugmans, Dr I.J., *Nederlands Indie Onder Japanse Bezetting* (Dutch East Indies under Japanese Occupation), Franeker, Netherlands, 1960.

Bullock, Cecil, *Etajima: The Dartmouth of Japan*, Sampson Low, Marston & Co. Ltd, 1942.

Campbell, Jim, *I Survived a Hellship*, Sydney, 1951.

Cooper, Eric S., *Tomorrow You Die*, E.S. Cooper & Sons, Huddersfield, 1995.

Cowling, Anthony, *My Life with the Samurai*, Kangaroo Press, Kenthurst, Australia, 1996.

Daws, Gavan, *Prisoners of the Japanese: PoWs of World War II in the Pacific – the Powerful Untold Story*, Robson Books, 1995.

Dower, John, *Embracing Defeat: Japan in the Aftermath of World War II*, Allen Lane, Penguin, 1999.

Dull, Paul S., *A Battle History of the Imperial Japanese Navy 1941–45*, Patrick Stephens Ltd, 1978.

Edwards, Bernard, *Blood and Bushido: Japanese Atrocities at Sea 1941–1945*, Brick Tower Press, New York, 1997.

Elphick, Peter, *Life Line: The Merchant Navy in World War II*, Chatham Publishing, 1999.

Fuller, Richard, *Shokan: Hirohito's Samurai*, Arms & Armour Press, 1992.

Goodwin, Michael J. (ed. Don Graydon), *Shobun: A Forgotten War Crime in the Pacific*, Stackpole Books, Pennsylvania, 1995.

Hamato, I. and Izawa, Y., *Japanese Naval Aces and Fighter Units in World War II*, Airlife, 1990.

Hamilton, Geoffrey C., *The Sinking of the Lisbon Maru*, Hong Kong, 1966.

Harvey, Robert, *The Undefeated: The Rise, Fall and Rise of Greater Japan*, Macmillan, 1994.

Henriques, Fernando, *Stews and Strumpets*, MacGibbon & Key, 1961.

Howard, Keith (ed.), *True Stories of the Korean Comfort Women*, Cassell, 1995.

Kelly, Terence, *Living with Japanese*, Kellan Press, 1997.

Lamont-Brown, Raymond, *Kamikaze: Japan's Suicide Samurai*, Arms & Armour Press, 1997.

——, *Kempeitai: Japan's Dreaded Military Police*, Sutton Publishing, 1998.

Lindsay, O., *At the Going Down of the Sun*, Sphere Books, 1981.

Lord, Walter, *Day of Infamy*, Longmans Green, 1957.

McEwan, James, *The Remorseless Road: Singapore to Nagasaki*, Airlife Publishing, 1997.

MacKay, James, *Betrayal in High Places*, Tasman Archives, New Zealand, 1996.

Peacock, Don, *The Emperor's Guest: The Diary of a British Prisoner-of-War of the Japanese in Indonesia*, Oleander Press, 1989.

Piccigallo, Philip R., *The Japanese on Trial: Allied War Crimes Operations in the East 1945–1951*, University of Texas Press, 1979.

Rivett, Rohan D., *Behind Bamboo: An Inside Story of the Japanese Prison Camps*, Angus & Robertson, 1946.

Russell, Lord, of Liverpool, *The Knights of Bushido: A Short History of Japanese War Crimes*, Cassell, 1958.

Satow, E.M. (ed.), *The Voyages of Captain John Saris*, Hakluyt Society, 1900.

Seagrave, Sterling, *The Yamato Dynasty: The Secret History of Japan's Imperial Family*, Bantam, 1999.

Stead, Alfred, *Japan by the Japanese*, Heinemann, 1904.

Tanaka, Yuki, *Hidden Horrors: Japanese War Crimes in World War II*, Westview Press/HarperCollins Publishers Inc., 1996.

Waterford, Van, *Prisoners of the Japanese in World War II*, McFarlane & Co., n.d.

Watts, Anthony J., *Japanese Warships of World War II*, Ian Allan, 1966.

Whitecross, R.H., *Slaves of the Son of Heaven*, Corgi Books, 1961.

Williams, P. and Wallace, D., *Unit 731*, Hodder & Stoughton, 1989.

INDEX

NB: For names of US Navy and Imperial Japanese Navy vessels mentioned in the text see under their respective countries. All other vessels are listed in the alphabetical sequence.